Data Warehouse
Project Management

Data Warehouse
Project Management

Sid Adelman
Larissa Terpeluk Moss

Addison-Wesley

Boston • San Francisco • New York • Toronto • Montreal
London • Munich • Paris • Madrid
Capetown • Sydney • Tokyo • Singapore • Mexico City

The publisher offers discounts on this book when ordered in quantity for bulk purchases and special sales. For more information, please contact:

U.S. Corporate and Government Sales
(800) 382-3419
corpsales@pearsontechgroup.com

For sales outside of the U.S., please contact:

International Sales
(317) 581-3793
international@pearsontechgroup.com

Visit us on the Web at www.awprofessional.com

Library of Congress Cataloging-in-Publication Data

Adelman, Sid.
   Data warehouse project management / Sid Adelman and Larissa Terpeluk Moss.
       p. cm.
   Includes bibliographical references and index.
   ISBN 0-201-61635-1
   1. Data warehousing. I. Moss, Larissa Terpeluk. II. Title.
   QA76.9.D37 A34 2000
   658.4'038'0285574--dc21

                                                              00-056943

This product is printed digitally on demand.

Third printing, November 2002

I dedicate this book to my parents, Evelyn and Meyer Adelman,
who taught me so much and gave me such good advice.
I wish I'd been a better listener.

Sid Adelman

I dedicate this book to my mother, Lydia Terpeluk,
whose strength and endurance I inherited,
and to my father, Fedir Terpeluk, whose desire to fight injustice
in the world has found its expression in my character.

Larissa Terpeluk Moss

About the Authors

Sid Adelman is founder of Sid Adelman & Associates, an organization specializing in planning and implementing data warehouses. He consults exclusively on data warehouse topics including assessments, determining requirements, project planning, establishing roles and responsibilities, metadata strategy, and organizational and cultural issues. Sid presents regularly at data warehouse conferences and conducts a Data Warehouse Project Management seminar. Sid is a founding member of the Business Intelligence Alliance. He jointly developed a methodology, MapXpert for Data Warehouse™, which provides a master plan for implementing data warehouses.

Larissa Moss is founder and president of Method Focus Inc., a consulting firm specializing in improving business information quality. She frequently lectures and speaks at conferences on various data management topics, such as data warehousing, data quality, data modeling, and data audit and control. Her articles on data warehousing, project management, data management, and data quality are regularly published in magazines such as *DM Review*. She also provides consulting services in data warehouse assessments, data warehouse methodologies, project management, data administration, data modeling, data quality assessment, data transformation and cleansing, and metadata capture and utilization.

Contents

CHAPTER 1   INTRODUCTION TO DATA WAREHOUSING   1

CHAPTER 4   RISKS   77

CHAPTER 5   SATISFYING THE USER   101

CHAPTER 6   COST BENEFIT   117

CHAPTER 9   METHODOLOGY   193

CHAPTER 10   DATA MODELS   229

CHAPTER 11   DATA QUALITY   255

CHAPTER 12   PROJECT PLANNING   287

APPENDIX   315

List of Figures

Foreword

If you have anything to do with a Data Warehouse . . . if you only work for an enterprise that is merely *thinking* about Data Warehouse . . . and if you have this book in your hands. . . and if you haven't yet taken personal possession of it, STOP! Go directly to the checkout counter and pay for it, or acquire it by whatever mechanism you must, because you have a real gem in your hands. You have struck it rich and you need to stake your own personal claim on it.

Anyone who finds *Data Warehouse Project Management* has found for themselves a veritable gold mine, a wealth of wisdom and experience from some real pros who have "been there and done that" from the early days of stored programming devices and transaction automation to the latter days of mega-data devices and knowledge manipulation. I have known these folks for many years and I personally can attest that Sid Adelman and Larissa Moss literally exude the authority that can only come from a lifetime of pressing the state of the art and learning from an intimidating array and variety of implementations.

There are five reasons why I think this book is so valuable.

First, I already mentioned. . . It was written by folks who really know what they are talking about.

This is not just some pontifications on interesting concepts and entertaining new ideas. No. This is real life on the street, the street of Data Warehousing, one of the most promising and yet most misunderstood information technology opportunities of the modern enterprise. It is sage advice from people in the "front lines" of implementation under the pressures of schedule, budget, politics and complexity; people who have been "shot at" by every manner of vested interest and technological impossibility. Take my advice to take their advice.

Second, it is honest.

Sid and Larissa are not telling you what you want to hear, they are telling you what you have to know, that is, what you have to know if you want to be among those who return from real work on real projects with sufficient credibility still intact to pass on wisdom to another generation. The whole world has run out of time and has gotten impatient with the idea of actual work! Everybody seems to want some kind of magic. It would be a lot easier, and I am sure it would sell a lot more books if Sid and Larissa were saying, "Sure, sure! Just go buy a bunch of tools and slap in a bunch of 'Data Mart quick fixes;' schedule and budget are a non-issue because anybody can do this in three weeks or less with a handful of trainees who have taken correspondence courses on SQL from the local grammar school." That kind of thing seems to be what the world wants to hear!

In contrast, what Sid and Larissa are saying is, in effect, "There is enormous benefit to be had for the enterprise from Data Warehouse; but the magic lies in the actual work, in the data models, in the understanding of the data (element by element), in the data quality, in the preparation of the users, in the management, in the project planning and project management, etc., etc. There is no substitute for thoughtfulness, creativity, thorough preparation and hands-on involvement." This is the reality, the truth of the issue!

If everyone who has ever been involved in Data Warehouse implementations had read this book first, there would have been an infusion of honesty that would have demystified Data Warehouse and clarified a lot of the misunderstanding that surrounds it. Further, there would be a lot more positive Data Warehousing experiences in a lot more enterprises.

The third reason I think this book is so valuable is because it is comprehensive.

Data Warehouse Project Management contains exhaustive, expository lists of every subject relevant for consideration in managing Data Warehouse projects including, for example, the list of reasons for doing Data Warehouse, list of benefits, list of costs, list of risks, list of participants, list of skills, list of data quality issues, list of tool types, list of methodological steps, etc., etc. What a valuable resource!

Some folks get overwhelmed by the complexity and just "throw in the towel." Others simply start making lists. Lists make complexity manageable because invariably, the lists are shorter than you anticipate and the specificity of a list enables you to work on one thing at a time without being intimidated by everything on the whole list. The key to list-making is clean lists (no "apples and oranges" on the list) and completeness. In *Data Warehouse Project Management* no relevant Data Warehouse list has been left out and every list is complete, certainly to the extent that I am capable of judging. It is the most thorough and thoughtful work on Data Warehouse projects I have ever read.

Sid and Larissa have done us an invaluable service by giving us clean and comprehensive lists from which to work!

The fourth reason this book is so valuable is because it is practical.

At the end of every chapter there not only is a summary, but there also is a workshop. They have provided a "fill in the blanks" template for everything they discuss in the book. The workshop portion starts with a sample illustration and ends with blank spaces where the reader can write in their own specifications. If every reader would simply be disciplined enough to read the book and do the suggested exercises, they would end up with a Data Warehouse project plan that would improve the probability of their success by orders of magnitude! All that would be left to do is to execute.

The book not only arms you with an understanding of the issues but guides you directly and concretely into implementation.

The fifth reason I think this book is so valuable is because it is so well written.

It is not only readable by a technical audience but by a non-technical, management audience as well. In fact, the management principles espoused in the book go far beyond simply "Data Warehouse." That is, it is useful for helping think through any project, not only Data Warehouse projects.

That Sid and Larissa can share such a wealth of experience in such a succinct fashion in so few pages is also a testimony to the clarity of their thinking and ability for conceptualization. They are not only people who clearly have learned by doing but in this literary project, they articulate their experience as effectively as they implement. I read a lot of manuscripts and have written forewords to a number of books, but seldom do I read such coherent, well-structured material. Although, by its very nature, it is addressing a very complex technical undertaking, the book so effectively communicates that anyone, technical or non-technical, mechanical or managerial, can read it, understand it, employ it and benefit immeasurably by it!

I hope you don't stop with reading this foreword, but that you get your own copy of *Data Warehouse Project Management*, read on, complete the workshop exercises, and proceed to realize the benefits of the sage advice that Sid and Larissa have so generously shared with us.

This is pure gold! Dig in!

John A. Zachman
Glendale, California

Preface

You have been a project manager for years and have successfully implemented many systems, but on your data warehouse project nothing seemed to work. All those proven techniques you've acquired over the years did not smooth the path. The methodology you so faithfully followed for years did not seem to help you as much in controlling the activities on the project. Tasks had to be repeated many times, and some new tasks that you had never considered before had to be performed. Roles and responsibilities assigned to your staff seemed inadequate and sometimes inappropriate. Your users had not planned on spending so much time on your project, and you had not realized what was going to be required of them. You knew your source files had some bad data, but you had not anticipated the impact it would have on the extract/transform/load (ETL) process.

Maybe you are just planning your first data warehouse project and you have heard that it will be different and difficult. In either case, whether you already managed a data warehouse project or you are planning your first data warehouse project, this book will help you pave the road for a successful implementation. But before you immerse yourself into the content of this book, we would like to explain how we organized the book and provide a roadmap to guide you.

PURPOSE OF THIS BOOK

The hardest aspect to data warehousing is to manage a highly dynamic project. Data warehouse projects are dynamic because the requirements are usually not as well defined as they are for an operational system, and the process of building a data warehouse often leads to adjustments of these requirements or to discovery of new ones. Furthermore, these projects are staffed with talented but often inexperienced personnel. The complexity and learning curve on the new technology components are often underestimated. Management on both the IT and the business side all too often do not understand the complexity of a data warehouse project and put unreasonable demands on the team and the project manager. In other words, these projects are extremely challenging to manage.

The purpose of our book is to address the typical challenges on a data warehouse project and to educate the project manager on how to recognize the roadblocks and pitfalls. We give examples of risks and failures where we've encountered them, and we offer suggestions for avoiding them, or at least for mitigating them. At the end of every chapter is a section titled "A Cautionary Tale" that briefly describes our own experiences. Each chapter concludes with a workshop to practice what you have learned.

WHO SHOULD READ THIS BOOK

If this is your first or second attempt at a data warehouse project and you are not familiar or accustomed to using a different approach to managing this type of project, this book will help you. If you have already managed a data warehouse project that has been less than successful and you would like to do better on your next project, this book will provide some explanations for the difficulties you've encountered as well as suggestions for avoiding or mitigating these difficulties.

This book is not meant to be a tutorial for basic project management. Instead, it is meant to be a guide for the experienced project manager who needs to know about the differences between a data warehouse project and a traditional project and who can use a helping hand from someone who has already been there.

HOW THIS BOOK IS ORGANIZED

Our approach to this book was to write each chapter in such a way that it could stand on its own because we recognized that some project managers will want to use it only as a reference. In order to accomplish this, it was unavoidable to include some overlapping material in various chapters. However, we present the overlapping material within the context of its chapter and hope that it will not affect the reading pleasure of those who wish to read this book cover to cover.

Every chapter begins with a short list of its topics, followed by our experience from the field, highlighting landmines to watch out for, and concludes with a summary and a set of workshops. Some chapters also have appendices, which may be templates or worksheets, or additional guidelines. The workshops as well as the templates and appendices are stored in electronic format on the CD to make it easier for you to reproduce them. We encourage you to make use of these templates. They will help you standardize the process within your organization and simplify your own job.

We made every effort to write this book in gender-neutral format. At times, however, when we did have to use a gender, we chose the masculine "he." We most certainly realize that there are many women project managers, but alternating genders or using terms like "he/she" interrupted the flow of the book. Therefore, we hope that our readers will forgive us for taking this shortcut.

This book is on a serious subject and is written in a serious tone—most of the time. However, to keep our readers entertained, we chose to interject some wit, occasionally purposefully avoiding political correctness. We hope that our readers will not be offended.

Whether you plan to read this book cover to cover or use it only for reference, we suggest you start with Chapter 1, "Introduction," in order to understand our mindset and our terminology. All of the topics presented in this book culminate in Chapter 12, "Project Planning," which brings together all the chapters into one completed picture for the project manager.

OVERVIEW OF CHAPTERS

Chapter 1, "Introduction to Data Warehousing," gives an overview of the data warehouse world. It compares traditional decision support to data warehousing and lists the differences between these two environments. This chapter also addresses the difficulties of managing these projects and explains the views and positions of the authors on this subject.

Chapter 2, "Goals and Objectives," has an in-depth discussion about the deficiencies of traditional decision support systems and addresses the short-term goals as well as the long-terms goals of data warehousing.

Chapter 3, "Indicators of Success," discusses the measures of success, describing the determinants by which a project has succeeded or failed. It also talks about critical success factors, which are the project characteristics that are necessary for the project to be successful, and how to measure results.

Chapter 4, "Risks," presents the types of failures that various data warehouse projects have experienced. It lists the inherent risks with all of their attendant horrors and then suggests techniques to deal with each of them.

Chapter 5, "Satisfying the User," emphasizes the importance of understanding the business and then examines all areas that either affect or are affected by the users, from gathering the requirements from them to communicating with them.

Chapter 6, "Cost Benefit," discusses the need for cost-justifying each data warehouse project. It deals with the typical costs and with the expected benefits and provides a template for you to develop the cost justification for your own project.

Chapter 7, "Selecting Software," presents categories of data warehouse tools, suggests how the tools fit in an organization's architecture, discusses the process of determining product requirements, and deals with weeding out the vendors you want to avoid.

Chapter 8, "Organization and Cultural Issues," examines the roles and responsibilities of team members on a data warehouse project. It explains the structure of data warehouse teams and discusses staffing issues, such as recruitment and retention, training and mentoring.

Chapter 9, "Methodology," explains why the traditional waterfall methodology is not applicable to data warehousing. It also describes the various parallel development tracks, such as the extract/transform/load (ETL) process, the data delivery process, and the metadata collection and navigation efforts.

Chapter 10, "Data Models," examines the analytical purpose and usefulness of a logical data model, the primary technique for data integration, as well as the database design purpose of a physical data model. It compares the traditional database design schema of a two-dimensional entity-relationship–based architecture to the popular multidimensional star schema–based architecture.

Chapter 11, "Data Quality," defines what data quality means in a data warehouse and explains the cost of existing nonquality data. It also defines the various dirty data categories found on source files and suggests some triaging steps for data cleansing.

Chapter 12, "Project Planning," coalesces the previous chapters into one cohesive picture for managing a data warehouse project and guides the project manager through the development of a project plan. It presents some estimating guidelines and tips on how to control the project on an ongoing basis.

Acknowledgments

No book is ever written without the support and contribution of family, friends, business associates, reviewers, and, of course, the publisher.

Our first acknowledgment goes to our families, without whose patience this book would not have been written. We are thankful to Melinda Ann Smith for knowing when to stay out of the way. And we are especially thankful to Donald Philip Sherman for spending days reviewing every revision of every chapter for readability and grammar and thereby becoming a pseudoexpert on data warehousing.

We also want to thank our friends and business associates for taking time out of their busy schedules to review the chapters for content and clarity. We received a great deal of very valuable input from Joyce Bischoff, Lee Donoso, David Foote, Pat Higgs, David Marco, Rachel Meyers, Frank McGuff, Pieter Mimno, Dori Ann Neuman, Clay Rehm, J. D. Welch, and Duncan Witte.

Our special thanks go to Jane Aubol and Ed Carstens, who helped us tremendously through some of the chapters. Their contributions have made a significant impact on the quality of this book. Jane not only spent countless hours, nights, and weekends reviewing every chapter and giving us ideas on how to improve them, but she also wrote some sections in part or in whole. We are also grateful for Ed's excellent suggestions for the "Project Planning" chapter.

We also want to acknowledge our publisher, Addison-Wesley, for making our book idea a reality. We thank Elizabeth Spainhour and Mary O'Brien for encouraging us every step of the way and paving the road for us, Mariann Kourafas for helping us with editing questions and coordinating the reviews, Sarah Weaver for helping us get the chapters ready for production, Jacquelyn Doucette for managing production, and Curt Johnson, who we hope will enthusiastically market this book in various countries. Our thanks also go to all the other staff members of Addison-Wesley who worked on various aspects of this book.

Finally, we would like to thank Jerry's Famous Deli in Studio City, California, for offering us the use of their most hospitable restaurant corners with large dining tables. It provided a relaxed and unhurried atmosphere for our numerous book meetings.

CHAPTER ONE

Introduction to Data Warehousing

Virtually everything in business today is an undifferentiated commodity, except how a company manages its information. How you manage information determines whether you win or lose.

—Bill Gates

Data warehousing is perceived as being a fairly new approach to decision support, but its concept has been around since the mid-1980s. The data management aspect of data warehousing has been around even longer than that. Many excellent books have been written on that subject in the past, from data administration books, to data modeling books, to data quality books. A more recent concept in data warehousing is that of new and innovative methods for data delivery. Here, too, in the last few years some excellent guides have been published on multidimensional database design, supplemented by a plethora of materials available from vendors on the use and usefulness of OLAP (online analytical processing) tools and Web-enabled tools.

There is one aspect of data warehousing, however, that has received less attention than it deserves, and that is the subject of project management. Many organizations assume that if they put their most experienced project manager on a data warehouse project,

1

nothing can go wrong. Yet, we find the most experienced project managers struggling with data warehouse projects because they treat a data warehouse like a traditional system, which it is not. This chapter covers the following topics:

- Traditional development
- Data warehousing
- The role of project management
- Difficulty of managing data warehouse projects

At the end of this chapter you may test your readiness for a data warehouse by taking our Data Warehouse Readiness Test.

1.1 TRADITIONAL DEVELOPMENT

For various control and efficiency reasons, organizations are structured according to their functional decomposition. The first layer in the hierarchy is the separation of business functions from technology functions. The business functions perform the actual operations of the organization, whereas the technology functions support those operations by automating manual processes.

Both sides of the organizational hierarchy, the business side and the information technology (IT) side, are then further subdivided into smaller, more manageable units. One or more of the IT units are then responsible for supporting one or more of the business units with automating their operational and their decision support functions, as illustrated in Figure 1.1. Regardless of how efficient this organizational hierarchy structure appears to be, there is an inherent flaw built into its effectiveness.

1.1.1 Swim Lane Development Approach

The flaw in the current development approach, which takes IT units and pairs them up with the business units, is that cross-functional integration is lost. It is lost because each business unit sees the organization only from its own viewpoint and builds systems to support only that viewpoint. Therefore, each pairing of a business unit and its corresponding IT unit(s) is operating independently of all the other pairings.

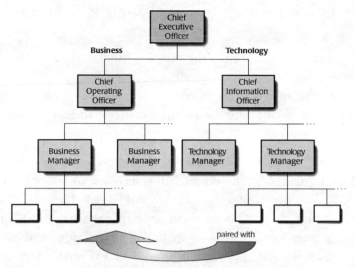

Figure 1.1: Typical Organizational Structure Chart

An analogy may be to imagine an Olympic-size swimming pool with many parallel swim lanes. Each swim lane represents one unique functional slice of the business. Each swim lane contains a business unit and its supporting IT unit(s), is independent and separate from all other lanes in terms of focus, scope, budget, staffing, and produces its own set of systems, operational as well as decision support, which only need to serve the users in that swim lane. See Figure 1.2.

There are some benefits to the swim lane development approach. The applications are much easier to develop because the functional scope is confined to one business unit. This makes them much less complicated than enterprise applications. Projects are much easier to manage because the scope is smaller, the number of users is smaller, and there is no integration required outside the swim lane. These systems can be developed faster and are therefore less expensive because communication is limited to the functional boundaries of one business unit.

1.1.2 Stovepipe Systems

If a data warehouse were to be developed using the swim lane development approach, it would produce a warehouse of standalone stovepipe databases and applications. While these stovepipe computer systems may be less expensive initially, this type of suboptimization makes the eventual cost to the organization more expensive because of the need to integrate them later.

During the early years when the support function of IT was restricted to simply automating business processes, stovepipe systems were not a problem. Operational systems have always been designed to perform a specific function or subfunction of the business, and they were usually not duplicated.

There is a decidedly different objective for decision support systems. Rarely does a business unit have such limited decision support requirements that it does not need to include any data created or used outside its own business function. Most decision support requirements do need to include data from outside their own business function, and, using the swim lane development approach, the same data is now being replicated everywhere.

To stay competitive in today's fast-paced business environment, all organizations must be able to see the complete integrated picture of their business, not just fragmented and isolated segments of it. Almost all organizations now find it very difficult to see that big picture of their business because the stovepipe systems were never developed for that purpose. Hence, for decision support, the data is still being replicated, sometimes hundreds of times, with the result of inconsistent data values.

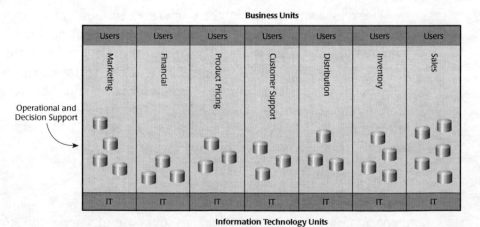

Figure 1.2: Swim Lane Development Approach

Many relationships between business objects have never been captured and can therefore not be recreated. The most common example of this is the difficulty to relate products with customers. This is demonstrated across all industries by the necessity for Customer Relationship Management (CRM) systems.

The relationship problem is compounded if portions or all of the processing has been outsourced and the primary keys of the unique business objects no longer match. An investment company was unable to ascertain customer profitability because the processing for their various investment branches, such as 401K funds, institutional retirement funds, direct investment funds, and so on, was outsourced to different companies. The same customer who had accounts in several investment branches was identified by different primary keys, which were assigned by the various outsourcing companies.

To address the shortcomings of isolated systems, many organizations are forced to build interfaces between them. These interfaces are now contributing to the existing data chaos (Brackett 1996) because they often evolve into separate systems, attempting to solve other relationship problems, capture additional data, or put a unique spin on some values as they are needed by some users. Not only are these interfaces expensive to build, they are even more expensive to maintain.

1.2 DATA WAREHOUSING

The data warehouse approach to decision support is based on a fundamentally different system development approach. Its strength is in the cross-organizational development approach, which has the integration of data at its core.

A cross-organizational development approach does not challenge the basic division of labor built into our traditional organizational hierarchy structures. It does, however, challenge the resulting swim lane approach to developing systems, and, more important, it challenges how we manage those projects. This challenge should, and hopefully will, eventually extend into the operational systems environment, but it is in the new data warehouse environment where organizations can start applying it right now.

1.2.1   Cross-organizational Development Approach

A cross-organizational development approach revolves around capturing the fundamental business pieces that have been scattered all over our stovepipe environment in one place and mapping existing and new applications to it. By business pieces we mean business data in terms of objects about which an organization stores data, such as customer or product, the relationships among the objects, the business actions performed on the objects, and the business intelligence imbedded in data values of those objects. In order to extract this fundamental business knowledge from our disparate operational as well as traditional decision support systems, the data from those systems must be gathered, examined, integrated, regrouped, and stored in a consistent and easy-to-access way.

The building of a cross-organizational data warehouse does not automatically translate into one and only one database for all. That would be ludicrous. It does, however, suggest that additional steps must be built into the development process to discover, communicate, integrate, document, and control the overlapping as well as the diverging functional views of all business units. See Figure 1.3.

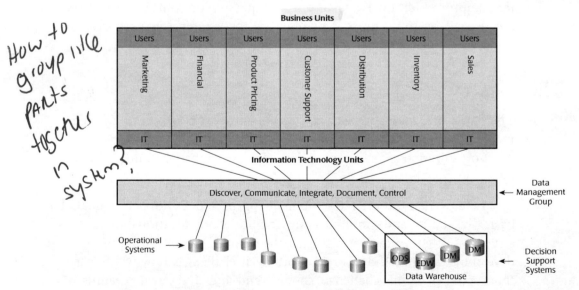

Figure 1.3: Cross-organizational Development Approach

The cross-organizational development approach will require some modification to the traditional organizational hierarchy structure, namely the introduction of one cross-functional data management group to coordinate the discovery, communication, integration, documentation, and control over the existing disparate data sources. This coordination is accomplished through the group's full-time involvement on all data warehouse projects. Their tasks and deliverables must be incorporated into the project plan.

Since cross-organizational integration on projects is a new concept for many IT teams, the purpose of the group's involvement is to help the project teams with data integration tasks and techniques. The following techniques are further explained in Chapter 9, "Methodology," and Chapter 10, "Data Models":

- Building an integrated logical data model over time
- Implementing a comprehensive metadata methodology (Marco 2000)
- Designing an integrated staging area for the extract/transform/load (ETL) processes
- Using conforming dimensions and facts (shared data) during database design (Kimball et al. 1998)
- Conducting comprehensive postimplementation reviews

The nature of the cross-organizational development approach will also require a slightly different team approach with some shifted roles and responsibilities, as well as some changes to the organization's traditional development methodology. All of these components are discussed in great detail in Chapter 8, "Organization and Cultural Issues," and Chapter 9, "Methodology."

Despite the obvious benefits of a cross-organizational development approach, it must be recognized that this approach impacts the data warehouse project in terms of scope, complexity, budget, time, staffing, and communication. These factors must be recognized, understood, and supported by all stakeholders. Stakeholders include team members, users, the project manager, the sponsor, IT management, and business management, as well as other participants on the periphery of the project, such as technical support and audit.

The project manager can minimize the impact of a cross-organizational development approach by controlling the size of the project, tightly managing change control, enhancing communication among all stakeholders, and educating the rest of the organization on data warehousing. Everyone in the organization must understand that even though there may be several data warehouse projects over the years, resulting in more than one database, the data warehouse environment should be considered *one* system.

1.2.2 Integrated Data Warehouse Databases

There has been much debate over the term *data warehouse*. To some people, a data warehouse is a database; to others it is a concept or an environment. The reason for this apparent confusion lies in the history of the data warehouse. In the beginning, the data warehouse database was the only target database in the data warehouse environment, so the term *data warehouse* was used interchangeably for both. See Figure 1.4.

The idea was that one integrated database would solve all the different users' data needs. Yet, the result was an overly complicated database structure, which was difficult for users to understand and navigate, and those who learned to navigate it experienced terrible performance.

The solution was to return to multiple, separate databases, each being designed and tuned to support only a few applications. These databases were called data marts. The popularity of multidimensional OLAP products furthered this solution along. The concept here was to use the data warehouse database to feed the data marts and have users access only the data marts.

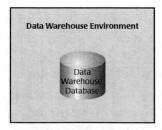

Figure 1.4: Original Data Warehouse Environment Target Database

Many organizations adopted a data mart solution by treating the data marts as totally independent applications. They developed multiple separate databases and populated them directly from the source files without going through the data warehouse database and without employing any other integration and reconciliation methods. By using this shortcut, these organizations ended up with stovepipe data marts, also known as legamarts (Hackney 1997), and are now faced with the extensive task of integrating them.

After the introduction of data marts, the data warehouse environment now consisted of multiple target databases (see Figure 1.5). However, the term *data warehouse* was still being used to mean two things. One meaning for the term was the data warehouse database, and the other meaning was the data warehouse environment, which now included data marts.

Over the years it has become accepted to use the term *data warehouse* to mean the data warehouse environment. For clarification, the data warehouse database was sometimes referred to as the wholesale data warehouse, and in recent years the term *enterprise data warehouse* has become the standard. In this book, we use data warehouse to refer to the data warehouse environment and Enterprise Data Warehouse (EDW) to refer to the data warehouse database.

One decision support problem remained to be addressed, namely the need for an integrated tactical and operational reporting database. The data warehouse was expanded again to include a new database called the Operational Data Store (ODS) (Inman, Imhoff, Battas 1995) (see Figure 1.6). Since this new target database contained integrated data from the operational systems, it was also a perfect feed for the enterprise data warehouse.

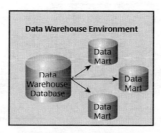

Figure 1.5: Expanded Data Warehouse Environment Target Databases

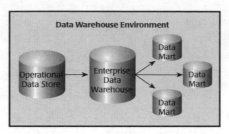

Figure 1.6: Current Data Warehouse Environment Target Databases

Some people question this architecture because not all organizations need all three types of databases for their reporting requirements. Why not just build the databases that are needed? There is nothing wrong with that idea, as long as the resulting databases are not stovepipe but are integrated and reconciled. This integration and reconciliation can be accomplished through the logical data model and enforced in the staging areas. See Figure 1.7.

Now organizations have the choice to implement in their data warehouse any combination of target databases that fits their needs and to control integration, redundancy, and reconciliation in the staging areas. A staging area is the physical environment where ETL programs and work files reside. The number of staging areas needed depends on the periodicity of database loads. If the ODS is a target database in the data warehouse, there would most likely be a daily staging area. If the enterprise data warehouse and/or data marts are the target databases in the data warehouse, there would most likely be a monthly staging area. These are not the only snapshot periods, but they are the most common ones.

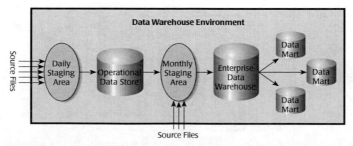

Figure 1.7: Staging Areas in the Data Warehouse Environment

Managing the ETL processes in the staging areas is one of the most critical tasks on data warehouse projects. This is addressed in Chapter 9, "Methodology."

1.3 THE ROLE OF PROJECT MANAGEMENT

Projects do not manage themselves, nor do the tools. Project managers manage projects (Corey and Abbey 1997). The role of project management has always been critical on any project, but it is especially crucial in this integrated and reconciled data warehouse environment, which has to support multiple target databases with various applications for a variety of users. On data warehouse projects, the project manager must embrace new tasks and deliverables, develop a different working relationship with the users, and work in an environment that is far less defined than the traditional environment (Adelman and Oates 1998). Data warehouse projects that start without a project plan and continue without stringent control procedures are usually short-lived. These projects are often late and over budget, the deliverables are of poor quality, and, most important, they do not give the users what they are expecting.

1.3.1 Traditional Project Management Techniques

A project manager is traditionally trained to deal with project plans, estimating, resources, schedules, change control, risk management, and communication. He learns through experience what tasks are critical and must be performed and what other tasks may be optional on certain types of projects. He understands task dependencies and people dependencies and knows, after some experience, how to "smell" trouble.

Because swim lane development is still allowed in the vast majority of organizations, inexperienced project managers continue to practice it, knowing how to do very little else. In a swim lane development approach the projects are predictable because each system is self-contained. Although there are small, medium, and large systems ranging from simple to very complex, within each category a project manager can fall back on his prior experience. This leads to shortcuts. For example, he may skip over some research activities because he had encountered a similar situation in the past and can plan the project based on that experience. He can put a project plan together fairly quickly because he can reuse the estimates from similar prior projects. He can delegate the ongoing controlling activities to a senior staff member because he expects very few unanticipated roadblocks.

On a traditional project, it is not unusual to see the project manager spend less than one week creating the project plan, assigning the work, setting up a formal status reporting procedure, and then letting the project run its course. The status reporting procedure requires staff members to submit their status reports at the end of each week. The project manager then summarizes the reported progress onto a higher-level status report, which he submits to management. The rest of his time is taken up with nonproject-related administrative activities, budgeting, attending meetings, and so on.

1.3.2 Data Warehouse Project Management Techniques

Traditional project management techniques will not work in data warehousing because data warehouse projects are different. They are much more dynamic, which means that some factors that are fairly stable and predictable on traditional projects change all too frequently on data warehouse projects. Items such as scope, performance of a tool, sponsorship, budget, and staffing, just to name a few, change more frequently and to a greater extent than on non-data warehouse projects. This is due to many factors. For example, an intermediate project deliverable may cause requirements to be refined or changed, which may affect the scope. Another example may be that staff resources are cut or reassigned to other projects due to a budget cutback in the organization.

There are other differences. The main purpose of the target data warehouse databases, with the exception of the ODS, is to enable strategic analysis, including trend analysis. This type of analysis should provide executives with information about the performance of their business and allow them to make decisions that affect the direction of their company. In order to support this type of analysis, storing many years of history is required. The result is that the target databases are usually extremely large, which means that the databases are designed differently, as explained in Chapter 10, "Data Models."

Since the data warehouse is *one* single environment, integration of data in its target databases is critical. That means integrating the logical data models and gathering comprehensive and accurate metadata are much more critical than on a traditional project. Dirty data in the source files becomes a big problem on data warehouse projects, because it makes the job of integrating and reconciling very difficult and time-consuming.

Requirements change often as the users see what can be done with the data warehouse and now ask for additional capabilities. That means that users are involved on the project much more directly and much more intensely. Put another way, without constant user participation it is not likely that the data warehouse project will deliver exactly what the users want and can use. Roles and responsibilities are shifted not only for users but also for analysts and programmers, and there are some new roles and responsibilities to incorporate.

The data warehouse evolves into a very complicated environment. It is not as predictable from project to project as the traditional stovepipe decision support environment, and it therefore needs strong and direct control procedures. This requires the project manager to be involved to a much higher extent than on traditional projects. If the data warehouse project is a large project, which most of them are, the project manager must either delegate other administrative responsibilities to an assistant, or he must delegate the managing of the data warehouse to a senior staff member. Managing a data warehouse project from his window office by reviewing weekly status reports will no longer work. Instead, the project manager must be involved on a daily basis, reviewing work in progress, adjusting tasks and deliverables, assigning new tasks, running interference for the team, and communicating to the sponsor and other stakeholders. He must also organize stakeholder review sessions, perform impact analyses on requested changes, perform cost benefit analyses for data that needs cleansing, and be prepared to change the direction of the entire project if an insurmountable roadblock is encountered.

1.4 DIFFICULTY OF MANAGING DATA WAREHOUSE PROJECTS

We have dedicated this entire book to help organizations manage their data warehouse projects with the highest chances for success. Here are just a few sections which will underscore our intent and our insistence for a full-time project manager.

1.4.1 Scoping

Scope creep is a constant threat to data warehouse projects. Not only do users change their minds on what they want as they see the capabilities of the new environment but programmers and analysts are often responsible for scope creep. During logical data modeling sessions, it is very tempting for a data modeler to pursue a discussion on a data element, which was mentioned in the session but is not really within the scope of the project. Programmers have often wanted to grab more data from a record, whether requested or not, just because they are already reading the file.

1.4.2 Estimating

Most project managers allow their staff to estimate their own work effort. If the staff members have performed the assigned task before, they will base their estimates on prior experience. If they have not performed the task before, the project manager will help with the estimating, taking the inexperience of the staff member into consideration. Estimating on warehouse projects is very difficult because each data warehouse project can be so different. If an organization is new to the Web, it will also be hard to estimate the time and effort to implement a robust and usable Web interface. Roadblocks encountered on one project may not be roadblocks on another, and on the flip side, just because one project went smoothly, that does not guarantee that the next project will go smoothly as well. Making allowances for unknowns and anticipating more roadblocks than usual help keep the schedule realistic.

1.4.3 Staffing

Every project manager tries to get the best people on his project. What constitutes "the best people"? There are three factors that put a person into that category. One factor is prior experience in the skill for which you are recruiting the person. The second factor is ability as well as desire to learn new things. The third, and maybe the most important factor, is that the person is a good team player with a positive attitude.

A good team player is someone who has great self-confidence and welcomes input from team members. It is someone who does not mind sharing responsibilities with another team member or taking over someone else's responsibilities. It is someone with a positive attitude, who likes sharing knowledge with other team members without being condescending and whose ego is not threatened by the teaching of others.

It is rare to have the entire team staffed with the "best people." But when you do, the project will be exciting and fun, regardless of how many roadblocks you encounter. The high spirits will keep the project running.

1.4.4 Shortage/Lack of Skills

A chronic problem on data warehouse projects is shortage of, if not lack of, skills. In this situation the blind are leading the blind. With enough money, this situation is not that difficult to remedy because you can buy the expertise from contractors and consultants. You should ensure that there is a knowledge transfer agreement in place with the expertise brought in from the outside to train your own staff in the three t's: technology, tools, and techniques. Your project plan must show the time for training, and since training does not equal experience, your task estimates must also allow for the associated learning curves.

1.4.5 Dirty Data

The degree of dirty source data is *always* underestimated. If you took your first estimate and quadrupled it, it would probably still be too optimistic. Dirty data is much more than typographical or programming errors. Mature organizations have most of their source data in old file structures and old hierarchical and network databases. Data in those structures does not lend itself to be converted into a relational structure easily. It has been consistently reported that 70 percent to 80 percent of the entire data warehouse development effort goes into cleansing and transforming data from source to target.

1.4.6 Control

By far your biggest challenge will be to stay in control of the project. What could get out of control? The list includes almost everything—the scope of the project, unrealistic user or management expectations, believed vendor promises, delayed hardware and software installations, overextended commitments, insufficient resource allocations, unreasonable demands, unrealistic schedules, inadequate budgets, lack of support and involvement from stakeholders. Daily assessments and, if necessary, daily adjustments are absolutely essential to stay in control.

1.5 SUMMARY

Organizations have been developing systems using a swim lane development approach, which pairs each business unit to a supporting IT unit, resulting in standalone stovepipe systems. These systems serve only the business units for which they were developed. They do not serve an organization's broader cross-functional decision support needs because they cannot provide a complete and integrated picture of the business.

Data warehouse projects should be based on a cross-organizational development approach, which requires some changes to an organization's hierarchy structure, to their old methodology, and to their old project management style. It basically requires a culture shift, which starts with the first data warehouse project.

A data warehouse is considered one integrated system, even though it has many databases supporting many applications. There are three target database categories in a data warehouse: the Operational Data Store (ODS), the Enterprise Data Warehouse (EDW), and the data marts. Integration and reconciliation of source data occurs in the staging areas during the extract/transform/load (ETL) process.

The role of project management has always been critical to every project. Because of the difficulties of managing data warehouses, old management techniques must be tightened with more stringent control procedures, and the project manager must be more directly involved in project activities on a daily basis.

A CAUTIONARY TALE

Building the Data Warehouse Using the Swim Lane Approach

Neither the project team nor the users really understood what data warehousing was all about. They had heard exciting things about new technology and new tools, and they were eager to try it out. There was no shortage of requirements, and users were enthusiastic about the new Web-enabled applications they were promised. They saw the product demos and couldn't wait to "slice and dice" their data to their hearts' content. Several projects were started at the same time, each project team developing a standalone system for their individual users the old-fashioned way, except now those systems were called *data marts*. After half a dozen of these so-called data marts were in operation, the users discovered that the data stored in those data marts was inconsistent and often redundant. Since each system had its own extract/transform/load process and put its own "spin" on the data, users found themselves no better off than before, except that IT now had six more inconsistent systems that had to be maintained. This organization ended up spending more money in sending their staff to more data warehouse conferences, hoping to learn how to integrate these standalone data marts.

1.6 WORKSHOP

If you are wondering if your organization is ready for a data warehouse, we encourage you to take the following data warehouse readiness test. After you have read the book and have started to prepare for your project, take this test again and compare your answers.

1.6.1 Readiness Test

For each of the 11 questions, give yourself a letter grade. *A* means that you are right on top of that subject and it is under control. *B* means that you are aware of that subject and you've started to address it. *C* means that you either didn't know about that subject or it is out of control. Once you've graded the 11 questions, give yourself 10 points for each *A*, 5 points for each *B*, and no points for each *C*.

The recommendations under each question suggest activities for the *C* answers.

Add the points, and compare your score with the following assessment results:

100 points	You probably cheated.
	If you didn't cheat, then unless a comet hits your installation, your success is guaranteed.
75–90 points	You are very well positioned for a successful implementation.
55–70 points	There are still some important issues to be addressed, but if they are addressed, your data warehouse project could well succeed.
30–50 points	You need to step back from an impending failure and understand that the data warehouse is not in the cards right now.
0–25 points	Reconsider the early retirement package.

READINESS TEST FOR THE DATA WAREHOUSE (DW)

1. **Have the mission and the objectives for the DW been defined?**

   A. Yes, completely.

   B. Partially. We are working on it.

   C. Management does not believe a mission and set of objectives are necessary.

   Recommendations:

   - Identify the sponsor of the DW.

   - Insist (strongly recommend) that the mission and objectives be defined prior to any serious activity.

   - Develop a draft for the mission and objectives, and propose it to the DW sponsor.

2. **Do the mission and objectives of the DW map to those of the enterprise?**

   A. Yes, the DW is expected to support and satisfy the organization's strategic direction.

   B. The DW will indirectly contribute to some of the organization's goals.

   C. No enterprise mission has been defined, or there is no mapping.

   Recommendations:

   - If there are no explicit enterprise objectives, there are probably assumed objectives to which most people in the enterprise would subscribe. These should be documented and mapped to the DW objectives.

   - If enterprise objectives exist but the DW does not support them, rethink what you are trying to accomplish with the DW.

3. **What is the quality of the source data?**

   A. The source data has some problems, but we will clean up most of it before it goes into the DW and identify suspect data.

B. We will clean the data as best we can.

C. The data has severe problems, or very little is known about the quality of the data.

Recommendations:

• If the quality of the source data is unknown, use a quality evaluation tool to help you determine just how bad things are. Identify operational data with quality problems to someone high in the organization (perhaps the CIO or the sponsor).

• Since the quality of the source data will be highly variable, try to convince the user to implement the cleanest data first (sometimes this will work).

• If the user insists on putting dirty data in the DW, at least flag the data in the data dictionary/repository indicating its level of quality (1 = pristine; 2 = questionable; 3 = dirty).

4. **Are the skills in place to support the DW?**

A. DAs, DBAs, application developers, and user liaisons have been identified, trained, and committed to the DW project.

B. We recognize the demand for skilled support, and we are working to staff the positions.

C. Management does not recognize that additional skills are needed.

Recommendations:

• Define the functional responsibilities of data administrators, database administrators, application developers, and user liaisons. Define the skill levels required for each of these positions.

• Sell management on the need to have skilled people on the DW team.

• Sell management on the need to have these people sufficiently dedicated to the project.

5. **Is an adequate budget in place?**

   A. Yes, the project has been budgeted and cost justified.

   B. Some money has been allocated, and we are working on getting the extra budget we need.

   C. An inadequate, bare-bones budget has been allocated, or no additional money has been appropriated to this project.

Recommendations:

- Compile industry publications, presentations, and so on that indicate what a DW will normally cost. Watch out for those who give figures for selected subsets of the effort or who disregard costs assumed by non-IT departments.

- Itemize each of the costs for your project. Don't pad the numbers, but don't underestimate just because you think the true cost will paralyze management.

- If the numbers are too high, consider a smaller project or one that does not require big-ticket items (a new DBMS, other expensive software, or major new hardware).

6. **Has supporting software (extract, cleansing, front-end tools, DBMS, etc.) been chosen and installed?**

   A. Yes, all the software is in place, has been tested, and has been incorporated in our DW architecture.

   B. We are now selecting software that will give us the most benefit.

   C. Very little has been budgeted for supporting software, or management does not recognize the benefit of such software.

Recommendations:

- Understand the benefit of each piece of software to the project. If it does not benefit this specific project, justification can be accomplished only if major follow-up projects will significantly benefit from its use.

- Quantify the costs of not using the software. These costs should include the additional effort to write the code, the ongoing costs to maintain the code, the costs of delay, and the potential for reduced quality of the implementation.

- Identify only the software that can make a major contribution. Avoid recommending a piece of software that is fun, leading edge, or a resume enhancer but does not make a significant contribution to the project.

7. **Has the source data been inventoried and modeled?**

   A. Yes, we have been using a modeling tool and have captured most of the anticipated source data. We know where the data comes from and have documented this metadata in a repository.

   B. We will be able to use some of our existing data models, and we plan to use a repository for our metadata.

   C. Modeling is not in the plan, or management does not recognize the value of modeling.

Recommendations:

- If source data has been neither inventoried nor modeled, it's probably because IT management does not recognize the importance of these activities.

- Any such recommendations would probably be seen as delaying the project. In fact, the inventory and modeling efforts are long and laborious. If management has not already recognized their benefits, it's unlikely that the DW project will sell them.

8. **Is there a strong, well-placed, and reasonable user sponsor?**

   A. Yes, in fact the user is driving the project.

   B. Users seem to be interested, but a sponsor for the pilot has not yet been chosen.

   C. No user has indicated an interest, or users are hostile to the idea of including their data in the DW.

   Recommendations:

   - Take your time. Make a list of sponsors that match the above criteria, and put the strongest ones on top. Research their decision support requirements, and determine which problems could be well served by the DW. Invite #1 to lunch, sell that user on the DW, outline what would be needed from them and from their department, and ask for their sponsorship.

   - If #1 is not agreeable, invite #2.

   - When you are down to "the user from Hell," stop, and do something else.

9. **Are the primary users of the data warehouse computer literate?**

   A. Yes, they are eager to try new software and have used their PCs for years.

   B. Many of the users are actively using their PCs, but some are still reluctant.

   C. Few users are computer literate and will need a great deal of training, or users are afraid to use computers and want nothing to do with them.

Recommendations:

- If your users are not computer literate, budget more money for user support.
- Allow more time for the target volumes to be achieved. Readjust your expectations.
- Revamp the training so as not to frighten the students.
- Provide mentors in the training process.
- Develop a more comprehensive set of predefined queries.
- Choose an extra-user-friendly front end (choose warm and fuzzy over power and function).

10. **Is the DW seen as a power grab by the DW Implementation Team?**

 A. No, the DW has been embraced by most of IT.

 B. Some developers are interested, but there are some resistance and concern about erosion of power basis within the application development community.

 C. The DW is being strongly opposed by powerful factions in IT.

Recommendations:

- Be sure it's not a power grab.
- Make the application developers an integral part of the DW Team.
- After they have been properly trained, make the application developers the primary contact with the users.

11. **What are the user's expectations for the DW?**

 A. The users are aware they will not be getting everything on the first DW iteration. They know there will be missing data and problems with the quality of the data, and they understand they will have to get training to be able to use the DW effectively.

 B. The users know it won't be perfect initially, but they still have some unrealistic expectations that need to be addressed.

C. Users have grossly inflated notions of what they will be receiving. Any suggestions of deferring their immediate wants are viewed as a reflection of IT incompetence.

Recommendations:

- Be honest. Don't misrepresent what the users will be getting, their required involvement, the costs, or the schedules.

- Never, never, never be coerced by anyone to accept unrealistic time frames or budgets.

- Document what the users will be getting and when (some installations ask the users to sign this document).

- Continue to remind the users of what they will be getting and when.

- If you have a user who is unwilling to accept your estimates, give someone else the opportunity to work with that user.

REFERENCES

Adelman, Sid, and Joe Oates. "Data Warehouse Project Management," *DM Review*, Volume 8, Number 5, May 1998.

Brackett, Michael H., *The Data Warehouse Challenge: Taming Data Chaos*. New York, N.Y.: John Wiley & Sons, 1996.

Corey, Michael J., and Michael Abbey. *Oracle Data Warehousing*. Berkeley, Ca.: Oracle Press, Osborne/McGraw-Hill, 1997.

English, Larry P. *Improving Data Warehouse and Business Information Quality*. New York, N.Y.: John Wiley & Sons, Inc., 1999.

Hackney, Douglas. *Understanding and Implementing Successful Data Marts*. Reading, Mass.: Addison-Wesley, 1997.

Huang, Kuan-Tsae, Yang W. Lee, and Richard Y. Wang. *Quality Information and Knowledge*. Upper Saddle River, N.J.: Prentice Hall, 1999.

Inman, William, Claudia Imhoff, and Greg Battas. *Building the Operational Data Store*. New York, N.Y.: John Wiley & Sons, 1995.

Kimball, Ralph, Laura Reeves, Margy Ross, and Warren Thornthwaite. *The Data Warehouse Lifecycle Toolkit*. New York, N.Y.: John Wiley & Sons, 1998.

Marco, David. *Building and Managing the Meta Data Repository.* New York, N.Y.: John Wiley & Sons, 2000.

Reingruber, Michael C., and William W. Gregory. *The Data Modeling Handbook: A Best-Practice Approach to Building Quality Data Models.* New York, N.Y.: John Wiley & Sons, 1994.

Simsion, Graeme. *Data Modeling Essentials: Analysis, Design, and Innovation.* Boston, Mass.: International Thomson Computer Press, 1994.

CHAPTER TWO

Goals and Objectives

"Would you tell me please which way I ought to go from here?"
said Alice.
"That depends a good deal on where you want to get to," said
Cheshire Cat.
"I don't much care where," said Alice.
"Then it doesn't matter which way you go," said the Cat.

—Lewis Carroll—Alice in Wonderland

The traditional decision support environment has failed to provide complete, accurate, integrated, and timely information to the organization. This chapter examines the inherent deficiencies of the traditional environment and offers solutions for reversing those deficiencies. It lists what the goals and objectives of a data warehouse should be and how to achieve them. This chapter covers the following:

- Deficiencies inherent in traditional decision support systems
- Data management solutions
- Data warehouse short-term objectives
- Data warehouse long-term objectives

At the end of the chapter you will have an opportunity to define your organization's data warehouse short-term and long-term goals and compare them with your company's strategic goals.

2.1 TRADITIONAL DECISION SUPPORT DEFICIENCIES

Shortly after manual processes were automated by the computer, management in all companies and across all industries started to ask for information from their newly automated systems. Their requests were heard and promptly put on the backlog because the main focus at that time was on automating processes. However, the hunger for data was so great, and the tools for manipulating that data were so limited, that it did not take long for data processing to split into two segments: operational systems and decision support systems (DSS).

What happened during the decades that followed is a familiar story to all of us. Decision support systems could not be built fast enough, a new market for DSS tools was created, business units started to hire their own programmers, and more recently some business units are even buying and managing their own technology platforms. Even the term *data processing* underwent some transformations to reflect the shift from *automating processes* to *providing information*. Data Processing (DP) became Management Information Systems (MIS), then Information Systems (IS), and now Information Technology (IT). Newer terms like Corporate Information Factory (Inman, Imhoff, Sousa 1998) and Business Intelligence (BI) are further indications of this shift.

On the surface it appears that all is well now, that all information needs are being met and that all participants are satisfied. Or are they? Let's look under the covers and see what's wrong with today's DSS environment.

Today's DSS deficiencies are so prevalent, and we have become so accustomed to them, that we accept them as part of the fabric of system development. Those involved may even think of the situation as "job security." As long as these deficiencies exist, there will always be a need to build another system, write another bridge between two systems, rewrite the system in another language, and buy another tool. However, if we seriously think about the impact of the situation, we realize the tremendous waste of time, money, and resources that we have been accepting without question all this time. When this tremendous waste is finally understood and felt, the goals and objectives of a data warehouse environment become very clear.

2.1.1 Departmental Views of Data

The speedy proliferation of traditional DSS environments happened in two ways:

1. *IT technicians dedicated to one or more business unit(s)*

   This is still the most common support model. One or more business units are matched up with an IT unit that is dedicated to solving the decision support needs for those business units. The IT unit may be a formal unit within the IT organization, or it may just be an informal group of two to three people whose priority is to serve those business units.

2. *Business units' own technicians*

   With the pervasiveness of client/server and Web environments, this support model is becoming more and more popular. Analysts and programmers are hired directly by the business units, and in many cases they develop and implement their systems on a hardware/software platform owned and maintained by their business unit.

In both cases, the technicians are exclusively supporting their business units. Independent from each other, they analyze the requirements, define the data, find the most suitable operational system from which to source their DSS, apply the most appropriate "spin" on the data, and basically cater in all ways to the business unit they are supporting. As we can see in Figure 2.1, this results in independently developed standalone systems.

As explained in Chapter 1, "Introduction to Data Warehousing," it is obvious that both models are "application centric" and result in numerous DSS deficiencies when looked at from an enterprise point of view. Yet, not only do most companies have this type of environment, but they continue to add to it.

2.1.2 Data Is Not Understood

This applies in a lesser degree to the original users of a DSS who had the system custom-built. They probably understood their data, or at least they thought they did. However, new users, either in the same business unit or from other business units, who want to use the data often do not have the same understanding of it. The data names are often reused and misleading, the data content has changed over the years, and how the

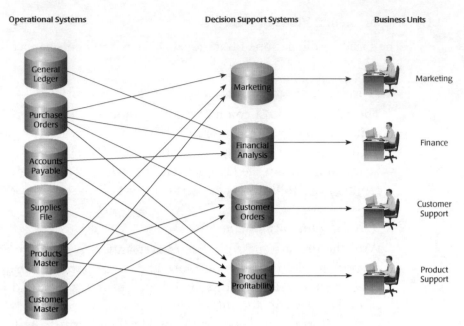

Figure 2.1: Traditional DSS Environment

data is used in reports may also not be self-explanatory. These new users must now take the time to search through documentation, if any exists, or ask other people who have been using the data to explain it to them. Most of the time the explanations given to these new users are again not documented, and this process has to be repeated with each new set of users. And if the explanations are documented, this documentation is seldom shared with other business units, it is seldom up-to-date, and its mere existence is often not known to others in the organization. The time spent by the new users and the staff assisting them to learn about the data is wasted time.

2.1.3 Users Disagree on Data Definitions

Since the traditional DSS systems are developed independently of each other by different people, data is interpreted and used in a business unit's view and not in an organizational view. Where it is possible and appropriate for different business units to have their own view on the data, the absence of reconciling and capturing these views in metadata leads to arguments between users about what the data means, what its values should be, and how it should be used. Again, a lot of unnecessary time is spent on these arguments.

2.1.4 Redundancy

An often underestimated or overlooked cost is the time and money spent on maintaining redundancy, both data redundancy and process redundancy. In most organizations today, the same data appears in hundreds of databases and is handled by hundreds of programs. That means that the same data is created, updated, and maintained hundreds of times, wasting disk space, requiring more computer resources, and wasting the time of people who reinvent the wheel by writing hundreds of applications that basically do the same thing. If an error is corrected in one application, the correction is rarely applied to the other applications, and in a very short time inconsistencies exist. The time to reconcile the inconsistencies is multiplied by the number of redundant databases and applications. Since the reconciliation effort is too great, most organizations simply write a new application and duplicate the data one more time to "fix" the problem.

2.1.5 Reports Are Inconsistent

When users don't even realize that they have a different interpretation and view of data, they may reject reports that show different totals or a different breakdown from their own. They will further label these other reports, along with the systems that generated them, as "bad," "wrong," "useless," "unreliable." Too often these labels spill over to the innocent staff that developed the other systems and reports. Not only is energy wasted on arguing about who is right and who is wrong, but the larger damage is done when different groups no longer respect each other and the work atmosphere is degraded. The impact is lower morale, which usually manifests itself as lower productivity and lower quality.

2.1.6 Users Do Not Trust the Reports

This is often the result when the communication between IT and users is limited and when IT develops the system with little or no user involvement other than gathering the original requirements. Here we have a situation where the understanding of data is different not only between business units but also between the business unit and its supporting IT staff. To make things worse, not only might IT lack understanding of the business view of the data, but the users often don't understand how the data is being captured and manipulated in the operational system. In this "us versus them" environment, users often try to handle their distrust by creating their own pseudo-IT environment. The impact of this solution

transforms low morale and low productivity into tangible costs for dupli-
cating technology platforms.

2.1.7   Data Is "Dirty"

This is a complaint we hear frequently from users and IT alike. Yet, when
faced with the task of analyzing the operational source data and cleaning
it up for the DSS, we equally frequently hear excuses such as

> "We are used to the dirty content in this field."
> "We are too busy with other things."
> "We will just write our queries to eliminate certain records."
> "We know how to interpret the bad data values."
> "It would take too much time to clean it up."
> "It would cost too much money to clean it up."
> "They will never tighten edit checks on the operational system."
> "It's really not that bad once you get used to it."

When confronted with the fact that every other person who does not
intimately know the dirty data would need a lot of time to learn how to
"eliminate certain records" or to "interpret bad data values," there are
usually two types of responses from the users:

> "They'll just have to take the time to learn. That's what we had to do.
> That's just how it is."
> "This is *our* data. No one else needs to access it. They should call *us*
> when they need our data."

Needless to say, the time it takes for many people to relearn the same facts
is not being taken into account, and neither is the associated cost considered. For detailed examples of "dirty data" their impact on the data warehouse and recommended transformations, refer to Chapter 11, "Data
Quality."

2.1.8   Data Is Not Shared or Is Shared Reluctantly

Because traditional DSS development has been *application centric,* it is no
surprise that data sharing is neither encouraged nor sought after. Users
who have full control over their systems in terms of data definitions, data
acquisition, data cleansing, data transformation, database design, and
tools used have no incentive to share what they develop. After all, since

the funding for their system came out of their own budget, they "have the right" to be in full control over what goes into the system, what comes out of it, and who uses it. And there certainly are no incentives to give up that control, especially if upper management is still holding them accountable for delivering the system in a very short time frame. Sharing means involving other users. Involving other users means reconciling their views of the data. Considering other views will slow down development. Slowed down development could result in missed deadlines. Missed deadlines will be remembered at performance appraisal time. An unfavorable performance appraisal will result in a small raise, or no raise at all, and most likely no bonus for the year. On the other hand, by keeping things separate, the raises and bonuses are safe, even though different users will spend time and money to reinvent the proverbial wheel.

We observed two other powerful reasons for reluctance to share data. One reason is fear of losing power. Knowledge is power. By letting others (presumably foes within the company) see their data, department heads give up power and leave themselves open to critical evaluation from their internal enemies. The second reason is fear of exposure. By holding onto their data, department heads have the ability to put a spin on the data, or actually to change the results before anyone else sees them. This does not usually imply a cover-up of a fraudulent activity, only a different interpretation or presentation of facts, which would put the department heads and their business units into a more favorable light.

2.1.9   Data Is Not Integrated

Even if there were a willingness to allow other users to share their data, as long as business units build their standalone systems based on their individual views, data between systems will not be integrated. Therefore, accessing data across multiple systems often involves writing complicated bridges between systems, a time-consuming and costly solution.

2.1.10   Historical Data Is Not Available

We cannot conclude this section without talking about another paradigm shift in DSS: the change from operational decision making to tactical and strategic. The user community of the DSS environment is also changing from business administrators to business analysts and executives from such business units as marketing, legal, finance, and human resources. The new focus on tactical, and especially on strategic, decision making brings a new requirement to DSS: the ability to compare data between time periods, geographic regions, and other business dimensions. This translates into the need for historical data that is as easily accessible as current data. Since traditional DSS do not typically store historical data in the same manner as current data, analysts end up creating new elaborate systems to accomplish their analyses. It can be weeks before an analyst can complete an analysis assignment because that is how long the process of extracting current data, merging it with historical data, running queries, and analyzing the query results may take each time. There have been reports of analysts spending up to 90 percent of their time gathering the data and only 10 percent performing the analysis.

2.2   DATA MANAGEMENT SOLUTIONS

Data warehousing is not the first attempt at tackling the types of data management problems discussed in the previous section, but if done correctly, it appears to be the most effective attempt so far. To be successful in the age of e-commerce and Web applications, it will be unavoidable to address the existing data chaos in our organizations once again. Only this time we must be more successful than we were in the past with the information engineering and the data administration functions.

2.2.1   Information Engineering

Data management became a major topic in most organizations in the early 1980s. Information Engineering was created as a new IT unit, chartered with developing and applying methods and techniques to manage the organization's data the same way as any other corporate resource is managed.

One of the first methods for managing data was the corporate data dictionary. Information Engineers spent years loading a central data dictionary with technical data from their operational systems. They ended up with thousands of data elements, hundreds of files, and hundreds and thousands of programs and job control language (JCL) procedures representing all of their systems. It took many more years to analyze and define all the accumulated systems-related data in the data dictionary. This was an honorable first attempt at gathering and maintaining metadata. However, the only visible benefit of this exercise appeared to be a tremendous understanding of corporate data by one or two IT analysts and not much else.

Most companies decided that this was not a cost-effective approach to solving their data management problems, and Information Engineering is now an affectionate memory of "the good old days."

2.2.2 Data Administration

Since the idea was good but the concept was unworkable, Information Engineers quickly reinvented themselves as data administrators. Their mission was the same, but their method was different. A new technique was gaining much popularity during the rise of relational database management systems. This technique was called Entity-Relationship modeling, or logical data modeling. There were some distinct benefits to the logical data modeling approach over the previous data dictionary approach.

1. *Top-down analysis*

   Logical data modeling was based on user participation. Having users involved in the analysis shortened the process considerably and made it more acceptable.

2. *Business-centric*

   The data was being analyzed from a business perspective and not from a technical perspective. The benefit was that users, not just one or two IT analysts, now had an in-depth understanding of corporate data.

3. *Relational database design (two-dimensional)*

   But what really saved data administration from becoming another "extinct IT species" was the direct applicability of a logical data model to relational (two-dimensional) database design. With few modifications to a logical data model we were actually able to implement the model as an application database.

Data Administration is still aiming for more than managing the data for isolated standalone application databases. The charter of Data Administration remains the management of corporate data across all business units and all systems in the organization.

2.2.3 Data Warehouse Administration

As mentioned in Chapter 1, "Introduction to Data Warehousing," a data warehouse is an integrated decision support environment and not simply another DSS database added to the existing collection of databases. A data warehouse is also not a database into which all of the operational data is thrown indiscriminately just to make it available online. That would be what we call the "suck and plunk" approach, where operational data is "sucked" out of the operational systems and "plunked" into the data warehouse database without analysis, without integration, without cleansing, without transformations, without much usefulness, and without business value.

Instead, a data warehouse is an environment of one or more integrated and reconciled databases designed to deliver consistent and reconciled business intelligence to all business units in the organization, to solve specific business pains, and to support the strategic goals of the organization, as depicted in Figure 2.2.

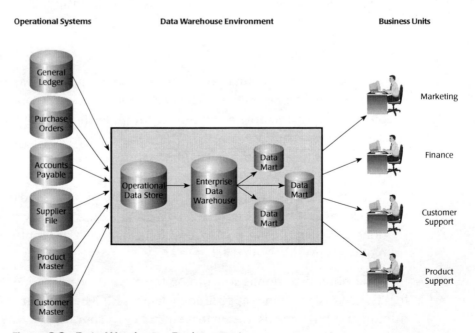

Figure 2.2: Data Warehouse Environment

The function of Data Warehouse Administration is to create and maintain that consistent and reconciled data warehouse environment. In order to do that, corporate data from internal operational sources, as well as data from external sources, must be analyzed, understood, integrated, transformed, and delivered. Therefore, Data Warehouse Administration must coordinate and oversee the development, delivery, management, and maintenance of the data warehouse environment.

Data Warehouse Administration should be involved with these issues:

- Prioritization of data warehouse projects—see Chapter 9, "Methodology"
- Negotiation of budgets, schedules, and staff—see Chapter 6, "Cost Benefit," Chapter 8, "Organization and Cultural Issues," Chapter 12, "Project Planning"
- Triaging data cleansing efforts—see Chapter 11, "Data Quality"
- Overseeing the establishment of the infrastructure, both technical infrastructure and development infrastructure—see Chapter 9, "Methodology"
- Overseeing the development and mapping of data models, both logical and physical—see Chapter 10, "Data Models"
- Coordinating the development and maintenance of the staging area(s)—see Chapter 9, "Methodology"
- Resolving disputes between users or escalating disputes to the advisory boards—see Chapter 8, "Organization and Cultural Issues"

2.3   DATA WAREHOUSE SHORT-TERM OBJECTIVES

After identifying the deficiencies in your current DSS environment and understanding the challenges of managing your organization's data, you should now define what your data warehouse objectives are or what they should be.

The main goal of any data warehouse should be to eliminate a business pain. A business pain could be loss of revenue, inability to keep up with competitors, high production costs, and inability to expand the market share. To achieve the desired results from your data warehouse, short-term and long-term objectives must be set.

To avoid the same calamity that befell Information Engineering when trying to correct all data management problems in one big-bang approach, you want to separate your data warehouse objectives into two categories: short-term objectives and long-term objectives. Short-term objectives are those you can realize with every data warehouse iteration. They provide immediate benefits to the users. Long-term objectives are achieved over time.

All of your short-term and long-term data warehouse objectives are for naught if they don't match the strategic goals and objectives of your organization. Let's say that one of your data warehouse objectives is to integrate data in order to get a better understanding of your customers' buying habits so that you can sell them more profitable products. On the other hand, your company's strategic goal is to reduce production costs. With this kind of mismatch between company goals and data warehouse objectives you will not get upper-management support for your data warehouse. The development of a data warehouse must support the strategic goals of your organization (Hackney 1997). As you are documenting the goals and objectives for your data warehouse project, keep asking yourself these questions:

- What is the business pain?
- Do your objectives address the business pain?
- Will the data warehouse contribute to the relief of that pain?

2.3.1 Improve Quality of Data

Since a common DSS deficiency is "dirty data," it is almost guaranteed that you will have to address the quality of your data during every data warehouse iteration. Data cleansing is a really sticky problem in data warehousing. On the one hand, a data warehouse is supposed to provide "clean, integrated, consistent, and reconciled data from multiple sources," and on the other hand, we are faced with a development schedule of 6 to 12 months. It is almost impossible to achieve both without making some compromises. The difficulty lies in determining what compromises to make.

Here are some guidelines for determining your specific goal to cleanse your source data:

- *Never try to cleanse ALL the data.*

Everyone would like to have all the data perfectly clean, but nobody is willing to pay for the cleansing or to wait for it to get done. To clean it all would simply take too long. The time and cost involved often exceed the benefit.

- *Never cleanse NOTHING.*

In other words, always plan to clean something. After all, one of the reasons for building the data warehouse is to provide cleaner and more reliable data than you have in your existing OLTP or DSS systems.

- *Determine the benefit of having clean data.*

Ask some questions about why you are building the data warehouse:

— Are you building it partly because you currently have inconsistent reports?
— What is the cause of these inconsistencies?
— Is the cause dirty data, or is it programming errors?
— What dollars are lost due to dirty data?
— Which data is dirty?

↓ constant Adjustments

on hAND

cost of lost inventry

receiving shipping removAL

- *Determine the cost for cleansing the data.*

Before you make cleansing all the dirty data your goal, you must determine the cleansing cost for each dirty data element. Examine how long it would take to perform the following tasks:

— how many weeks?

— Analyzing the data
— Determining the correct data values and correction algorithms
— Writing the data cleansing programs
— Correcting the old files and databases (if appropriate)

- *Compare the cost for cleansing to dollars lost by leaving it dirty.*

Everything in business must be cost justified. This applies to data cleansing as well. For each data element, compare the cost for cleansing it to the business loss being incurred by leaving it dirty. Determining business losses due to the impact of dirty data can be a difficult task, like estimating the business loss resulting from a tarnished reputation of a company with its customers and suppliers. The task of calculating business losses involves many steps, some of which are researching the

"if we have 1, will have to so" check

Not Knowing exactly what is on hAND At all times

How much
at
inventu

company's past performance, measuring its ongoing performance, calculating customer lifetime value, and projecting lost profits (English 1999). Once you have calculated your business losses, compare them to the cost for cleansing the data and decide whether to include it in your project's data cleansing goal.

— If dollars lost exceed the cost of cleansing, put the data on the "to be cleansed" list.

— If cost for cleansing exceeds dollars lost, do not put the data on the "to be cleansed" list.

• *Prioritize the dirty data you considered for your data cleansing goal.*

A difficult part of compromising is balancing the time you have for the project with the goals you are trying to achieve. Even though you may have been cautious in selecting dirty data for your cleansing goal, you may still have too much dirty data on your "to be cleansed" list. Prioritize your list.

• *For each prioritized dirty data item, ask, "Can it be cleansed?"*

You may have to do some research to find out whether the "good data" still exists anywhere. Places to search could be other files and databases, old documentation, manual file folders, even desk drawers. Sometimes the data values are so convoluted that you may have to find some "old-timers" who still remember what all the data values meant and who will help you write the transformation logic. Then there will be times when, after several days of research, you find out that you couldn't cleanse a data element even if you wanted to, and you have to remove the item from your cleansing goal.

As you document your data cleansing goal, you want to include the following information:

— Degree of current "dirtiness" (either by percentage or by number of records)

— Dollars lost due to its "dirtiness" — *adjustments* *backorders.*

— Cost for cleansing it   — *wages*

— Degree of "cleanliness" you want to achieve (either by percentage or by number of records)
   — *100 %.*

2.3.2 Minimize Inconsistent Reports

Addressing another common complaint about current DSS environments—namely, inconsistent reports—will most likely become one of your data warehouse goals. Inconsistent reports are mainly caused by misuse of data, and the primary reason for misuse of data is disagreement or misunderstanding of the meaning or the content of data. Correcting this problem is another predicament in data warehousing because it requires the interested business units to resolve their disagreements or misunderstandings. This type of effort has more than once torpedoed a data warehouse project because it took too long to resolve the disputes. Ignoring the issue, however, is not a solution either.

We suggest the following guidelines for each project dealing with a set of inconsistent reports:

- *Identify the data in dispute.*
  Examine carefully how the disagreement or misunderstanding of the data contributes to producing inconsistent reports.

- *Determine the impact of the inconsistent reports.*

  — How seriously are they compromising business decisions?
  — What dollars are lost due to bad decisions?
  — Are the differences significant?
  — How easy are the reports to reconcile?

- *Determine the cost for resolving data in dispute.*
  Estimate how long it would take to do the following:

  — Get the involved business units to commit to the process of resolving their disputes
  — Analyze the data disputes and model the different user views
  — Separate the consistent views from the inconsistent views
  — Come to an understanding on definitions and content of data for the consistent views
  — Create new data for the inconsistent views
  — Come to an understanding on definitions and content of the new data

- *Perform cost-benefit analysis.*

Compare cost for data resolution to dollars lost by leaving data disputes unresolved.

A cost benefit must be demonstrated before including the resolution of a data dispute in your goal.

All loses exceed costs.

— If dollars lost exceeds the cost of resolution, put the data dispute on the "to be resolved" list.

— If cost for resolution exceeds dollars lost, do not put the data dispute on the "to be resolved" list.

- *Prioritize the data resolutions you consider tackling.*

Anyone who has ever participated in a data resolution session knows how time-consuming it can be. Your project schedule may not allow you to resolve all the data in dispute. You should therefore prioritize your list.

As you did with your data cleansing goal, you want to document the following information for your "minimize inconsistent reports" goal:

— Degree of impact on business decisions
— Dollars lost due to data disputes
— Cost for resolving the disputes
— Degree of "resolution" you want to achieve

  Examples: Do all users have to agree, or only the two main users?

  Do the totals have to agree 100 percent, or is a 5 percent variance acceptable?

  If resolution cannot be achieved in X days, can the data be dropped?

2.3.3 Capture and Provide Access to Metadata

Metadata until now has always been considered the dirty "D" word: documentation. However, in data warehousing, metadata is the nice "N" word, navigation, because it is indispensable for data sharing and data navigation.

Data Sharing

As we discussed before, most data is not being shared today for a number of reasons. Besides the turf war reasons, one reason is not understanding the data, and another reason is not trusting the data content. We already established that in order to correct this problem, users have to discuss their views of the data and discover their commonality and differences. Two major goals of this discussion are commonly agreed-upon data definitions and commonly agreed-upon domains (valid data values). Because these two goals are often misunderstood and declared as unattainable and a waste of time, we must be clear on what we mean by these goals.

The process of achieving commonly agreed-upon definitions and domains does not mean that hundreds of users are arguing ad infinitum about who is right and who is wrong. It also does not mean that the desired result is a declaration of victory by the most powerful user having forced his opinion on the other users. The process involves a small group of people, usually five or six, consisting of a facilitator, the data owner, and one authoritative representative from each business unit that is using the data to make critical business decisions. In organizations that do not have a strong data management commitment, it may not be possible to get representatives from the business units to attend the sessions. In those cases the project team and the user must define the data and send it out to the business units for review. A feedback loop and review procedures must be established to process any disagreements.

When strong disagreements about the meaning or content of the data surface, it is an instant indication of high probability that all of the disagreeing parties are "right" and that more than one data element exists. This probability is explored within a predefined short time frame, usually no more than a few days, and a new data element is created, named, and defined by the group. If the exploration does not yield a new data element, the data owner makes the final decision on definition and content. Assuming there is no turf war between the disagreeing parties, the definition and content will, to some extent, include any reasonable variations perceived by the other involved business units. The now agreed-upon definitions and content for the original and for the new data elements are documented in a metadata repository and made available to all other users in the organization.

Data Navigation

We like to think of metadata as the nice "N" word: navigation. Once the source data has been cleansed, transformed, aggregated, summarized, and dissected in numerous other ways, the users will never find it again in the data warehouse without the help of metadata. Capturing the metadata, both business metadata, such as the data definitions and the domains, and technical metadata, such as the algorithms for transforming the source data, the columns and tables, and all the other technical components, is only half of the solution. The other half is making metadata easily accessible and useful to the users.

2.3.4   Provide Capability for Data Sharing

If data sharing is one of your data warehouse goals, you will most likely have to include some data cleansing, data dispute resolution, and metadata access components as means of achieving the goal. These components are prerequisites to data sharing because in order to be able to share data, the data has to be clean and consistent and have the same meaning to every user. Two other vital components are database design and database access.

Database Design

After the requirements have been analyzed, the requested data has been logically modeled, and the related metadata has been captured in the repository, the next step is database design. Designing a standalone database for one business unit is different from designing a shared database for multiple business units. It isn't just a matter of granting access to more users but a matter of designing a database based on (1) the lowest level of detail and granularity necessary to satisfy all the different data needs and (2) the type of access required by the different business units.

There are many design choices, depending on the mix of requirements. When you define data sharing as a goal, you must be specific about the following factors:

- Technical literacy level of users
- Business knowledge
- The level of detail data required by all users
- The types of summarization and aggregation requested

- The types of queries each user will write
- The periodicity needed—daily, weekly, or monthly snapshots

Database Access

As with metadata, getting the data into the database is only half the battle. Providing easy access to it is the other half. Not all users are created equal. There are power users—some of whom may even qualify as programmers—and there are technophobes who want only pull-down menus and radio buttons to run some standard reports and canned queries. Then there are all the competency levels in between. You need to accommodate a wide spectrum of users with multiple different query and reporting tools and easy Web access for all.

When you document your data sharing goal, describe the users in terms of the following:

- Overall technical literacy level
- The types of queries they are capable of writing
- Whether they will need to manipulate query results
- What summary views they need
- What report-writing capabilities they might need
- How often they will access the system
- Whether they have prior experience with a query or reporting tool
- Their proficiency level with a query or reporting tool
- Their ability and speed of learning new tools

This information will be most valuable for tool evaluation and selection, as well as for training.

2.3.5 Integrate Data from Multiple Sources

This is another primary goal for all data warehouses because it is a primary deficiency in current DSS. A frequent lament is "It takes me days to merge data manually from four different systems because there is no common key between the files." Standalone systems, which have the same data identified by different keys, are only one of many reasons why data integration does not exist in most companies. Some other reasons are that the data content in one file is at a different level of granularity from that in another file or that the same data in one file is updated at a different time period from that in another file. In a shared data environment the requirements from different business units regularly include data relationships that do not exist in current systems. This often means that the necessary foreign key to implement the requested relationship does not exist in the source files.

Before you define your data integration goal, review your current DSS deficiencies and analyze the source systems you have identified as possible feeds to your data warehouse. Document the following:

- Whether the keys for the same data have the same data type, length, and domain
- Whether the same data is identified by the same key value
- Whether new data relationships can be implemented
- The granularity of the data content
- Periodicity of data updates

2.3.6   Merge Historical Data with Current Data

A typical data warehouse objective is to store history in order to perform trend analysis. This objective comes with its own challenges. Historical data is seldom kept on the operational systems, and even if it is kept, rarely will you find three or five years of history in one file. First of all, historical data is not of as much use to the daily operational processing of a business function as it is to decision support. Second, operational files do change over time, and reloading historical data to match the new records layouts would not be cost justified. Third, operational history is a point-in-time transaction history, not a periodic snapshot in time. Point-in-time transaction history means a record is written to the file each time a transaction (change) occurs. Periodic snapshot means a record is written to the file once for each period (daily, monthly, etc.) regardless of how many transactions occurred within that period.

Having said all that, you must define the following detail for your goal to merge historical data with current data:

- The number of years for which you wish to keep history
- Whether history will be collected from this point (initial loading) forward or whether you will load "X" number of past years
- Whether the history files have the same record layout

- Whether the format of the data has changed over time
- Whether the meaning of the domain (valid values) has changed over time
- Whether the organizational hierarchy has changed over time
- How much history is actually available on disk or on tape

2.4 DATA WAREHOUSE LONG-TERM OBJECTIVES

The long-term data warehouse objectives resemble many of the original data management objectives from the early 1980s. If you follow the steps outlined in the data warehouse methodology, as described in Chapter 9, "Methodology," while focusing on your short-term objectives during your data warehouse iterations, your long-term objectives will almost assuredly be realized.

2.4.1 Reconcile Different Views of the Same Data

If your short-term goals include minimizing inconsistent reports and providing the capability for data sharing, you are already addressing this reconciliation effort to some degree. We say *to some degree* because in order to complete your project within the scheduled time frame and within the budget, you may have to restrict your reconciliation efforts to those differences that have the highest impact for your user. This means that you may not achieve complete reconciliation of all the different views of the same data all at one time. However, as your data warehouse grows with each iteration, more and more different views of the same data will be addressed and resolved.

If your organization is committed to achieving the highest level of maturity in terms of data management, your Data Administration unit is most likely chartered with the task of reconciling the remaining different views of the same data. However, this activity is outside the scope of a data warehouse project. As project manager your involvement in this activity ends with your communication to Data Administration about the following information:

- All the different views of the same data you have discovered
- The views you are planning to reconcile in your project
- The views you are not addressing in your project

2.4.2 Provide a Consolidated Picture of Enterprise Data

One of your project deliverables will be a logical data model of the data within the scope of your project, as described in Chapter 9, "Methodology." As you add new data and new requirements to the data warehouse in future iterations, you will expand the logical data model. Over time, this model will grow into a consolidated picture of enterprise data within the scope of the data warehouse.

An organization trying to achieve the highest level of maturity in terms of data management will have chartered the Data Administration unit with the task of completing that picture. We have to remember that even a fully completed and populated data warehouse will not have all of the operational data used by the organization. To complete the picture, Data Administration will create or obtain the logical data models from all other systems and merge them into a high-level enterprise model. Clearly, this activity is outside the scope of a data warehouse project. As project manager your only involvement is to share your logical data model with Data Administration.

2.4.3 Create a Virtual "One-Stop Shopping" Data Environment

One-stop shopping means that the following features are in place:

- All the data in the data warehouse environment is accessible through one common interface or "point of entry."
- A suite of standard query and reporting tools is available and easy to use.
- The physical location of the data is transparent to the users.
- The data is integrated, clean, and consistent, or at least reconcilable.
- The query results are consistent, or at least reconcilable.

In order to achieve this long-term objective, two types of architectures must be very well designed and redesigned with every data warehouse iteration: the technical architecture and the data architecture.

Technical Architecture

There are many parts to technical architecture, but in this context we will address only three: the application layer, data access tools, and database structure.

Application layer. This is a "store front," a point of entry. It can be a home-grown application written in a conventional programming language with a desktop icon to launch it, or it can be a purchased software package or a Web application. All data warehouse components are "hooked" into it and are launched from it. This type of an application layer could even be expanded to provide user access to systems other than the data warehouse.

Data access tools. The second tier in this architecture is a suite of data access tools. This should include a query library of prewritten queries using these tools or written in native SQL.

Database structure. Also part of the second tier are the actual database files. Their physical placements on one server or another, in one physical location or another, will be completely transparent to the users. All the communication and synchronization between the physical files are handled by the database management system (DBMS) or middleware.

If these three components are designed properly, it will ensure that all the data is accessible through one common interface, that a suite of standard tools is easy to use, and that the physical placement of data is transparent to the users.

Data Architecture

There are two parts to data architecture: the logical data architecture, which is a logical data model, and the physical data architecture, which is composed of the physical data model as well as the actual physical databases, as explained in Chapter 10, "Data Models."

Logical data architecture. Data issues are addressed at the logical level with a logical data model and metadata. The logical data model will help attain data integration and data sharing, and the metadata will help achieve sanctioned definitions and domains.

Physical data architecture. Access and performance issues are addressed at the physical level with the appropriate database designs. Since one logical data model can, and often will, be implemented as two or three differently designed databases, it is important to capture the mapping between the logical and physical data architectures as metadata.

If these two data architectures are well designed, it will ensure that all the data is integrated, clean, and consistent and that all query results are consistent, or at least reconcilable.

2.5 SUMMARY

Our traditional decision support systems are application-centric, which means they were built to support specific needs of small business units and not the entire organization as a whole. There are many inherent deficiencies with our traditional DSS environment, such as data that is not understood, inconsistent reports, data redundancy, and process redundancy. These data management problems are often responsible for IT's inability to provide business executives with complete and reliable business information about their organization. One of the goals of data warehousing is to address these data management issues.

Data warehouse objectives can be grouped into short-term objectives and long-term objectives. Examples of short-term objectives are improving data quality, minimizing inconsistent reports, providing access to metadata, enabling data sharing, integrating data from multiple sources, and providing historical data. Examples of long-term objectives are reconciling different views of data, providing a consolidated picture of enterprise data, creating a virtual one-stop shopping data environment. All data warehouse objectives must match and support the strategic company goals.

A CAUTIONARY TALE

"Suck and Plunk" All Your Operational Data into One Database

The CEO read an article in an airline magazine about a data warehouse in his industry, and he thought it would be a cool idea if he had one, too. He told the CIO to give him a data warehouse. The users had trouble articulating their information needs, and the project manager didn't want to be caught not having some data the users might want. So the project manager decided to "suck" all of the operational data, even remotely related data, and "plunk" it into the data warehouse (disk is cheap, right?). Unfortunately, because there was so much data to deal with, there wasn't enough time or resource to understand and document the data fully, and practically no time to clean it up. The end result was a very large data warehouse that was misunderstood, dirty, inefficient, and practically useless to the business. The CEO got a data warehouse but not one that would ever be written about—except as a case study of how *not* to do it.

2.6 WORKSHOP

In this workshop you will list the deficiencies of your current DSS environment. You will also itemize your data warehouse short-term and long-term objectives. And finally you will match the data warehouse objectives to the strategic goals and objectives of your organization.

2.6.1 Traditional DSS Deficiencies

List all the deficiencies in your current DSS environment that have led to the decision to transition to a data warehouse environment. Refer to Section 2.1 for examples of traditional DSS deficiencies.

For example:

1. Product Services and Corporate Finance disagree on "Monthly Liability Amount." The algorithms and data elements used for their calculations are not consistent.
2. The "Location Opened Date" and "Location Closed Date" are unedited fields. In many records these dates appear to be switched.
3. Only one business unit has access to the product category hierarchy.

Now list your own.

1. _____
2. _____
3. _____
4. _____

2.6.2 Data Warehouse Short-term Objectives

List all the short-term objectives you are hoping to accomplish with your data warehouse project. Be sure you include the following:

- The degree of deficiency—how severe and widespread the problem is
- The dollars lost due to the deficiency
- The cost for correcting the deficiency

Calculate the cost by multiplying the time by the fully burdened rate for the individuals who would be performing the tasks. You may also consider the cost that continues to be incurred for not solving other business needs that these individuals would be working on if they weren't involved in the tasks to correct the deficiency.

- The degree of "cleanliness" you want to achieve

Refer to Section 2.3 for examples of short-term objectives.

For example:

	Short-term Objective	Degree of Deficiency	Dollars Lost Due to Deficiency	Cost for Correcting	Degree of Cleanliness
1.	Minimize inconsistent report totals for "Monthly Liability Amount."	100 percent	$200,000 per month	$150,000	99 percent desired 95 percent required
2.	Give access to product category hierarchy to three more business units.	90 percent of users have no access now.	$400,000 annually	$300,000	50 percent of users will have access.

Now list your own.

	Short-term Objective	Degree of Deficiency	Dollars Lost Due to Deficiency	Cost for Correcting	Degree of Cleanliness
1.					
2.					
3.					
4.					

2.6.3   Data Warehouse Long-term Objectives

List all the long-term objectives for the data warehouse environment at your organization. Indicate how your project addresses each of these objectives, and document what your project will not address. If you are delegating any portion of attaining a long-term goal, specify which person or department you delegate it to. Refer to Section 2.4 for examples of long-term objectives.

For example:

Long-term Objective	Percent Addressed with Project	Percent Not Addressed	Delegated to Person/ Department
1. Reconcile different views of Product Category rollup.	Hardware products only, approximately 40 percent of all products.	60 percent of products not addressed.	Product Services
2. Create One-Stop Shopping environment.	80 percent with this DW project.	20 percent of effort is Web application.	Web Development Unit

Now list your own.

Long-term Objective	Percent Addressed with Project	Percent Not Addressed	Delegated to Person/ Department
1.			
2.			
3.			
4.			

2.6.4   Matching the Company Strategic Goals

Finally, you must identify how the data warehouse objectives will match the strategic goals of the organization. In the following matrix, list the Company Strategic Goals next to the data warehouse objectives.

For example:

DW Objective	Short-term / Long-term	Company Strategic Goal
1. Give access to product category hierarchy to three more business units.	Short-term	Increase staff efficiency and reduce duplication of effort.
2. Access for all business units.	Long-term	Increase staff efficiency across the entire organization.

Now match your own.

DW Objective	Short-term / Long-term	Company Strategic Goal
1.		
2.		
3.		
4.		

REFERENCES

Inman, W. H., Claudia Imhoff, and Ryan Sousa. *Corporate Information Factory.* New York, N.Y.: John Wiley & Sons, 1998.

English, Larry P. *Improving Data Warehouse and Business Information Quality,* New York, N.Y.: John Wiley & Sons, 1999.

Hackney, Douglas. *Understanding and Implementing Successful Data Marts.* Reading, Mass.: Addison-Wesley, 1997.

CHAPTER THREE

Indicators of Success

Success is a science; if you have the conditions, you get the result.

—Oscar Wilde

This chapter consists of three main sections:

- Section 3.1, "Measures of Success," describes the determinants by which a project has succeeded or failed.
- Section 3.2, "Critical Success Factors," lists the factors or characteristics of the project and the infrastructure that are necessary for the project to be successful.
- Section 3.3, "Measuring Results," deals with how to measure the product and the results of the project: activity, performance, and customer satisfaction.

You probably want to know if your project will be a success. The Workshop at the end of this chapter will give you that chance. You will be asked to identify what constitutes success and failure for your project. You will identify your critical success factors and then be asked to score your organization's and your project's compliance to those factors. Finally, you will indicate how you intend to measure your project's success.

3.1 MEASURES OF SUCCESS

There has been much heated discussion over the failure rate of data ware-houses. Luminaries disagree on the percentage of those that have suc-ceeded. The problem may be with the definition of success and failure. In fact, very few organizations have identified up front what for them will be success or failure. That being the case, any industry-wide numbers on failure are meaningless.

Compared to industry-published failures, we may not be sure if our data warehouse is a success, but we will always know when we have failed. We have all seen projects that are grossly over budget and years behind schedule, delivering a fraction of the promised function. The following are some other indications of failure:

1. Funding has dried up.
2. Users are unhappy with the quality of the data and with their query tools.
3. Only a small percentage of users takes advantage of the data ware-house.
4. Performance is poor.
5. There is no ability to expand data warehouse data that is not inte-grated.
6. Extract/transform/load (ETL) steps do not fit in the batch window.

For a more complete discussion of failures, see Chapter 4, "Risks."

For various reasons, some of these projects have been declared a suc-cess accompanied with promotions, industry and publication awards, and bonuses for all involved. The problem is that we have no accepted definition for *success*.

List your measures of success, and have that list approved by both IT and the business sponsor so that everyone is working toward the same set of goals and you are legitimately able to declare victory. There are a num-ber of examples of success indicators. Let's take a look at some measures of success.

3.1.1 Return on Investment (ROI)

ROI (Kaplan and Norton 1996) is the amount of return from an investment. In this case the investment is the money spent on implementing the data warehouse. See Chapter 6, "Cost Benefit." ROI can be increased in a number of ways:.

- *Lower cost*

  Costs could be lowered through better inventory management, fewer dollars spent on unproductive activities, product promotions, and so on.

- *Improved productivity*

  Greater productivity could be expected from both IT and the user. Today user analysts may spend up to 90 percent of their time gathering data and only 10 percent analyzing the data. A successful data warehouse should reverse those numbers. IT will still be responsible for developing complex reports as well as writing reports for production systems. The data warehouse can provide reporting tools with a well-documented, clean, and easily accessible database. This capability should significantly improve IT productivity.

- *Increased revenue*

  This could be as a result of greater market share and increased sales, as marketing is able to target customers more effectively and to provide the right products at the right time to the right market.

The effects of costs and revenues may be difficult to assign to the impact of the data warehouse. As the data warehouse is being implemented, the organization is not standing still. There are both internal and external factors that impact both costs and revenues, and therefore the actual benefits of the data warehouse may be difficult to isolate.

3.1.2 The Data Warehouse Is Used

One of the easiest categories to understand can be measured by the number of users and the total number of queries and reports generated. If queries and reports are run regularly, it's a good indication that the users are achieving some benefit. There have been a number of data warehouse implementations where the users have disliked the interface, have found the system difficult to use, or have preferred their old way of doing things. In some cases, IT built the warehouse with little input from the users. These implementations usually resulted in an abandoned and unused warehouse.

3.1.3   The Data Warehouse Is Useful

The data warehouse may be used, but the users may find the benefits to be marginal and illusive. It's important to ask the users what they see as the benefits of the data warehouse, how it has changed the way they do business, how it may have improved their productivity, and how it may have improved the quality of their decisions. Some users easily articulate the usefulness of the data warehouse, whereas others either have great difficulty or are reluctant to identify specific benefits other than the time saved in producing a report or an answer to an important question.

3.1.4   Project Is Delivered on Time

This measure is problematic, as schedules are often set without an understanding of what is involved and how long each project task will take. "On time" is relevant only if a realistic schedule is the basis for comparison. "On time" must take agreed-upon changes into account. A detailed project plan with reasonable time estimates and dependencies is a requisite for a realistic schedule. Anticipate small delays; they should not eliminate a project from being considered a success.

3.1.5   Project Is Delivered within Budget

This criterion may be difficult to achieve, since the total costs of a data warehouse are difficult to determine. You must consider all of the following factors to avoid severely underestimating the budget:

1. How many users to expect, how many queries and reports they will generate, and the complexity and resources used by the queries and reports.
2. How large the data warehouse will be or how many indexes and summary tables will be required and desired.
3. The potential need for a larger CPU.
4. The possibility that the software is more difficult than the vendors represented and that teams of software consultants will be required.
5. The need to upgrade your network to support the increased line traffic.
6. The need to raise the salaries of the data warehouse team or the increased cost of recruiting the talent required to make the project a success. "Within budget" is relevant only if a realistic budget is the basis for comparison.

3.1.6 Improved User Satisfaction

Users may be internal, external, or both. In all cases, the goal is to have users who are happy with the features and capabilities, the performance, the quality of data, and the level of support. User satisfaction should closely map to how well the project agreement is fulfilled. See Chapter 12, "Project Planning," in its discussion of the project agreement.

3.1.7 Additional Requests for Data Warehouse Functions and Data

You'll know you were successful if other user departments are beating down your door with requests for access to the data warehouse. This means that the reputation of the data warehouse and what it can do is circulating through your halls and around your water coolers. If current users are requesting new data and functions to be added to the existing data warehouse, it means they are actively engaged in running queries and discovering new opportunities for making better decisions.

3.1.8 Business Performance-based Benchmarks

This is the most subjective of all the measures and will become the most controversial. Most industries have sets of industry averages as well as benchmark (the best) companies against which they make comparisons. For example, the industry average for building a car may be ten worker days. With better information, a car manufacturer in the middle of the pack may have a goal to manufacture a midsize sedan, using eight worker days. The data warehouse may be able to provide improved, more complete, and timelier information, and with this information the auto manufacturer may be able to achieve its productivity goals.

How many shipments per day?

3.1.9 Goals and Objectives Are Met

In Chapter 2, "Goals and Objectives," we discussed goals and objectives of the data warehouse, and in the Workshop you developed goals and objectives for your organization. Success will be defined by how well these goals and objectives were met. No doubt, not all were met or were only partially met. A scorecard will give you an initial and then an ongoing measure of your project's success. Use Section 3.5.3 in the Workshop to score your results.

3.1.10 Business Problems Are Solved

The data warehouse was developed for some specific reason. Perhaps marketing was unable to identify customer demographics for target marketing, and you wasted postage, printing, and trees with a blanket mailing to all your customers for an offering that would be of interest to only a small subset. Home improvement loans are of little interest to apartment dwellers. If the data warehouse now provides this targeted marketing capability, it should be considered a success.

3.1.11 Business Opportunity Is Realized

Most organizations have identified specific business opportunities that have not been implemented due to lack of resources but more often to lack of information. The identified opportunity might have been the ability to provide information to suppliers through the Web so they would be able to respond more quickly to your demands for components you need for your manufacturing process. If the supplier now has fewer stock-outs, the project is successful.

3.1.12 The Data Warehouse Has Become an Agent of Change

The world is changing, and the rate of change is accelerating dramatically. Successful organizations must be able to respond and respond quickly. Faster decisions must be made, but this can happen only with better and timelier information. There can be some fundamental changes to the business in the manner and speed in which decisions are made, and the data warehouse can be the vehicle for that change. As an example, some drug companies are analyzing the data in their data warehouse to screen out and eliminate a large number of expensive and invasive animal tests. These companies are speeding up the process, reducing costs, and minimizing the number of animals involved in the testing.

3.2 CRITICAL SUCCESS FACTORS

If a factor or characteristic is critical to the success of a project, we call it a critical success factor (CSF). The absence of that factor or characteristic dooms the project. CSFs provide a measure for the completion and quality of the project. By knowing and understanding what is very important, the project manager can make a case for adequate budget, resources, schedule improvement, and management commitment. The next sections discuss the CSFs that are mandatory for a successful data warehouse project.

3.2.1 Expectations Communicated to the Users

IT is often unwilling or afraid to tell the users what they will be getting and when.

- *Performance.* Users must know that not all of their queries will have subsecond response time. A query joining two tables of ten million rows each will take minutes, or even hours, and the users should expect such.
- *Availability.* Expectations of availability include the time and days (for example, 6 A.M. to 11 P.M., Monday through Saturday) the system is scheduled to be accessible, as well as the percentage of time planned for availability (for example, 97 percent availability during scheduled hours). A service level agreement (SLA) will normally document an availability agreement.
- *Function.* Function includes what data will be accessible and what predefined queries and reports are available. It also means the level of detail data, as well as how the data is integrated and aggregated.
- *Historical data.* For trend analysis, users need data from previous periods. Users need to know, for example, that monthly data will be kept for just two years.
- *Level of difficulty.* The expectation of simplicity is the ease of use. Users do not want a complex system.
- *Accuracy.* The expectations of accuracy are for both the cleanliness of the data as well as an understanding of what the data means.
- *Timeliness.* Timeliness is both when the data will be available (such as three days after the end of the month), as well as how frequently the data will be refreshed (daily, weekly, monthly).
- *Schedule.* Schedule expectations involve when the system is due for delivery. Since not all the users will be getting access on the first implementation, each user needs to know when he or she will get a turn.
- *Support.* The expectation for support comes into play as the users have problems. Where will they go for help, how knowledgeable will the support be for the query tools, and how well will they understand the data?

All these expectations should be documented in the project agreement discussed in Chapter 9, "Methodology." Besides the project agreement document, every opportunity must be seized to clarify expectations for the users, especially when a casual comment may create a misunderstanding of what they can expect.

3.2.2 Ensured User Involvement

There are three levels of user involvement:

1. "Build it; they will use it."
2. Solicit requirements from the users.
3. Have the users involved all the way through the project.

   This means that the users would participate not just in the requirements and testing phases but in all phases in between. (The ideal arrangement is to have a project co-managed by a project manager from IT and one from the business.)

Number 3 is by far the most successful approach, whereas number 1 almost always results in failure. A commitment by the users to the project is critical to the project's success, and the users' involvement is an excellent indicator of that commitment.

3.2.3 The Project Has a Good Sponsor

The best sponsor is from the business side, not from IT. The sponsor should be well connected, willing to provide an ample budget, and capable of getting other resources needed for the project. The sponsor should be accepting of problems as they occur and not use those problems as an excuse to either kill the project or withdraw support. Most important, the sponsor should be in serious need of the data warehouse's capabilities to solve a specific problem or gain some advantage for his department.

3.2.4 The Team Has the Right Skill Set

Without the right skills dedicated to the team, the project will fail. The emphasis is on "dedicated to the team." It does little good to have skills somewhere in the organization if they are unavailable to the project. The critical roles should be reporting directly to the project manager. Matrix management does not allow the project manager to control these resources. Without this control, there are no guarantees that the people will be available when needed. See Chapter 8, "Organization and Cultural Issues," for a description of the skills necessary for a data warehouse project, a more complete discussion of the roles, and a recommended reporting structure.

3.2.5 The Schedule Is Realistic

The most common cause of failure is an unrealistic schedule, usually imposed without the input or the concurrence of the project manager or the team members. Most often, the imposed schedules have no rationale for specific dates but are only means to "hold the project manager to a schedule." Those imposing the schedule usually have little concept of the tasks and effort required. Chapter 9, "Methodology," describes those tasks in detail, and Chapter 12, "Project Planning," will provide the project manager with the data needed to negotiate a reasonable schedule.

3.2.6 The Project Has Proper Control Procedures (Change Control)

Project managers are familiar with change control and know how to document and evaluate prospective changes. There will always be changes in the scope of a data warehouse project, but the scope must be controlled, and change control must be implemented just as it is in transactional systems.

3.2.7 The Right Tools Have Been Chosen

The first decisions to be made are the categories of tools (extract/transform/load, data cleansing, OLAP, ROLAP, data modeling, administration, etc.). See Appendix 7.E for a list of the tool categories. Many of these tools are expensive, not just for their initial and maintenance costs but in training contractors, consultants, and the internal people required to implement and support the tool. The tools must match the requirements of the organization, the users, and the project. The tools should work together without the need to build interfaces or write special code. See Chapter 7, "Selecting Software."

3.2.8 Common Data Definitions

Every department has its own set of definitions for business terms, which are often defined differently by each department. The definitions in most organizations make the Tower of Babel look communicative. To make matters worse, these departmental definitions are rarely documented. Department heads assume that everyone shares their understanding of the business and their definitions of the major business terms. Not wanting to appear ignorant, most employees do not question the meaning of business terms. While it is not possible to gain definitional concurrence among departments, each project must have a glossary of the business terms used in the project.

3.2.9 Well-defined Transformation Rules

As the data is brought over from the source systems to the data warehouse, much of the data will be transformed in one way or another. The data may be specifically selected, recoded, summarized, integrated with other data, or changed in some other way. The rules for the transformations are critical to the users getting what they expect and need.

3.2.10 Properly Trained Users

In spite of what the vendors tell you, users must be trained, and the training should be geared to the level of user and the way each user plans to use the data warehouse. In addition to the tool, users should learn about the availability of predefined queries and reports. Users must learn about the data, and the power users should have more in-depth training on the data structures. Just-in-time training will solidify and reinforce the skills learned in class as the students immediately begin using the data warehouse at the conclusion of the class. Some organizations include tests to determine if the students should graduate from the training program. No one likes to take tests, but just knowing the test is a prerequisite for graduation and for using the system should command more attention from the students. A test is also a good way for the trainers to know if they are being effective.

3.3 MEASURING RESULTS

Monitoring and measuring the project are the only ways to know if you have been successful. The measurements are both subjective and objective. Just like certain medical tests, some of these measures are invasive and may have negative consequences, such as an impact on performance or the stability of the system. Some measures are costly; they require knowledgeable people and machine resources to carry them out. The clever project manager will select the appropriate metrics by evaluating both cost and impact. The next sections discuss metrics that should be considered.

3.3.1 Functional Quality

Do the capabilities of the data warehouse satisfy the user requirements? Does the data warehouse provide the information necessary for the user to do his job?

3.3.2 Data Quality

If the data warehouse data is of poor quality, the users will reject it. There are three means of measuring quality:

1. Ask the users if their reports are accurate—they may not know.
2. Use a software tool to provide a scorecard on the quality of the data.
3. Ask users always to run "reasonableness checks" on their results.

Be aware that the software tools cannot evaluate all types of data quality. See Chapter 11, "Data Quality."

3.3.3 Computer Performance

There are four indicators of computer performance that you should consider:

1. Query response time
2. Report response time
3. Time to load/update/refresh the data warehouse
4. Machine resource

Some organizations have established benchmark performance numbers for known queries and reports, and they exercise and measure these benchmarks periodically, looking for impending performance problems. There are a number of tools that measure performance. Most of the database management systems have imbedded capabilities to measure database performance. Third-party utilities supplement this capability. A number of the query and report tools have response time metrics.

3.3.4   Network Performance

The ability of the network to handle the data traffic will directly impact response time. Network software measures both line load and line traffic and indicates conditions where an activity was waiting for line availability. Besides the software, network administrators must be available to analyze the results and take appropriate action.

3.3.5   User Satisfaction

Users should be polled shortly after they receive the data warehouse capability and then polled periodically to identify changes in their level of satisfaction and to detect trends. Appendix 5.F is a sample user satisfaction questionnaire and can be easily tailored to your organization.

3.3.6   Number of Queries

Many of the query tools provide metrics on the number of queries executed by department and by individual. Management will want this measure—even if they don't ask for it.

3.3.7   What Data Is Accessed

Many organizations have data that is never accessed. This is the result of inaccurate or incomplete requirements gathering or users changing their minds. Sometimes IT loads all of the source data, fearing the user will ask for something not anticipated in the requirements-gathering phase. IT has been beaten up often by the users who "want all the data, want to keep it forever, and want the system delivered yesterday." See Chapter 5, "Satisfying the User," on how to deal with such problems. There are tools that will identify what data is actually being accessed and how often.

3.3.8   Project Agreement Satisfaction

The Project Agreement discussed in Chapter 9, "Methodology," documents what functions the users will be getting and when. It is appropriate to review the Project Agreement document and determine which functions might not have been satisfied and why.

3.3.9   Benefits Achieved

Before the project began, you estimated the benefits, both tangible and intangible, for your project. They included your ability to create new reports faster, as well as the improved productivity of creating those reports. See Chapter 6, "Cost Benefit," for more discussion of benefits. Now you need to measure the tangible benefits and make some approximations for the intangibles. Since the benefits will not materialize the first day the system is installed, measurement should wait at least two months after implementation.

3.3.10 Balanced Scorecard

A balanced scorecard measures success by a number of factors that go beyond the traditional measure of profit. It includes the financial measures of return on investment, profitability, revenue growth, and cost reduction. The scorecard has the customer metrics of acquisition, retention, and satisfaction. It has internal measures of employee satisfaction, retention, and productivity. It also has measures of innovation and learning, such as information systems, employee capabilities, motivation, and empowerment. The data warehouse, besides providing access to data to help improve the financial results, can support the decision-making process to serve customers and employees better. The data warehouse can be the primary vehicle to store and disseminate information and provide internal measures that support the balanced scorecard.

3.4 SUMMARY

In any project, but particularly with a data warehouse, you have to know where you are going and what constitutes success. Some project managers display those measures of success for all to see and to help the project manager remain focused. It is especially important to know the Critical Success Factors, the ingredients that you must have in place for the project to succeed. By understanding what needs to be in place, the project manager can legitimately request resources. The value of the project must always be demonstrated to management, so you must be able to measure success by showing the benefits and results.

A CAUTIONARY TALE

New Team Taking Over the Project—The "New Broom" Philosophy

The sponsor lost faith in the team. The original team was eventually replaced; a new team was brought in and, of course, redid everything. The source data in its existing form would not support the data warehouse. The project was saddled with making major corrections to the source operational data that added an unanticipated burden to the work and the schedule. The new project manager wanted to establish his territory and so discounted much of the good work that had already been done. He questioned the choice of tools and the choice of an architecture. Management was still expecting the project to be delivered on time. This "new broom" philosophy meant the project was further delayed, and most of the original budget was wasted.

3.5 **WORKSHOP**

In this workshop you will develop your measures of success, identify your CSFs, and determine how you will go about measuring success, including mapping to your original goals and objectives.

3.5.1 Measures of Success

List all the measures by which your project will be judged. Some measures are more easily collected than others, whereas other measures will be far too costly or even impossible to collect. The difficult and impossible measures deserve inclusion but should be flagged with a note that the measure will not have an objective metric. The list is always created in partnership with those who will provide the accolades or the tomatoes. Refer to Section 3.1 for examples of measures of success.

For example:

1. The data warehouse is delivered by July 1, 2001.
2. The total budget does not exceed $5,000,000.
3. The data warehouse is used by 75 percent of marketing analysts.

Now list your own.

1. _____
2. _____
3. _____
4. _____
5. _____

3.5.2 Critical Success Factors

List all the factors or characteristics that must be in place for your project to be a success.

Refer to Section 3.2 for examples of critical success factors.

For example:

1. Users will be available as needed.
2. Ron Robinson will be the sponsor.
3. All users will be trained on the tool prior to their having access.

Now list your own.

1. _____
2. _____
3. _____
4. _____
5. _____

Identify those factors that are outside of your control along with who is the controlling party.

For example:

1. Availability of users depends on the completion of their current marketing campaign. Responsibility for releasing them is with Ron Robinson.
2. Training depends on scheduling by Betty Rising.

Now list your own.

1. _____
2. _____
3. _____
4. _____
5. _____

Specify the steps you plan to take to assure the controlling party's cooperation.

For example:

1. Will follow up with Ron Robinson on a weekly basis.
2. Schedule a meeting with Betty Rising for next week to discuss training schedule.

Now list your own.

1. _____
2. _____
3. _____
4. _____
5. _____

3.5.3 Measuring Success

Identify the tasks and the tools you plan to use to measure your project's success.

Include costs and resources required, and indicate if those resources are part of your group or if you will have to beg for money and resources.

For example:

Tasks

1. Send out user satisfaction surveys.
2. Create procedures for monitoring data quality on an ongoing basis.

Tools

1. Data cleansing/assessment tool

Now list your own.

Tasks

1. _____
2. _____
3. _____
4. _____

Tools

1. _____

2. _____

3. _____

4. _____

Finally, take the goals and objectives identified in Chapter 2, "Goals and Objectives." Score how well these goals and objectives were achieved.

For example:

Goal	**Achievement**
1. Provide the data warehouse to 12 users in the accounting department.	Thirteen users in the accounting department now have data warehouse access.
2. Minimize inconsistent reports.	Inconsistent reports somewhat minimized (no quantitative numbers available).
3. Respond to 90 percent of the requests for new reports within five working days.	Ninety-two percent of requests for new reports were delivered within five working days.

Now list your own.

Goal	**Achievement**
1.	
2.	
3.	

Take the benefits you project in Chapter 6, "Cost Benefit," and score how well these benefits were realized.

For example:

Benefit Projected	**Achieved**
1. Improve the productivity of the accounting department by 20 percent. Savings projected: $200,000	Productivity was improved by 14 percent. Estimated savings: $140,000
2. Reduce the requests to IT for ad hoc reports by 40 percent. Savings projected: $400,000	Requests were reduced by 50 percent Estimated savings: $500,000
3. Reduce mailings by targeting market segments. Savings projected: $200,000	Savings achieved: $230,000 the first year

Now list your own.

Benefit	**Achieved**
1.	
2.	
3.	

REFERENCES

Kaplan, Robert S., and David P. Norton. *The Balanced Scorecard.* Cambridge, Mass.: Harvard Business School Press, 1996.

CHAPTER FOUR

Risks

My God, Thiokol, when do you want me to launch, next April?
—Lawrence Mulloy, NASA, January 27, 1986

They couldn't hit an elephant at this dis. . . .
—General John B. Sedgwick, the general's last words at the
Battle of Spotsylvania, 1864

This chapter provides you with the ability to identify the potential risks within your project and to address those risks before they become major problems. Risk is inherent in any project, but the risks involved in a data warehouse project seem to be greater than most others, and there are different types of risks. This chapter presents the following:

- The types of failures that have been experienced by various data warehouse projects
- The inherent risks, with all their attendant horrors, and techniques for dealing with each of them
- The risk associated with the types of people you will want to exclude from your team
- A Workshop where you can identify the risks that may be lurking in your own project

4.1   TYPES OF FAILURES

There is disagreement over the failure rate of data warehouse projects. Rather than contribute to the debate, we will detail the types of situations that could be characterized as failures and leave it to the reader to decide if they truly constitute failure.

4.1.1   The Project Is Over Budget

Depending on how much the actual expenditures exceeded the budget, the project may be considered a failure. The cause may have been an overly optimistic budget or the inexperience of those calculating the estimate. The inadequate budget might be the result of not wanting to tell management the bitter truth about the costs of a data warehouse.

Unanticipated and expensive consulting help may have been needed. Performance or capacity problems, more users, more queries, or more complex queries may have required more hardware or extra effort to resolve the problems. The project scope may have been extended without a change in the budget. Extenuating circumstances, such as delays caused by hardware problems, software problems, user unavailability, change in the business, or other factors, may have resulted in additional expenses.

4.1.2   Slipped Schedule

Most of the factors listed in the preceding section could also have contributed to the schedule not being met, but the major reason for a slipped schedule is the inexperience or optimism of those creating the project plan. In many cases it is management's eagerness to "put a stake in the ground" by choosing an arbitrary date for delivery in the hopes of giving project managers something to shoot for. The schedule becomes a deadline without any real reason for a fixed delivery date. In those cases the schedule is usually established without input from those who know how long it actually takes to perform the data warehouse tasks. The deadline is usually set without the benefit of a project plan. Without a project plan that details the tasks, dependencies, and resources, it is impossible to develop a realistic date by which the project should be completed. Chapter 12, "Project Planning," describes the process of creating a realistic schedule.

4.1.3 Functions and Capabilities Not Implemented

The project agreement specified certain functions and capabilities. These would have included what data to deliver, the quality of the data, the training given to the users, the number of users, the method of delivery (such as Web-based), service level agreements (performance and availability), predefined queries, and so forth. If important functions and capabilities were not realized or were postponed to subsequent implementation phases, these would be indications of failure.

4.1.4 Unhappy Users

If the users are unhappy, the project should be considered a failure. Unhappiness is often the result of unrealistic expectations. Users were expecting far more than they got. They may have been promised too much, or there may have been a breakdown in communication between IT and the user. IT may not have known enough to correct the users' false expectations or may have just been afraid to tell them the truth. We often observe situations where the user says, "Jump!" and IT is told to say, "How high?" Also, the users may have believed the vendors' promises for grand capabilities and grossly optimistic schedules.

Furthermore, users may be unhappy about the cleanliness of their data, response time, availability, usability of the system, anticipated function and capability, or the quality and availability of support and training.

4.1.5 Unacceptable Performance

Unacceptable performance has often been the reason that data warehouse projects are cancelled. Data warehouse performance should be explored for both the query response time and the extract/transform/load time.

Any characterization of good query response time is relative to what is realistic and acceptable to the user. If the user was expecting subsecond response time for queries that join two multimillion-row tables, the expectation would cause the user to say that performance was unacceptable. In this example, good performance should have been measured in minutes, not in fractions of a second. The user needs to understand what to expect. Even though the data warehouse may require executing millions of instructions and may require accessing millions of rows of data, there are limits to what the user should be expected to tolerate. We have seen queries where response time is measured in days. Except for a few exceptions, this is clearly unacceptable.

As data warehouses get larger, the extract/transform/load (ETL) process will take longer, sometimes as long as days. This will impact the availability of the data warehouse to the users. Database design, architecture, hardware configuration, database tuning, and the ETL code—whether an ETL product or hand-written code—will significantly impact ETL performance. As the ETL process time increases, all of the factors have to be evaluated and adjusted. In some cases the service level agreement for availability will also have to be adjusted. Without such adjustments, the ETL processes may not complete on time, and the project would be considered a failure.

4.1.6 Poor Availability

Availability is both scheduled availability (the days per week and the number of hours per day) as well as the percentage of time the system is accessible during scheduled hours. Availability failure is usually the result of the data warehouse being treated as a second-class system. Operational systems usually demand availability service level agreements. The performance evaluations and bonus plans of those IT members who work in operations and in systems often depend on reaching high availability percentages. If the same standards are not applied to the data warehouse, problems will go unnoticed, and response to problems will be casual, untimely, and ineffective.

4.1.7 Inability to Expand

If a robust architecture and design is not part of the data warehouse implementation, any significant increase in the number of users or increase in the number of queries or complexity of queries may exceed the capabilities of the system. If the data warehouse is successful, there will also be a demand for more data, for more detailed data, and, perhaps, a demand for more historical data to perform extended trend analysis—for example, five years of monthly data.

4.1.8 Poor Quality Data/Reports

If the data is not clean and accurate, the queries and reports will be wrong, In which case users will either make the wrong decisions or, if they recognize that the data is wrong, mistrust the reports and not act on them. Users may spend significant time validating the report figures, which in turn will impact their productivity. This impact on productivity puts the value of the data warehouse in question.

4.1.9 Too Complicated for Users

Some tools are too difficult for the target audience. Just because IT is comfortable with a tool and its interfaces, it does not follow that all the users will be as enthusiastic. If the tool is too complicated, the users will find ways to avoid it, including asking other people in their department or IT to run a report for them. This nullifies one of the primary benefits of a data warehouse, to empower the users to develop their own queries and reports.

4.1.10 Project Not Cost Justified

Every organization should cost-justify its data warehouse projects. Justification includes an evaluation of both the costs and the benefits as described in Chapter 6, "Cost Benefit." When the benefits were actually measured after implementation, they may have turned out to be much lower than expected or later than anticipated. The actual costs may have been much higher than the estimated costs. In fact, the costs may have exceeded both the tangible and intangible benefits.

4.1.11 Management Does Not Recognize the Benefits

In many cases, organizations do not measure the benefits of the data warehouse nor properly report those benefits to management. Project managers, and IT as a whole, are often shy in boasting about their accomplishments. Sometimes they may not know how to report on their progress or on the impact the data warehouse is having on the organization. The project managers may believe that everyone in the organization will automatically know how wonderfully IT performed and that everyone will recognize the data warehouse for the success that it is. They are wrong. In most cases, if management is not properly briefed on the data warehouse, they will not recognize its benefits and will be reluctant to continue funding something they do not appreciate.

4.2   TYPES OF RISK

All projects have risks, and many of the ones discussed here are relevant
to operational systems as well as to the data warehouse. Nonetheless, they
must be addressed because you are likely to encounter these problems in
one way or another.

4.2.1   No Mission or Objectives

Neither the mission nor the objectives for the data warehouse have been
defined. This is a boat without a rudder. It is not clear where the data
warehouse is going or what business problem it is supposed to solve. Cli-
ches may be used, but they may have no real meaning to either management or the team. An example is "Empower the user." To avoid this
situation, we suggest the following remedies:

Identify the data warehouse sponsor. The sponsor—usually on the business side—is someone who has a strong stake in the success of the data
warehouse. It may be a department head that desperately needs the information the data warehouse will provide. Occasionally it is an IT executive
who, aligned with an important business requirement, has a career stake
in the success of the data warehouse.

Define the mission and objectives first. Insist—or strongly recommend—that the mission and objectives be defined prior to any serious
activity on the project. This is an issue of what comes first. Management
may want you to get started, and perhaps, they see defining the mission
and objectives as an activity that is not contributing to moving the
project along. Now is the time to bring out the examples of those projects
that failed or got delayed because their direction was not clear.

Develop a sample set. The fastest way to build and get approval for a
set of missions and objectives is to develop a sample set of missions and
present this set to the IT Advisory Board and the Business Advisory
Board and ask for their approval. Expect discussion, disagreement, and
changes to this set.

Convene a committee. Bring together a small group of people who
have a strong interest in the data warehouse and where it is going. This
will take a little longer than the previous approach but should result in
more support from the troops. The list of missions and objectives would

still need the approval of the IT and Business Advisory Boards. Chapter 8, "Organization and Cultural Issues," discusses the responsibilities of the advisory boards. Carefully select the members of the committee and avoid the "poison people" described in Section 4.3. There will be some important influencers and decision makers who will not have time for the committee, but be sure at least to copy them on drafts and to solicit their input.

4.2.2 Data Warehouse Mission and Objectives Do Not Map to Those of the Enterprise

Document explicit enterprise objectives. These objectives can be found in the chairman of the board's letter to the shareholders. It can also be found in the organization's mission statement, vision statement, and documents outlining the strategic direction. Here are some examples:

- Outstanding customer service
- Superior quality products
- Low-cost provider
- Fastest delivery to the market

Document implicit enterprise objectives. If there are no explicit enterprise objectives, there probably are implicit or assumed objectives to which most people in the enterprise subscribe. These should be documented and mapped to the data warehouse objectives.

What if the data warehouse does not support the enterprise objectives? If enterprise objectives exist but the data warehouse does not support them, rethink what you are trying to accomplish with the data warehouse, and consider data warehouse applications that do support the strategic objectives of the enterprise.

4.2.3 Quality of the Source Data Not Known

In most organizations, the quality of the operational data is either unknown or grossly overestimated. Organizations often do not even know how to assess the quality of their source systems. Chapter 11, "Data Quality," gives detailed examples of source data that need transformation. The effort involved in transforming and cleansing the source data can be significant. Without knowing about the source data quality, it is impossible to estimate the effort and time to cleanse the data.

Data quality analysis tool. Use a quality evaluation tool to determine just how bad things are. Identify operational data with quality problems to someone high in the organization—perhaps the CIO but definitely the business executive who owns the data. Identify the impact of the dirty data on the reliability of decision making, determine the cost for cleansing, determine the benefits for cleansing, prioritize the cleansing effort, and negotiate time, effort, cost, and scope with the user and the owner of the data.

Implement the cleanest first. There are often multiple files and databases that can be used for the source data. Choose the cleanest source. The data warehouse is always implemented in phases, which are discreet deliverables handed over to the users. Different phases will be using different source data. Try to structure the phases so that the first phase is able to use the cleanest source data.

Metadata reflecting quality. Quality indicators can be stored as metadata in the repository. You may choose to assign one of four categories to each data element: "Pristine," "Questionable," "Dirty," and "Not Evaluated."

4.2.4 Skills Are Not in Place

It is rare that the team initially has the right number of people in the right roles with the right skills and that they are available at the right time. To mitigate the risks associated with shortage of skill, we recommend the following:

Define responsibilities. Define the functional responsibilities of data administrators, database administrators, application developers (both back-end ETL developers and front-end delivery developers), user liaisons, and any other required roles, as outlined in Chapter 8, "Organization and Cultural Issues." Define the skill levels required for each of these positions.

Develop a project plan. By defining the resources required and when they are needed in the project plan, you will be able to identify explicitly the need for the right people with the right skills. Without such a plan, the project manager has nothing to support the requests.

Identify candidate resources. List all candidate staff members who are being considered for the data warehouse team, and evaluate their skill levels. If there is a shortage of skills in the organization, consider supplementing the team with contractors and consultants.

Convince management. Management will often ask you to get by with a substandard team—inadequate resources and skills. You have to sell management on the need to have skilled people on the data warehouse team. You also have to convince management of the need to have these people sufficiently dedicated to the project. Management may ask you to use a person who is 100 percent committed to another project. This will not work. This is the time to bring out your notes from your discussions with references on how many experienced and trained people it required to implement their data warehouse as discussed in Chapter 7, "Selecting Software." Based on size and project complexity, you should be able to extrapolate and provide management with a realistic resource requirement.

If you are unable to convince management of the need for resources, hire an expensive consultant (management doesn't listen to low-cost consultants), and ask him to either present or write a resource recommendation.

4.2.5 Inadequate Budget

It is often difficult to know ahead of time how much a data warehouse will cost. Data warehouse budgets are often underestimated.

Research. Compile industry publications, presentations, and consultant reports that indicate what a typical average data warehouse will normally cost. Watch out for those that give figures for selected subsets of the effort, those that do not count software or hardware already in place, or those that do not include costs assigned to some other departments.

Estimate the costs. Itemize each of the costs for your project. Follow the steps outlined in Chapter 6, "Cost Benefit." Don't pad the numbers, but don't underestimate just because you think the true cost will cause management paralysis.

Think smaller. If the costs are too high, consider a smaller project or one that does not require some expensive items (a new RDBMS, fancy tools, or major new hardware).

4.2.6 Lack of Supporting Software

In many cases, supporting software (extract, cleansing, front-end tools, RDBMS, etc.) have not been chosen or installed in time.

Evaluate software benefits. Understand the benefit of the software to the project. If it does not benefit this specific project, justification can be accomplished only if major follow-on projects will significantly benefit from its use. However, if it does not benefit your project, don't waste your time and energy justifying the software.

Cost of not using the software. Quantify the costs of not using the software. These costs should include the additional effort to write code or operational procedures, the ongoing costs to maintain the code, the costs of a delayed implementation, the increased risk, and the potential for reduced quality of the deliverable.

Choose the big hitters. Identify only the software that can make a major contribution. Avoid recommending a piece of software that is fun, leading edge, and a resume enhancer but does not significantly contribute to the project's success.

4.2.7 Source Data Not Understood

Most organizations do not have a documented understanding of the source data. The knowledge is probably in someone's head or is documented on his laptop, but this information is generally unavailable to the rest of the organization.

Inventory and model source data. If source data has been neither inventoried nor modeled, it is probably because users and IT management do not recognize the importance of these activities. Any such recommendations would probably be seen as delaying the project. In truth, the inventory and modeling efforts are long and laborious. If management has not already recognized their benefits, it's unlikely that the data warehouse project will support it either. Standalone systems can get by without this type of analysis and documentation, but integrated systems cannot. Do not try to model the entire organization, but you must analyze and model those data elements that are targeted for the data warehouse as part of your project. Integration cannot occur unless the data relationships are known and can actually be built from the source data.

Reverse engineering. If a CASE tool that has reverse engineering capability (the ability to take database definitions [DDL], capture them in the CASE repository, and generate rough models) is in place, this reverse engineering could be the least costly and most acceptable starting point. Unfortunately, many existing databases are unintelligible, and the reverse engineering process will require significant effort to make the documentation on those databases useful.

4.2.8 Weak Sponsor

For the project to succeed it needs a strong, well-placed user sponsor who makes reasonable decisions.

Solicit the best. Take your time. Make a list of sponsors that match the criteria outlined in Chapter 8, "Organization and Cultural Issues," and put the strongest ones at the top of your list. Research their decision support requirements and determine which problems could be well served by the data warehouse. See Appendix 4.A. Invite the top candidate to lunch, present your research results to that user, and try to sell him on the benefits of a data warehouse. Explain to him what he would be getting, outline what would be needed from him and from his department, and ask for his sponsorship.

Solicit the second best. If the top candidate is not agreeable, invite the second on the list. As you progress down the list and when you are down to "the user from hell," stop and do something else. In fact, it is not productive to go *too* far down the list.

4.2.9 Users Not Computer Literate

There will always be users who, based on their experience and their willingness, will be open to try something new. However, there will be other users who may not be computer literate, or at least not literate with your desktop operating system, and who may be reluctant to use new technology.

Expand user support. If your users are not computer literate, budget more money for user support. You will be getting many more calls, and explaining how to use the system will take longer than it would if you were supporting power users.

Adjust expectations. Computer illiterate users will generate fewer queries. Your projections of the volume of queries may have assumed users who were more comfortable with the system. Allow more time for the expected volume of queries to be achieved. Allow more time for the users to be satisfied with the system and to be able to use the system productively. Readjust your expectations and those of the sponsor.

Training. Slow down the training so as not to frighten the students. Be sure the students are successful in their workshops. Provide mentors in the training process.

Predefined queries and reports. Develop a more comprehensive set of predefined queries and reports, and communicate their availability to the user community. Take the initiative to add predefined queries and reports to the library.

User-friendly front end. Choose an extra-user-friendly front end. Choose "warm and fuzzy" over "power and function." It does not matter about the wonderful features of the tool if the users are afraid to use it. The ideal tool is both easy to learn and easy to use.

4.2.10 Political Problems, Turf War

If the data warehouse is being developed outside of IT, the data warehouse project could be seen as a power grab by a user department or as a way to keep IT out of the data warehouse process. If the data warehouse is being developed within IT, the project could be seen as a power grab by the data warehouse team.

Involve all of IT. Involve all of IT in the project. You will need them. The involvement must extend to the CIO so that IT and all the contributing groups get joint credit for success. IT must have a strong stake in the success of the project.

4.2.11 Unrealistic User Expectations

The users usually have unrealistic expectations of the data warehouse, what they will be getting and when, how much it will cost, and how easy it will be to use.

Be honest. Don't misrepresent what the users will be getting. Be sure to tell them how much of their time will be needed for the project, along with who from the user department needs to be involved. Give them the estimated costs and your real estimate of the schedules.

Realistic time frames and budgets. Never be coerced by anyone to accept unrealistic schedules or budgets. If you do, it will catch up with you at the end of the project, and your reputation, as well as that of the data warehouse, will be destroyed.

Document. In the project agreement you will capture what the users will be getting and when, as outlined in Chapter 9, "Methodology." This document should be developed jointly by IT and the users and should be signed by both. Continue to remind the users of what they will be getting and when. If you have a user who is unwilling to accept your estimates, give someone else the opportunity to work with that user.

4.2.12 Architectural and Design Risks

If the data warehouse is successful, the database will grow and grow much larger than most people would have expected. The size of the database, the number of users, and the complexity of the queries may exceed the capabilities of the platform, so you may be forced to migrate from one platform to another—never a fun process.

A very large database (VLDB)—defined here as anything over 500 gigabytes of raw data—will have performance problems. (The perception of just what is a VLDB is rising fast, so please increase the 500 gigabyte definition by 25 percent for every year after the date of publication of this book.) The larger the database, the greater the risk as a result of the size. A VLDB will take longer to load, longer to back up, and longer to recover and, as a result, will have poorer availability than a smaller database. It will usually result in poorer query response time. A VLDB will require smarter and more experienced DBAs to design, monitor, and tune the database; a VLDB is much less forgiving of mistakes. A VLDB will also require a more sophisticated and robust RDBMS.

4.2.13 Scope Creep and Changing Requirements

Scope creep is one of the major risks in any project. The scope (functions, data, users) often gets expanded, but the schedule remains the same. IT's most frequent complaints about their users are that they are not sure of what they want, but they are sure about the due date, they move around their priorities, and that they constantly add, delete, and change their requirements. Chapter 12, "Project Planning," has a comprehensive discussion of scope creep and changing requirements.

Scope creep control. Controlling scope creep works only if you have already established a relationship with the sponsor—who is probably the one asking for the new function. Earlier in your discussions with the sponsor, you described the four variables in a project:

1. Function—what the users will be getting
2. Time—how long it will take to deliver the function
3. Resources—people, skills, and budget
4. Quality

In those discussions you made it clear that putting more people on a project will not always shorten the project; it may actually lengthen it (Brooks 1995).

Remember the project agreement you developed with the sponsor? Three of the key dimensions of the agreement were time, data, and function, and they were derived from the project plan. If the sponsor understands the project plan, he will realize that if he wants new function, the deadline must be extended or some of the original function must be eliminated or postponed to subsequent phases. There are a few situations where additional budget would allow some scope creep, but be very careful—this is usually not the right solution.

4.2.14 Vendors Out of Control

By this we mean out of *your* control. They are calling on the users and selling to them directly. The risk is that the users will either buy a product or force IT to buy a product that does not fit the data warehouse architecture or that IT cannot adequately support. If it is the wrong product, you must take the time to justify why the product is not being considered. The other risk is the users believing the vendor hype about how easy and fast it is to implement and to use their product. This now becomes your benchmark for success. Chapter 7, "Selecting Software," discusses ways to control the vendors.

4.2.15 Multiple Platforms

Multiple platforms means more than one operating system and/or more than one RDBMS for the data warehouse. As the number of platforms increases, you will need more people, each trained and knowledgeable on a particular platform, or you will need the same people trained on more than one platform. It is rare that one person can be as expert and productive on multiple platforms as he can be if he had only one platform to support. With multiple people supporting multiple platforms, a significant amount of time and effort will be spent communicating among them. The risk is high that communication may break down or that misunderstandings may occur. Many of these disparate operating systems and RDBMS have their own terminology that can lead to further miscommunication.

Multiple platforms means that interfaces, or middleware, whether you buy them or build them, must be in place. These interfaces allow the operating systems and RDBMS to talk to each other and to transfer data. Each additional interface is another possible source of breakdown and failure. Sometimes, the standards for the systems are different enough that perfect correspondence and tie-outs are impossible.

You cannot always avoid multiple platforms, but there should be a preferred or designated architecture that specifies a single platform. With architectural standards, multiple platforms should be implemented only with a special dispensation from the architecture committee.

4.2.16 Key People May Leave the Project

The data warehouse is a hot market for talent, and some of your key people may be lured away by money or the promise of promotion. The lure may come from within your organization as well as from outside. However, the prime reason for leaving a project is, more often than not, dissatisfaction with an immediate manager or the organization's management in general. Dissatisfaction often comes from frustration with not knowing where the data warehouse is going and what it is supposed to do for the organization. Dissatisfaction also comes from continual changes in direction and priority so that the staff never knows if what they are working on today will have any merit tomorrow. Dissatisfaction may come from demands to work unreasonable hours or to work on meaningless activities. All these factors can cause key people to leave the team.

Do not confuse staff size with capabilities. You are much better off with a smaller staff that has more skills and experience and whose team members work well together than with a larger staff with fewer skills and experience.

4.2.17   Loss of the Sponsor

The sponsor pays the bills, supports the project when there are problems, and gets the necessary resources to keep the project on schedule. The sponsor deals with the political problems, neutralizes the assassins, and promotes the project with upper management. If the sponsor leaves, the project is in jeopardy, and failure is imminent.

Back-up sponsor. You should anticipate losing your sponsor during the course of the project. What you must do is cultivate back-up sponsors who also have a strong interest in the project's success. The sponsor's second in command or the heir apparent to the sponsor is a good choice, but that person may also leave along with the sponsor; executives often bring along their lieutenants. A second backup is a good insurance policy.

4.2.18   Too Much New Technology

It is a big mistake to bring in a large number of new and complex data warehouse products to support the project, as explained in Chapter 7, "Selecting Software." Each new major tool requires your people to learn the tool and to make some mistakes along the way. Installing and integrating each new tool carries risks, including bugs in the software, incompatibilities with your environment, performance problems, and nonacceptance by the users and by IT.

Leverage existing technology. Buying a new tool should require justification that includes the time, effort, and cost of implementing the product. This should help to minimize the number of new products and force the organization to take a close look at existing software. In many cases, the existing tools can satisfy most if not all of the data warehouse software requirements.

4.2.19   Having to Fix an Operational System

It sometimes becomes apparent that there are severe problems in the operational systems, which makes the source data difficult or even impossible to use without a Herculean effort. The effort to fix the data will undoubtedly be far in excess of the time and resources allocated in the initial project plan.

Reevaluate the project direction. At the point of such a discovery, it is appropriate to reevaluate the project to determine if it should progress. The cost and effort to deal with the data should be reentered in the cost/benefit evaluation. There may be other source data that could be used rather than the original source data. If other source data is not available and the cost justification no longer makes the cut, the project should be killed.

4.2.20 Geographically Distributed Environment

Most database administrators will agree that a distributed database is at least three to four times as complex to design and administer as one that is centralized. If the data warehouse is distributed, the risks also increase proportionately. Decentralization should still be considered, but it means the additional time, effort, and cost should be weighed against the benefits of decentralization.

4.2.21 Team Geography, Language, and Culture

When the team is not all in the same physical location, their productivity will be impacted. Communication problems and not having all the key people together for important meetings increase the risks. The greater the distance and the greater the number of time zone differences, the greater the risk. Different native languages also increase the risk of miscommunication. Cultural differences that may cause a reluctance to confront or disagree will minimize the chances for an important problem to be identified and resolved.

4.3 POISON PEOPLE

One of the biggest risks to any project manager is having on the team people with the wrong attitude, bad work habits, or incompatible skills. Do not accept them on your team, even temporarily—a temporary assignment may outlast your tenure and is likely to if you accept these people. Your job is not to rehabilitate but to implement your project. Before you accept the job as project manager, have a clear understanding with your boss of what your job really is. Your boss will be successful only when you are successful, so your boss should support your efforts.

The Poison People are not just deadwood; they infect the entire team, hurting morale and work habits. They will require time from both you and the other team members to deal with them, their problems, and their incompetence. Good workers do not want to be on the same team with these people.

1. Retired-on-the-Job Rudy. Rudy may in fact be close to retirement or just a nonperformer. Whatever skills he once had (autocoder and board wiring) are either rusty or of little use on your project.

2. Bad Luck Bob. Bob has never worked on a project that has been successful. Disaster seems to follow him wherever he goes. His bad luck will undoubtedly rub off on the project.

3. Obstructionist Orville. Orville finds fault with every approach suggested and will argue every minor point that could be debated. By the time he is finally convinced (and then not convinced, but he grudgingly acquiesces), the project is way behind schedule or has been canceled.

4. Learning Lena. Lena believes she can take on her assignments only if she attends classes (all scheduled in resort locations) for the next six months.

5. Researcher Russ. Russ believes that we should not move forward until we have thoroughly evaluated every tool on the market, brought each one in for extensive evaluation and testing, and visited all the reference sites.

6. Incompetent Ernie. Ernie couldn't find his mouse at high noon with both hands.

7. Oldie Goldie. Goldie has been with the company since the company was founded. She knows everything and everyone. She manages to stay employed by playing the politics very well and by working the minimum time. She does manage to look busy. It doesn't matter what you assign her; she still works only on tasks she enjoys doing. She has seen many project managers come and go and is willing to take her chances that she will outlast you.

8. Gunslinger Gus. Gus doesn't believe in following standards, rules, or anything else. Version control is an annoyance and cramps his style. He's pretty confident of the quality of his code, so his motto is "Testing is always an option."

9. Water Cooler Walt. Walt loves to discuss everything with the team, whether it's relevant to the work or not. Unfortunately, he doesn't just

do it at the water cooler; he drops into the other team members' cubicles and wastes their time, and they don't know how to get rid of him, politely or otherwise.

10. Big Idea Bernie. Bernie has read everything—and he believes everything he reads. He knows every Web site, and he attends every conference. Unfortunately, he's too busy actually to do anything productive.

11. Internet Ida. Ida surfs the Net for everything. Very little of it applies to her job. She is an Internet junky, and, even though she has been urged to, she has not yet joined the 12-step program for Internets Anonymous.

12. Safe Stan. Stan has some mysterious connections that protect him from ever being fired. He may be the CIO's wife's idiot son (by a previous marriage), or he may have some pictures that the board's chairman would not want on the front page of the *Evening Bugle*.

13. Insensitive Igor. Whenever Igor opens his mouth, he manages to offend everyone, and those who seem to be the most offended are the users. You hate to bring him to meetings because you know you will have to make amends later on.

14. Saboteur Sam. Sam hates everything and everybody. He has an ax to grind and thinks the company has done him wrong. He does his best to sabotage every project he is on.

15. Heat-seeker Henry. Henry knows no fear. He will try anything and everything as long as it is new and technical, even if he brings down a few systems in the process.

16. Reminiscing Rena. Rena remembers the Good Ol' Days, and she reminds you of them constantly. Nothing ever lives up to her expectations, and it takes an act of God to get her to try something new.

So, you say, you can't get rid of these people. What to do? Establish a gulag; separate them from the productive workers. Make the separation physical as well as by task. Separate them from the mainstream project. Give them work to do that will keep them out of trouble, will not detract from your project, and will minimize contact with the rest of the team. Give them tasks such as reviewing all the code and reporting on standards violations a complete review is always required when anyone makes even the slightest change in the code. You might also assign them to research obscure tools that have no chance of ever being chosen, but be sure that the activity does not take up the vendors' time as well.

4.4 SUMMARY

There are many ways for a data warehouse project to fail. The project can be over budget, the schedule may slip, critical functions may not be implemented, the users could be unhappy, and the performance may be unacceptable. The system may not be available when the users expect it, the system may not be able to expand function or users, the data and the reports may be of poor quality, the interface may be too complicated for the users, the project may not be cost justified, and management might not recognize the benefits of the data warehouse.

The data warehouse has inherent risks that need to be understood and addressed as early as possible. The project may not have any defined mission or objectives, and, if there is a mission, it may not map to the mission of the enterprise. The quality of the source data may not be known, and you may not understand the source data. You may not have the appropriate skills, and there may not be enough money in the budget to fund the project properly. There may not be the necessary tools to implement effectively, your users may not be computer literate, and there may be political problems associated with the project. There may be unrealistic user expectations, and there is always the risk of changing requirements resulting in significant scope creep. The architecture may not be well defined, and there may be too much new technology for your staff to absorb. Key people, including the all-important sponsor, may leave the project. Finally, if the vendors are out of control, you may be spending much of your time answering questions that contribute nothing to the work of implementing a data warehouse.

By knowing the types of failures others have experienced, you are in a position to avoid those failures. You must know what risks to anticipate with the data warehouse if you are going to deal with those risks and head them off before they sink your project. The most important activity of a project manager is picking the right people and avoiding those who can and will hurt the project.

A CAUTIONARY TALE

Terrible Load Time

A daily load that took 27 hours: The deadline was much too short, and the team did not have the time to find out what data the users actually needed, so they extracted everything they could possibly think of (the "suck and plunk" method). The DBAs did not have the time to design the warehouse properly, so the database structure did not lend itself to a good performing design. Since the DBAs did not know how the users would access the data warehouse, they put an index on almost everything. The technical people and the DBAs did not have the time to establish a parallel environment, and so the load was single thread.

4.5 **WORKSHOP**

4.5.1   Identify Your Risks

As we said before, any data warehouse project has serious risks. Identify all
the risks you can think of for your project. For each of the risks, determine the
seriousness of the risk on a scale of 1 to 5, with 5 having the *greatest* impact
on the success of the project. Individually, estimate the probability of that risk
being relevant for your organization.

For example:

Risk	Impact	Probability of Occurring
1. Loss of sponsor	4	20 percent
2. Scope creep	5	90 percent
3.		
4.		
5.		

Now list your own.

Risk	Impact	Probability of Occurring
1.		
2.		
3.		
4.		
5.		

4.5.2   Mitigate the Risks

Now that you have identified your own risks, develop solutions and actions
you can take now and in the future to minimize the impact of those risks if
they should occur. Consider multiple solutions for each risk.

For example:

Risk	Mitigating Steps
1. Loss of sponsor	Mitigate impact of loss of sponsor by lining up an alternate sponsor for the same project scope.
2. Scope creep	Mitigate scope creep by implementing strict change management procedures.
3.	
4.	
5.	

Now list your own mitigating steps.

Risk	Mitigating Steps
1.	
2.	
3.	
4.	
5.	

REFERENCES

Brooks, Frederick P., Jr. *The Mythical Man Month*. Reading, Mass.: Addison-Wesley, 1995. ISBN 0-201-83595-9.

CHAPTER FIVE

Satisfying the User

If you don't have good input from the business, you'll merely end up putting up bad systems faster and cheaper.

—*Earl Hoskins*

If we could just get the user out of the way, we could get some serious work done.

In this chapter you will learn the following:

- Techniques to understand the business
- How to differentiate and support different types of users
- Modes of communicating with the users
- How to gather requirements
- How to sell the project to your organization

The Workshop has a set of templates for communicating, including a newsletter, presentations and demonstrations, briefings, and networking. The appendices have user validation templates, a sample letter to interviewees, an interview template, and a user satisfaction survey.

5.1 UNDERSTANDING THE BUSINESS

If you think of yourself only as a technologist, your perception must change. You must understand the needs of the business, the direction of upper management, and the strategic vision of the enterprise. As much as possible, the data warehouse must support those needs, those directions, and that vision. Without a solid understanding of the business, your project will surely fail. This section suggests how to gain an understanding of the business.

5.1.1 Terminology

Whatever the language of the business, be it banking, retail, manufacturing, insurance, health care, or education, it is imperative that you know the industry-specific terminology and feel comfortable using it. Assuming you and your team are more technically knowledgeable than the users, must never flaunt this technical knowledge. Users hate technobabble. They normally see it as a way technologists use to distance themselves. Never speak in a condescending fashion. If technology must be explained—and it doesn't always *have* to be explained—do it in a way users will understand, and do it without talking down to them or boring them.

5.1.2 Learn What Drives the Business

You must know the concerns and problems of the users, their goals, their priorities, and what keeps them up at night. If your organization is publicly traded, review the chairman's letter to the stockholders. Your CEO has probably made statements internally and to the press about your organization's vision and where it is going. Follow the trade and business press on articles about your company, your industry, and national as well as global conditions that affect your organization.

5.1.3 Educate Yourself

It is important that you know your organization from the perspective of the users. There are classes, seminars, conferences, books, and periodicals for your industry. Familiarizing yourself with industry information is time and money well spent. If you are supporting the marketing department, hang out at their watering hole—you will hear their concerns, better understand the power structure, and learn what really drives them and what they care about. If you are supporting the actuarial department, attend their interdepartmental actuarial meetings.

5.1.4 Educate the Team

Some of the technical people on your team may balk at having to learn anything that is not specifically IT related. However, to be able to talk to the users, they must know the business, not to the level the users do but in enough depth so that the users will accept them. IT needs to understand that it is the business that ultimately pays the bills. They need to understand that without user support their best efforts will be wasted. Their efforts would be like putting on a stage play to an empty theater.

5.2 TYPES OF USERS

Not all users are created equal. There is no "average" user. They have different levels of skills, experience, desire to learn, comfort with technology, and patience. Treating them all the same is a mistake. You must understand each type of user and customize your approach, training, and type of support. You must allow different amounts of time for different users to become capable of using the system. Appendix 5.G can help you categorize your users. The following are different types of users:

5.2.1 Technophobe

This user has been dragged, kicking and screaming, into the technological twenty-first century. He looks at any and all problems associated with the project as justification for his membership in Luddites-R-Us.

You are going to have to make it very easy for him to use the system. He will prefer very simple over increased functionality and additional information.

5.2.2 Tech Wienie

This user carries a cell phone, an electronic organizer, and a pager. The Internet is his primary source of information—about everything. He manages his life electronically, loves technology, and believes that all the opportunities and challenges in both professional and private life (much to the dismay of his spouse) are technical.

The tech wienie will choose the technologically elegant solution, even though it is inappropriate for the business. This user will frequently want to get involved in making all the technical decisions, even though most should not concern him and he is not qualified to make the decisions.

5.2.3 Hands Off

This user wants all decisions to be made by someone else, usually IT. Even though this user defers to others on decisions, he is still willing to assign blame when a poor decision is made. While most IT choices do not necessarily require input from the users, there are some choices, specifically the query/analysis tool where users' input is important. Most users will want to participate to some extent. If they abdicate this responsibility, they must be willing to live with a system that may not be totally to their liking.

5.2.4 Control Freak

This user wants to control everything about the project, not just for the business, but for everything IT does that relates to the project. He wants to be involved with every decision, big and small, and to validate everything. If he is not invited to every meeting, he feels left out and will retaliate.

An understanding of the data warehouse roles is mandatory. This user needs to understand that his bandwidth could probably impact the schedule; he should neither take on tasks beyond his area of expertise nor delay the project while everyone is waiting for him to make up his mind.

5.3 COMMUNICATING WITH THE USERS

The user sponsors are not there for your convenience. They are busy, and you must respect their time and use their time efficiently.

5.3.1 Listen

User sponsors will inundate you with requirements. It's very important to capture and document these requirements. The requirements should be validated with the sponsor for clarity, specificity, priority, and accuracy. The sponsor will want to know you heard what was said. It is also important that you ask your sponsor to prioritize the requirements in case the scope turns out to be too large and you have to break out data and functionality into implementation increments.

5.3.2 Status Reports

Let's face it: Most of us hate writing status reports, and those who do like writing them probably have some genetic deficiency. We need to change the way we look at status reports. Start to view them as an efficient way of communicating with the users as well as with your management and your sponsor. The status report will have "Accomplishments," "Next Period's Planned Activities," and "Issues."

The status report is not the place to exaggerate your accomplishments, but it does provide an opportunity to give credit to team members and others involved with the project. The status report is a vehicle to give notification of problems, indication of the need for more resources, and advanced warning of actions that must be taken to overcome roadblocks. Management hates surprises and hates not knowing what's going on, especially when everyone else in the organization appears to know of impending doom. It makes them look bad.

> On one project, any "issue" had to be explained to the CIO, along with a complete plan on how the issue was to be resolved. Needless to say, this procedure was much too threatening, and as a result, very few issues were reported—that is, until it was too late for management to correct the problem. Management was kept in the dark for as long as possible. In fact, project managers were instructed not to put any issues in their status reports. The CIO's objective of staying in touch with the problems did not succeed. This was clearly a case of upper management "choosing" to cut off upward communication.

5.3.3 Meetings

Meetings can be a time-efficient means of communicating, discussing problems and options, and getting resolution and concurrence to decisions. Meetings can also be an incredible waste of time. Be sure that your meetings are in the first category. You will get a reputation for the types of meetings you run. There are some standard rules for good meetings:

1. There is an agenda—preferably sent out ahead of time so that people can decide whether to attend. Be prepared for the topics on the agenda and for their assigned responsibilities.
2. The meeting starts on time and ends on time.
3. Time is not taken from the meeting to brief a tardy participant.
4. The agenda is followed. Topics not relevant to the discussion are tabled for future meetings.
5. There is only one person speaking at a time.
6. Responsibilities for activities are assigned, and those to whom they are assigned are called on to report on the progress of their activities.
7. Minutes of the meeting are distributed as soon as possible after the conclusion of the meeting.
8. A person other than the person running the meeting should take minute notes during the meeting.
9. The person who called the meeting controls unruly participants and brings the discussion back to the published agenda.
10. Coffee and donuts are available. An informal study found that when people know there will be coffee and donuts, attendance improved by 22.638 percent. Knowing there will be donuts and that the good ones are gone early also encourages people to be on time.

5.3.4 Validation and Concurrence

During project development, many decisions are purely technical and need no validation from the users. Examples might include the choice of a data modeling or ETL tool. Other decisions absolutely need user validation. Examples include a specific business definition for a data element and the allowed access to the data from another department. In these latter cases, ask for validation and provide a deadline for the validation. Appendix 5.B has a template for user validation.

In meetings and conversations, the user sponsor will often make statements, address issues, and make decisions. It's very important that those utterances be captured and validated. You may have heard incorrectly, or the importance of what was said may be either much more or much less significant than your perception. Document the sponsor's statement, pass it back as a memo of understanding, and ask for the sponsor's validation.

5.3.5 Informal Communication

This is the information received in the elevator, by the coffeemaker, and in the rest room. Informal communication comes from a spouse who works somewhere in the organization, from peers, from people in your old department, and from your well-established network. This is often how IT management or a business sponsor finds out that the project is in trouble. Sponsors and other management don't like bad news, but, again and more important, they really don't like surprises.

5.3.6 Lining Up Support

Before going in to a meeting where you are scheduled to make an important, and possibly controversial, proposal, have discussions with the key players prior to the meeting, discuss your plans, solicit their comments, and ask for their support.

5.3.7 User as a Co-Project Manager

The most effective means of communicating with the users is to have "one of them" do the communicating. Read Chapter 8, "Organization and Cultural Issues," to get ideas for co-managing the project. If a user co-manages the project, he will be able to talk and write to the user departments in their language and do so with unmatched credibility.

5.4 REQUIREMENTS

5.4.1 User Interviews

This is the most common way of finding out what the users need and want. A two-person team works best—one to lead the questioning and ask the majority of the questions and the other to take notes. The interviewers may be internal personnel, outside consultants, or a mixed team.

A letter coming from a high-level and well-respected sponsor of the project should briefly describe the project, introduce the interviewees, describe the interview process, and notify the prospective interviewees that they will be contacted to have their interviews scheduled. See Appendix 5.D for a sample letter.

There is no excuse for requiring clarification just because you do not know the terminology of the industry. This means that the interview team must do their homework before the interview. They must familiarize themselves with the industry and the organization.

It is sometimes best to interview one person at a time; he is usually more candid and open than if his peers are in the room. However, when you get together several people who are at the same level, they tend to bounce ideas off each other, they can discuss their different views, and you may even discover some business conflict that needs to be addressed. The interviewer should be flexible and able to "change direction" if one approach doesn't work. A manager may want one or more of his staff to attend, but subordinates are sometimes intimidated by their manager and may not be as candid as they would be if interviewed alone or with their peers. On the other hand, subordinates sometimes see the interview as an opportunity to impress their manager. This wastes time and may mislead the interviewing team. This means that it is normally best not to interview a manager with his subordinates.

The interviews should be scheduled for approximately one hour. Busy managers are reluctant to give you more time, and we have found that more than one hour at a time is exhausting for both the interviewees and the interviewers.

Prior to the interview, the interview team should review any previous notes relevant to the interviewee, understand the interviewee's position in the organization, and get information on any factors that could be influencing the interviewee or his department. Examples of these factors are the interviewee's real power in the organization, political currents, history within the organization, reputation, plans for retirement, and professional and personal relationships with other movers and shakers in the organization (those who go to church together, golf together, drink together, and sleep together).

5.4.2 Joint Application Development (JAD)

Joint Application Development is the process of bringing the users into a session with the system designers and the data modelers. Detailed requirements are captured, and (almost) immediate feedback is given to the users to validate their requirements. These highly interactive sessions are excellent for clarifying issues, establishing priorities, and identifying the appropriate data sources. Detailed analysis and modeling activities can best be performed in JAD sessions.

5.4.3 Documenting the Requirements

The notes may be handwritten or captured on a laptop. With either means of documentation, the process should not be slowed down because of the scribe's inability to take notes quickly. Occasionally, the scribe may have to ask for clarification or for the spelling of a name. Time should be scheduled between interviews so that the scribe can complete and correct the notes with the help of the lead interviewer. Appendix 5.E has an Interview Results Template.

5.4.4 Validating the Requirements

After the notes are corrected, captured in machine-readable form, and made intelligible, they should be sent back to the interviewee for corrections and additions. This gives the interviewee the opportunity to correct any misunderstandings and to amplify on any points he wishes to make. The interviewee will occasionally tone down his comments because he does not want to appear negative or appear to denigrate some other department or person. You may want to keep two sets of notes so as not to lose your original comments and unexpurgated notes that could provide important insights into the politics and critical dynamics of the organization. If you do so, treat these as confidential, and do not share them outside the interview team.

5.4.5 Project Agreement

In some organizations, the Project Agreement is known as the scope document, document of understanding, or statement of work. The Project Agreement describes what will be delivered, when, and by whom. While you might deliver something in addition to the deliverables described in the agreement, you'd better at least deliver what's on paper. The full content of the Project Agreement is described in detail in Chapter 9, "Methodology," but here are some specific sections that relate to users.

Functions and Capabilities

This is what the user will be getting. These are the actual deliverables the users will be able touch and use, the capabilities, the format of the data, and the user interface. This section includes the amount of data, the data sources, and the number of historical periods maintained by the data warehouse. The numbers of users (this can change) are specified in this section. There is a big difference between delivering the system to 10 users and delivering it to 500. The user training would be outlined, as would the nature of the help desk and the support structure. The query and reporting tools and OLAP tools are documented. The capabilities for Web delivery are specifically defined. Functions and capabilities include the number and types of canned queries and canned reports.

Schedule

The schedule specifies the committed dates for the major milestones and the date of delivery of the test system as well as the full system. The project manager should establish these dates after the functions and capabilities are defined and after receiving input from the project team. It's ironic that the majority of data warehouse project schedules have been set by management who know exactly when they want the system delivered—even though they are not sure what they want in the system, and they have no understanding of the effort required to develop the system. Under no circumstances should an externally imposed schedule be accepted before the scope and the resources are analyzed.

Service Level Agreements

The service level agreements specify which hours each day and which days each week the system is scheduled for availability. The service level agreement would commit to the percentage of time the system is available during scheduled hours. Data warehouse systems usually do not have service level agreements for query response time, as response time is exceptionally variable in an ad hoc environment.

User and IT Responsibility

Users have an important role in any data warehouse implementation along with serious responsibilities. These responsibilities are elaborated on in Chapter 8, "Organization and Cultural Issues." It's very important that the users understand their roles including the need to be timely in response and completion of tasks. Appendix 5.A has a problem related to user responsibilities.

The Project Agreement is not a document to write and forget about. If the project has a dedicated war room, it is a good idea to put the Project Agreement content up on a wall or a board in that room and encourage team members to read it often. The data warehouse project manager should reread the Project Agreement every Friday at 3:00 P.M. Following the agreement keeps the project on track and helps minimize the dreaded scope creep.

5.5 INTERNAL SELLING

5.5.1 The Necessity to Sell

"If you build a better mousetrap, the world will beat a path to your door." This works pretty well for mousetraps; it doesn't work for data warehouses. Let's assume you have built a good data warehouse; the users use it, and they like it. You have to measure and document the benefits, and then you have to make the organization aware of those benefits.

The best person to sing the praises of the data warehouse is the user sponsor. The sponsor has credibility with the business side of the organization and is in the best position to know what it has done for his department.

You need to make management aware of what the competition is doing—nothing gets management's attention like when they hear about their main competitor's data warehouse. You also need to make management aware of future possibilities for the data warehouse and for killer applications that should be considered for the next iteration. See Appendix 4.A.

5.5.2 Evaluating Results and Benefits of the Data Warehouse

Chapter 6, "Cost Benefit," addresses the benefits of the project. Now the question is how to identify and measure those benefits and how to be sure management accurately understands those benefits. A key measurement is user satisfaction. Appendix 5.F has a sample questionnaire for measuring user satisfaction. Some users see the questionnaire as a vehicle to vent displeasure with the system. That's acceptable. If you don't know what the users think, you will not know where to put your efforts to improve the system. The data warehouse is not like an operational system; it requires continual improvement and enhancement.

5.5.3 Modes of Presentation and Communication

Appendix 5.C has some suggestions about terminology, words, and phrases to use, as well as terminology, words, and phrases that should *not* be used.

Executive Presentations

This is the opportunity for upper management to hear about and actually to see a demonstration of the system. A business user should be the one to give the demonstration; the demonstration should not be given by IT. Management continues to harbor the concern that what IT delivers can be effectively executed only by IT and that IT systems are too complicated for the users.

Internal Publications

Many organizations have internal newsletters, some in print and some electronic. The organization's Intranet can easily carry information about the project. The editors are always looking for material. The article should describe the project, the department, and the users. Quotations from users and sponsors will round out the article.

Lunch and Learn

Some organizations have informal sessions, often over lunch, where specific topics are discussed. Called "Lunch and Learn" or "Brownbag Session," they are usually sponsored by IT either on a monthly schedule or as topics and interest dictate. These sessions are ideal for presenting and demonstrating the status and results of the project.

Trade Press Articles

The trade press and especially the vendors are always looking for data warehouse success stories. The reputation of an organization can be enhanced by success stories. These are particularly effective if they are published in the industry press, not just in the computer press. Industry analysts who make recommendations on publicly traded companies and recommend buying and selling the company's stock read industry publications. However, this is a two-edged sword. Favorable articles can boost morale on the team and provide an organization with a reason to feel good about itself. It can provide recognition to an individual, often the team leader or the business user, but these articles are also fraught with peril. Feelings that the recognition was not spread fairly or that the person featured in the article was grandstanding and taking all the credit for the project can lead to bad feelings and can hurt morale. If the article exaggerates the accomplishments of the project, a cynical reaction is often the result.

Unfortunately, these articles provide leads for headhunters looking for data warehouse talent with proven experience. The headhunters will attempt to recruit those associated with the project. The article may result in the loss of some of your key people.

5.6 SUMMARY

Satisfying the users is one of the critical success factors of implementing a data warehouse. Regardless of how good a job you think you have done, if the user is not satisfied with the capabilities of the system, the quality of the data, the response time, the timeliness of the data, or the availability, your project will be seen as a failure. You must understand the business. You must be aware of and support different types of users and communicate well and often with them. A Project Agreement will keep you on track and help to prevent misunderstandings. You must be able to sell the project to management to get the budget and resources you will need to continue to enhance the data warehouse.

 A CAUTIONARY TALE

Ugly Interface

An ugly interface was much too difficult for the users, and they didn't use the system. The query tool selection team was composed of people from IT and power users from the business side. The team members were all comfortable with the interface. They were able to navigate and write queries, and they felt good when they were able to solve a challenging problem and work out ways around difficulties with the tool. When the less-than-power users took the training, they were overwhelmed with the function, and they never did learn how to use the tool to answer their own questions. Only the power users made use of the tool.

5.7   WORKSHOP

Communication Plan Templates

5.7.1   Newsletter

The newsletter will be distributed _____ (monthly, quarterly, whenever we get enough to fill it).

The newsletter will be distributed _____ (in hard copy, by e-mail, on the Web)

The newsletter will be distributed _____ (just within our department, to the whole organization, just to business users, etc.).

These people will be on the distribution list:

_____

_____

_____

_____

_____

These people will be contacted to solicit experiences, success stories, hints, and tips:

_____

_____

_____

These people will be on the Newsletter Advisory Board, contributors, and so forth:

_____

_____

5.7.2   Presentations/Demonstrations

What is the presentation/demonstration called? _____

Brief description

_____

_____

_____

What do we expect to accomplish in this session?

_____

_____

Who is the session sponsor? _____

Who is running the session? _____

Who are the active participants in the session?

_____

_____

_____

Who is invited?

_____

_____

_____

Postsession review

What was the reaction of the audience?

_____

_____

_____

What did we learn? What can we do better next time?

_____

_____

_____

5.7.3 Briefings and Networking

Who are my stakeholders and sponsors?

_____

_____

_____

What is my plan for formal and informal communication with my sponsors and stakeholders (periodic briefings, coffee, lunch, drinks)?

_____

_____

_____

If I only had thirty seconds of my sponsor's time, what would be my current "thirty-second message"?

_____

_____

_____

CHAPTER SIX

Cost Benefit

Project manager's fairy tale: We don't have a budget yet for the data warehouse, but don't worry—you have a blank check. Spend whatever you need to.

In 1803, Thomas Jefferson commissioned Meriwether Lewis to explore and map the upper reaches of the Missouri River and to look for a water passage to the Pacific. At that time, the sovereignty in this area was being contested. Parts of this territory were claimed by France, Great Britain, Russia, and Spain, as well as by the United States. Jefferson did not know what would be found. The territory explored is now a major part of the United States. The expedition may have proven fruitless, and the expense of the expedition ($2,500 was authorized; $38,000 was spent) may not have been justified. By most measures, the cost of this project did not exceed the benefits.

Not every data warehouse project will initially be cost justified. Many have been implemented without really knowing how much they will cost. Many will be authorized without even estimating the potential benefits. Projects are often started because a sponsor has the need for information and has the budget. This chapter discusses the need for cost justification. It will deal with costs and with benefits. The Workshop provides a template for you to develop a cost justification for your own project. Appendix 6.A has a sample set of cost/benefit analyses for health care, and Appendix 6.B has one for finance.

6.1 THE NEED FOR COST JUSTIFICATION

Budgeting. Without cost justification, projects will always be in jeopardy. During future budget cycles, management will be looking for ways to reduce cost, and if there is no documented reason for completing the project, they are likely to forget that first flush of excitement that accompanied the project's initiation.

Staffing. Without cost justification, staffing with the right people may be difficult. By having some real dollar numbers to back up a request, the request is more likely to be satisfied.

Prioritization. Without a cost/benefit analysis, project prioritization is difficult, and management has little to compare projects other than a gut feeling that one is more important than another. Without cost/benefit analysis, the line-of-business manager with the most power is likely to get his project approved. The project that is most important to the enterprise may never be implemented.

Measuring Success. By documenting the estimated costs and anticipated benefits, we have a solid measure of success when the costs are not exceeded and the anticipated benefits are measured and realized.

6.2 COSTS

6.2.1 Controlling Costs

Costs can and must be controlled. It is the project manager who has the responsibility for controlling costs. Adhering to the Project Agreement is a major start for controlling costs. The Project Agreement is described in Chapter 9, "Methodology." The Project Agreement specifies the data that will be in the data warehouse, the periods for which the data is kept, the number of users, and the predefined queries and reports. If not held in check, any one of these factors will increase the cost—and probably the schedule—of the project. A primary role of the project manager is to control scope creep.

6.2.2 Additional Support

User Support staff or the Help Desk staff will be the users' primary contact when there are problems. The roles of User Support and Help Desk are described in Chapter 8, "Organization and Cultural Issues." Providing adequate user support will require more people and more training of those people to answer questions and help the users through difficult situations. The cost for the additional people, the training, and possibly an upgrade in the number and knowledge level of the staff answering the phones must be added into the data warehouse costs.

6.2.3 Consultants and Contractors

Consultant and contractor expenses can balloon a project's cost. As we mention in Chapter 8, "Organization and Cultural Issues," consultants are used to supplement the lack of experience of the project team, and contractors are used to supplement the lack of skilled personnel. There are two types of consultants/contractors.

1. *Product-specific contractors.* These people are brought in because they know the product. They either can help or be primarily responsible for installing the product. They can tune the product and customize it if necessary. The product-specific consultants may either be in the employ of the tool vendor or be independent. An example of their services would be installing and using an ETL tool to extract, transform, and load data from your source files to the data warehouse. In this activity they may be generating the ETL code on their own or working with your people in this endeavor. To control costs, the most important thing is to have the right people on your staff, working with the contractors and absorbing their knowledge and understanding the process. The acquired knowledge would allow your staff to perform this work in the future and to maintain what has already been done. Your goal is to make your staff self-sufficient as soon as possible.

2. *General data warehouse consultants.* These consultants may have a specific niche such as data modeling, performance, data mining, tool selection, requirements gathering, or project planning. They will typically be involved for a shorter period of time than the product-specific consultant/contractor. They have two roles that are equally important. The first is working with your people to complete a task, such as

selecting a query tool or developing a project plan. The second is the knowledge transfer to your staff so they can perform the activity the next time on their own. Just as in the case of the product-specific consultant/contractor, your goal is to make your staff as self-sufficient as soon as possible.

Very often, contractors and consultants are asked to participate in activities beyond their original statement of work. These may or may not be useful activities, and they may or may not contribute to the success of your project. Keep the contractors and consultants focused on their stated objectives and on your project, and, if they are working on something other than your project, be sure some other department is paying for them.

You didn't marry the contractors and consultants. They are not there until death do you part (or when the project is canceled). Don't let them get too comfortable. Watch their time, their activities, and their deliverables. By having specific deliverables associated with their contracts, they are more likely to complete their projects on time and within your budget. Do not bring them in too early, and do not keep them beyond the time when they no longer make significant contributions to your project.

6.2.4 Products

The software products that support the data warehouse can be very expensive. The first thing to consider is which categories of tools you need. Chapter 7, "Selecting Software," deals with these categories. Do not bring in more categories of products than you need. Do not try to accomplish everything with your first implementation. Be very selective.

Hopefully, you have someone in your organization experienced in dealing with vendors and understanding their contracts. You will be working closely with this person. He will know the things to watch out for in a contract, but you will need to give him some help to acquaint him with data warehousing. You will also have to give him some warning if you heard anything negative about the vendor. Your contract people will know how to include protection in the contract to keep the vendor from arbitrarily raising prices. They will know how to control maintenance costs. They will know about protection if the vendor sells out to a less-accommodating company. They will know about enforcing satisfactory service from the vendor. If you do not have anyone in your company who can perform these functions, engage a procurement consultant.

Most of the products have base prices and many add-ons. For example, add-ons with the ETL tools could include additional costs for each different type of source file or target database. The tools are often priced based on the platform (MVS, Unix, and NT) and the size of the platform. For the query tools, they are based on the number of seats, and these could either be designated users or concurrent users. When you talk to the references (refer to Chapter 7, "Selecting Software"), you will want to ask them what they planned to buy from the vendor and what they eventually had to buy. There often are surprises.

Anticipate growing your environment. The growth will be in the number of users (Web delivery could significantly increase the number of users), the size of the database, much more machine resources necessary to perform the more complex queries, an extension to users beyond your enterprise (for example, customers and suppliers through an Internet capability), and possibly the need to migrate to a more robust and better-performing platform. Be sure your contract allows for these types of growth factors and that the growth, while it may increase, does not explode your costs.

6.2.5   Existing Tools

Your organization most likely already has an RDBMS. Should you have to pay for it as part of your data warehouse project? If there is a site license, there may be no charge to your department, or you may have to pay a portion of the site license. You may have to pay if the data warehouse will be on another CPU and if the RDBMS is charged by CPU. You may have to pay an upgrade if the data warehouse requires going to a larger CPU and if there is an additional cost for the larger CPU.

What if you already have a site license for a query tool or report writer? You may have to pay a proportional percentage of the cost or at least a proportional percentage of the yearly maintenance fee. A reasonable method of assigning proportionality is by the number of users your project supports.

6.2.6   Capacity Planning

Capacity planning for a data warehouse is extremely difficult for the following reasons:

- The actual amount of data that will be in the warehouse is very difficult to anticipate.
- The number of users will also be difficult to estimate.
- The number of queries each user will run is unknown.
- The time of day and the day in the week when the queries will be run are difficult to guess (we know there will not be an even distribution, expecting more activity at month's end, etc.).
- The nature of the queries, the number of I/Os, and the internal processing are almost impossible to estimate.

All these unknowns mean that whatever hardware is chosen, it must be scalable. It must be able to scale and grow to at least three times the largest anticipated size.

The turnpike effect may cause you to underestimate the resources needed. (The number of lanes needed for turnpikes was based on the traffic in the area. When the turnpikes were built, more traffic was attracted because of the road's convenience. This meant the turnpikes were underbuilt.) If the data warehouse is successful, it will be used more than anticipated, and an increasing number of users will want to use it. It will be used for more functions than were originally considered. More data will be desired. The data will be expected at a more detailed level, and more historical periods (five years instead of two years) will also be desired.

6.2.7   Hardware Costs

For the data warehouse, you will need CPUs, disks, networks, and desktop workstations. The hardware vendors can help size the machines and disks. Be aware that unanticipated growth of the data, increased number of users, and increased usage will explode the hardware costs. Existing desktop workstations may not be able to support the query tool. Do not ask the query tool vendor for the minimum desktop configuration. Ask for the recommended configuration. Call references to find out if and how they had to upgrade their desktop workstations.

6.2.8   Raw Data Multiplier

There are many debates over how much disk is needed as a multiplier of the raw data. Besides the raw data itself, space is needed for indexes, summary tables, and working space. Additional space may be needed for replicated data that may be required for both performance and security reasons. The actual space is very dependent on how much is indexed and how many summary tables are needed. The summary tables may be created as you learn more about what the users are asking for and how often they ask. From this information, you will be creating summary tables one at a time. Considerable disk space will be required for the staging areas where the raw data is prepared and then loaded to the target data warehouse databases. The RDBMS vendors should be able to help you with estimates of how much working space you will need. We did a study of what other data warehouse installations were using as a multiplier. It was highly varied, but we arrived at a five-times multiplier—if you have 100 gigabytes of raw data, you should provide for 500 gigabytes of disk space.

6.2.9   Existing Hardware

How should you account for existing hardware that can be used for the data warehouse? It may mean you do not have to buy any additional hardware. The Y2K testing required hardware that is now redundant and perhaps unused. Should that be included in your data warehouse cost? It is a safe assumption that your organization will need additional hardware in the future. By using the redundant hardware for the data warehouse, it means that additional hardware for non-data warehouse purposes must be purchased sooner. You may be able to defer the cost of the redundant hardware, but you will eventually have to pay. In the future when hardware is purchased, it will undoubtedly cost less than it does today.

6.2.10   Controlling Hardware Costs

Your ability to control hardware costs will depend primarily on whether your organization has a chargeback system. Even though department heads are supposed to have the best interests of the organization at heart, what they care most about is meeting their performance objectives. These, of course, include the costs assigned to their department. If department heads are paying for what they get, they will be more thoughtful about asking for resources that may not be cost justified. We had an experience with a user asking to store ten years' worth of detailed data. When he was presented with the bill (an additional $1.5 million), he decided that two years' worth of data was adequate.

6.2.11   Internal People Costs

These people are getting paid anyway regardless of whether we use them on this project or not. Why should we have to include their costs in our budget? We have to assume these people would be working on other productive projects. Otherwise, there is no reason for the organization to keep them employed. Count on having to include the fully burdened costs of the people on your project. Keep in mind that you are much better off with a small team of highly skilled and dedicated workers than with a larger team of the type of people who should be avoided, as we outline in Chapter 4, "Risks."

6.2.12   User Training

User training is usually done on the premises and not at a vendor site. There are four cost areas for user training that must be considered:

1. The cost to engage a trainer from the outside or the time it takes for your in-house trainer to develop and teach the class.
2. The facilities, including the desktop workstations for the workshop.
3. The time the users spend away from the job, attending class, and the time it takes them to become proficient with the tool.
4. If not all the users are in the same location, travel expenses for either the users or the trainer must be included.

Training may be simplified if the delivery is Web based.

6.2.13   IT Training

Generic training may be appropriate. Examples are classes in logical data modeling, data warehouse project management, or star schema database designs. Data warehouse conferences and seminars can provide an overall perspective as well as training in specific areas. IT will need to attend training on the complex tools and products. IT will also need enough time to work with the products to become proficient. The cost of training is sometimes included in the price of the tool.

6.2.14 Ongoing Costs

Most organizations focus on the cost to implement the initial data warehouse application and give little thought to ongoing expenses. Over a period of years, the continuing cost will very likely exceed the cost of the initial application. Backup and recovery are always resource expensive. The data warehouse will grow in size, in the number of users, and in the number of queries and reports. The database will not remain static. New data will be added, sometimes more than for the initial implementation, the design most likely will change, and the database will need to be tuned. New software will be introduced, new releases will be installed, and some interfaces will have to be rewritten. As the data warehouse grows, the hardware and network will have to be upgraded.

User support of the data warehouse will be an ongoing expense, both from the maintenance team and from the Help Desk. Desktop workstations will need to be upgraded, as will the software on those workstations, although the cost may be significantly reduced by deploying Web-based systems.

6.2.15 Total Cost of Ownership

The total cost of ownership (TCO) includes all the direct and the indirect costs. Examples of direct costs are the software and hardware purchased specifically for the data warehouse project, training costs, and consultants. Examples of indirect costs are internal costs related to improving standards, procurement time, and management attention. TCO includes costs that are normally hidden from a budget, such as the additional time the users spend working with the data warehouse directly, assuming that in the past they sent their requests to IT. TCO includes costs you incur initially as well as costs in future periods. If your recruiting requires using placement agencies, their fees must be included. Insurance, tax, floor space, and utility costs will all be part of the TCO. The TCO should be calculated for the initial implementation and for projected costs in later years for the enhancement and sustenance of the data warehouse.

6.3 BENEFITS

This section discusses benefits, but we have found that business managers are often reluctant to commit to hard dollar cost reduction, revenue increase, customer recruitment, or customer retention. They know these commitments will appear in their department's performance plans.

> The difficulty lies in measuring the benefits. The greatest benefits come from added insights managers and number crunchers gain, and how effectively these revelations are implemented (Christianson, 1999).

As you enumerate the benefits, be sure to do so in business terms. If some of the benefits are specific to IT and technology terms are required, put these benefits in a separate section.

Benefits fall into two categories: tangible and intangible. The guys with the green eyeshades want tangible numbers, and you will be able to provide them. Does this mean the intangible benefits should be excluded from consideration? Absolutely not! To take that position is to say that your organization's reputation is unimportant or that your relationship with your suppliers is irrelevant—both benefits being intangible. Of course, these are important, but they are difficult or even impossible to quantify. The difficulty of quantifying the benefits is usually getting the users to agree to and give their backing to dollar benefits. The most you may be able to hope for from the users is anecdotal information. ("It took us only two hours to produce and deliver that report. In the past it took two weeks.") They may be reluctant to provide hard numbers because they may expect any quantification they give to be charged against their department in next year's budget.

Some of the benefits that are classified as tangible may seem intangible, and vice versa. It is ultimately up to you and your management to decide which of these benefits can translate into real money.

6.3.1 Tangible Benefits

The tangible benefits are those to which you can assign hard dollars.

Improved Productivity

Analysts now spend 50 percent to 90 percent of their time gathering data; the remaining time is spent actually performing the analysis and reporting the results. A data warehouse should reverse these percentages, giving the analysts far more time to perform productive work.

It has been estimated that 50 percent of requests to IT are for new reports and changes to existing reports. By giving users the ability to create their own reports, the productivity of both IT and the analysts should increase.

Increase Revenue

With a marketing data mart you will be better able to market to your customers. By understanding their buying behavior, offering them complementary products, anticipating their life event needs, and by cementing your relationship with your customers, you will be able to sell them more products. Improved marketing can result in more revenue per customer and a greater share of the customer's wallet. The increase in wallet share will be at the expense of your competitors.

Increase Profits

Profits can be increased by marketing higher-margin products, by focusing on the more profitable customers, controlling costs, improving quality, and using more cost-effective channels to deliver services. Profits can also be improved by avoiding ineffective marketing programs.

Increase the Number of Customers

This would include recruiting new customers and retaining old customers. Assuming the new customers and the retained customers are profitable, the net new customer margins would translate into real dollars. The cost of recruiting new customers should be allocated over the expected customer retention life. The cost of recruiting a new customer is far more than the cost of retaining an existing customer. You will be able to retain your customers by keeping them happy with your services, products, prices, and attention to their individual needs.

Improving Quality

The cost of poor quality is usually not understood except in specific instances such as the cost of servicing a warranty. The automobile manufacturers in the United States were slow to learn the lesson of quality. It became apparent to them only as they saw their market share erode. The cost of a supplier's poor quality may be severe penalties or the loss of an important customer.

The quality of service is no less important. Consumers are willing to pay more money for excellent service and will leave a provider if the service is unacceptable. Companies are now tracking their level of service and need some way to view and analyze the data. The data warehouse is the appropriate vehicle for the analysis of how customers perceive your level of service.

Fraud and Abuse Detection

The data warehouse and specifically data mining have been used to detect fraud with credit cards and with insurance claims. Data mining has identified profiles of usage that often indicate that the credit card is stolen. Analysis of claims has identified fraudulent health and workers' compensation claims connected with specific doctors and lawyers. The types and patterns of the claims flag the investigators, who then conduct a more thorough audit to uncover fraud and abuse.

Cost Control

While revenue must be balanced with the cost required to produce that revenue, cost savings flow directly to the bottom line. The data warehouse can help to control costs in a number of areas.

- By having a better understanding of customer purchasing patterns, timing of purchases, and the specific products that will be purchased, an organization is in a much better position to minimize its inventory. By having more information about the manufacturing process and the need for parts from suppliers, an organization can minimize the quantity of parts carried in stock.
- By knowing more about the suppliers, their products, and how much you buy from them, you are in a better position to negotiate price, delivery, and terms.
- By knowing more about your employees, their productivity, and contribution to profit, you are in a better position to negotiate contracts with the unions. You are also in a better position to make Human Resources decisions regarding head count and use of temporary services.
- By having better information about your employees, you are better able to negotiate contracts with your health maintenance providers.
- By having better information about your employees and their financial position and desires, you are able to structure more cost-effective pension and retirement plans that should better serve your employees.

- By having better data on costs and revenues, you are better able to document—and not overpay—state and federal taxes. By having better data on fixed assets and their location, organizations with large fixed assets will be better able to control their property tax payments.

Improving the Processes

Organizations are constantly looking for ways to improve the way they do business. Data on productivity, quality, and timeliness is critical to making the right decisions on changing the processes. These first need to be captured and then analyzed. "What If" scenarios can be evaluated to determine the effectiveness of changing the various processes. The data warehouse should be the agent of this change.

Quickly Exploiting Opportunities with the Right Information

Our world is rapidly changing, and the rate of change is accelerating. Without the right information and without timely information, an organization is not in a position to respond quickly to a fast-moving business environment. The response will be with new products—getting them to market faster. The most appropriate responses may include different methods of delivering products and services. The response will be with new services for customers and varying prices and terms. An organization must know its costs, its ability to deliver, its profit margins, and its quality trade-offs.

Organizations must be able to evaluate different options before they are presented to suppliers and customers. Without the right information, organizations may be reluctant to make what would otherwise be profitable proposals, with the result of making proposals that are far from optimal for both the organization and the customer or supplier.

6.3.2 Intangible Benefits

Intangible benefits are, by definition, difficult to quantify. There are two approaches to applying hard dollars to the benefits in this section.

1. Evaluate the funding of projects. As an example, if users are willing to fund a project that will give them more timely information (and nothing else), the amount of the funding may be considered as the benefit the user places on improved timeliness.

2. Ask the users what they would be willing to pay for specific capabilities. The users may be wary that what they answer will be charged to their department. Make it clear to them that this information will be used only for prioritizing the projects and for determining the usefulness of the data warehouse. For example, they could be asked what they would be willing to pay for the following:

- Getting their reports two days earlier than they are getting them today
- Receiving cleaner data than they are getting today (this would have to be done with specific examples of higher-quality data)
- Access to information that will allow them to make decisions based on specific facts
- The capability of analyzing alternatives without actually first having to implement them

Note: Be careful. Suggest these possibilities only if you feel they can be accomplished and accomplished in a reasonable period of time.

The following are intangible benefits.

Competition

Does the competition know about your customers? Will they be able to deliver better products than you can? Will they be able to develop products more quickly than you can? Are they able to make better decisions? Do they have access to better data than you do? If the competition has a good data warehouse, the answer is probably yes. It is very difficult to quantify the edge we would relinquish to the competition, but it is definitely a major factor in many decisions to initiate a data warehouse.

One intangible benefit of having a data warehouse is that you will not be overwhelmed and buried by your competition. The majority of organizations in the United States and in many industrialized countries have some form of data warehouse. Those that are using them effectively put you at severe risk. Your competitors with an effective marketing data mart will steal your best customers. Your competitors with an effective manufacturing data mart will produce higher-quality products at a lower cost. Those with an effective Human Resources data mart will have lower labor costs and higher employee morale. Morale could be improved by better understanding employee preferences for specific benefits packages and being able to evaluate multiple benefit options. Your competitors with a financial data mart will be able to tap the capital markets more effectively and deliver a higher price/earnings ratio on their stock. Your competitors will be able to develop successful products and get them to market more quickly than you.

The data warehouse has the ability to combine internal data with data about your competitors that you can buy or research (all legal and ethical). The competitive intelligence is what your analysts are able to discover (that tells you how you are doing compared to your competitors). The comparisons include percentage of the market by region, product, and so on, your profit margins compared to theirs, and your costs compared to theirs. Competitive intelligence tells you what companies your competitors are selling to and what they are charging.

Consistent Answers to Queries and Consistent Reports

Organizations spend an enormous amount of time reconciling inconsistent reports. The data warehouse should provide one accepted source of data. With the correct operational controls on the ETL process and proper metadata, reports and queries should be consistent.

More Timely Information

The goal is to make the information available sooner than you are getting the data today. You must be careful because the ability to load the data warehouse is dependent on the availability of the source data. If the operational systems that create the source data do not complete their processing until the 15th of the month, the load cannot start until the 15th, so users may not see their data any sooner than they do today.

Reputation of the Organization

Organizations are evaluated in a number of ways. The quality of management is given great weight as analysts determine a company's value. Lately, the technological capability of a company has become one of the major indicators of a company's worth and its ability to compete and survive. The price of a company's stock is strongly affected by analysts' and the stock market's views of technological capabilities. A number of CEOs have indicated that the way they are measured is by the price of the stock. CEOs are often compensated based on the stock price, and many have lost their jobs when the stock price has not kept up with that of the competition. The ability of an organization to make effective use of information has become a major topic in computer and industry publications, and this has had a strong impact on the organization's reputation. The data warehouse is the vehicle for providing information effectively.

Better Relationships with Suppliers

Rather than an adversarial relationship, the connection with suppliers has become critical for companies that depend on timely and high-quality supplies. This is not just for manufacturing organizations. Many organizations depend on information and services provided by outside enterprises. Organizations buy data; others have outsourced all or portions of their operations. The quality of material supplies, data, and the service provided by outsourcers is critical to an organization's success.

By providing information to these suppliers, an organization should be receiving higher-quality and more timely supplies and services. A case in point is an automobile manufacturer that relies on a large number of parts manufacturers. The quality of these parts has a tremendous impact on the overall quality of the cars manufactured. The automobile manufacturer gives the supplier access to its data from the manufacturer's data mart. The data is captured in the assembly process and during warranty work. The supplier is given access only to his own data, not to the data of his competitors. This information (date of manufacture, plant of manufacture, team responsible for building the part, etc.) helps the supplier build higher-quality parts that, in turn, raise the overall quality of the manufacturer's cars. The automobile manufacturer is now able to negotiate reasonable quality goals with the suppliers, and these goals are based on actual experience, not just on wishful thinking. The Internet is the preferred delivery vehicle for organizations outside of your own.

Better Relationships with Wholesale Customers

Using the previous example of the automobile parts supplier, this time from the position of the supplier, the customer is the automobile manufacturer. The supplier is anxious to provide the best service and the highest-quality parts and to lock in the customer as much as possible. This can be done by providing the customer access to information about the supplies that would encourage the customer to buy products from this supplier and not from the competition. The customer is given access only to his data, not to that of his competitors. The most effective delivery of this information would be through a highly secured Internet connection.

IT Relationship with Users and Management

For the last 20 years, IT has had a terrible relationship with users. Users are unhappy with long backlogs for their requests. They are unhappy with IT not understanding their requirements. They are generally unhappy with the services from IT. Some wag suggested that IT was the second most-disliked department in most organizations—Internal Auditing taking the top spot. The dissatisfaction with IT is one of the primary reasons that IT functions have been outsourced and that departments are building their own IT capability. When these departmental data marts are built, they rarely follow any standards, and the ability to share data within the organization becomes very difficult.

The data warehouse provides an opportunity for IT to redeem itself. With the data warehouse, IT can deliver information quickly and accurately to the users. Users have always expected, and always will expect, instant gratification. The data warehouse will not be instant, but it will deliver much faster than the two-year backlog the users were getting. With this change in service come respect and trust. This should bring the user departments back into the fold and minimize further outsourcing and decentralization that come from departments building their own systems.

By outsourcing, organizations have given away much of the ability to respond quickly to competition and to the marketplace. Both outsourcing and departmental decentralization have foreclosed opportunities to integrate cross-departmental data. By healing the relationship between IT and the users, there is much more opportunity to integrate data, to understand customers better, and to support the strategic goals of the organization better.

Recruiting Good People

Computerworld publishes a list of the "100 Best Places to Work in IT." People choose where they want to work—especially in a market where competent people are in short supply—based on a number of factors, but a key factor is the organization's reputation for being at the forefront of implementing interesting systems. Data warehouse is interesting and important and should be a major selling point to the potential employee.

6.3.3   Postproject Review

It would be unusual if the resulting benefits were as predicted. It is important to review the benefits to determine the accuracy of the predictions. Armed with the results of the review, more accurate predictions can be made in each category, and the prediction process can be improved with more accurate benefits projected for future projects. The data warehouse lends itself to iterative development, and this then allows us to measure the costs and benefits of each new iteration. More accurate benefits analysis can aid in prioritizing data warehouse projects.

6.4   SUMMARY

Costs are more difficult to estimate with decision support systems than with operational systems because at the beginning we do not know the size of the data, the number of users, the number of queries and reports they will be writing, and the complexity of the activity. We would like to develop an estimating capability that would help with prioritizing and budgeting projects.

While costs are difficult to estimate, they are more tangible than many of the benefits we expect to achieve with the data warehouse. Management needs to be aware and accepting of the intangible benefits, for without them, the data warehouse may never be cost justified.

Most organizations forego the very important step of measuring both the costs and benefits of their projects. Without this feedback information, the wrong projects will continue to be chosen, the data warehouse will not be improved, and it will go the way of the woolly mammoth.

A CAUTIONARY TALE

Hardware Requirement Underestimated

The hardware to run the system was grossly underestimated. The data warehouse team had no idea how to size the system, and they didn't want to scare management with what the system might really cost. They based their estimates of the amount of disk on little more than the size of the source data. They did not take into account indexes, summary tables, or working space. There were no measurement tools to monitor usage, response time, or resource usage. The users complained of terrible response time. The hardware vendor had a solution—a bigger box. Later the number of users tripled. The hardware vendor had a solution—a bigger box. More data sources were requested. The hardware vendor had a solution—a bigger box. In the final analysis, they bought a much bigger computer than they had originally planned and budgeted for.

6.5 WORKSHOP

6.5.1 Costs

Expense	Calculation	Dollars
CPU		
Maintenance		
Internal support		
Disk		
Maintenance		
Internal support		
Network		
Maintenance		
Internal support		
Desktops		
Maintenance		
Internal support		
Products/Tools		
RDBMS		
Maintenance		
Internal support		
Modeling tool		
Maintenance		
Internal support		
Query/Report		
Maintenance		
Internal Support		

continued

Expense	Calculation	Dollars
ETL		
Maintenance		
Internal support		
Other tool 1		
Maintenance		
Internal support		
Other tool 2		
Maintenance		
Internal support		
Contracting		
Consulting		
Internal people cost	Fully burdened rate × number of people on the project	
IT training	• Direct training expense • Travel and living • Training + learning curve time	
User training	• Direct training expense • Travel and living • Training + learning curve time	
Total cost		

6.5.2 Tangible Benefits

Benefit	Calculation	Dollars
Marginal return from increased revenue	Increased revenue minus increased cost to produce the revenue	
Lower costs		
User productivity increase	Less head count	
IT productivity increase	Less head count	
More customers	Additional customers × profit/customer	
Higher profitability/customer	Increased profitability/customers × number of customers	
Higher-quality product	Change in number of returns × cost of return	
Total tangible benefits		

6.5.3 Intangible Benefits

Benefit	Explanation or Narrative	Dollars or Other Benefit
Reputation		
Better relationship with suppliers		
Better relationship with customers		
Better relationship between IT and users		
Facilitate recruiting		
Improved morale		
Total tangible benefits		

REFERENCES

Christianson, Robin K. "An Inside Look at Warehouse," *Public Utilities Fortnightly*, Winter supplement, 1999.

CHAPTER SEVEN

Selecting Software

*Some people grasp technology as a drunk grasps a lamppost—
for support, not illumination.*

—*Howard Exton-Smith*

*Technology may have a direct effect on competitiveness and the
bottom line, but few companies have developed good strategic
plans [to be able to use this technology].*

—*Joe Barrett*

This chapter guides you through the process of determining what you need, helps you develop criteria for evaluation, presents a process to select vendors and tools, and provides a way to justify your selection. Don't be surprised if not everyone will approve of the choices.

This chapter has four main sections:

- Categories of data warehouse tools
- How the tools fit an organization's architecture
- The process of determining product requirements
- Weeding out vendors who are difficult or provide poor support

In the Workshop, you will be asked to identify which categories of data warehouse tools you need now and which ones you will need in the future and when. You will be asked to develop your own set of criteria for evaluation. You will then weigh your criteria against your prioritized requirements.

Appendix 7.A suggests the types of references you want to speak with as you evaluate the tools and the vendors; Appendix 7.B has a list of questions for the references and an outline for a trip report; Appendix 7.C identifies vendor rules of engagement, rules by which the vendors must play if they are to market to your organization. Appendix 7.D has a list of tasks you need to accomplish to select the tools, and Appendix 7.E has a list of the data warehouse product categories.

7.1 DATA WAREHOUSE TOOLS

There are over 400 data warehouse tools and products, and, depending on how you categorize the products, there may be as many as 29 different categories. No organization needs every category. It's important to focus on the categories that provide the most benefit for the least effort and cost.

7.1.1 Main Product Categories

There is an order to the main categories, a sequence in which the tools would be used.

Modeling Tools

Sometimes called computer-aided software engineering (CASE) tools, these are relatively inexpensive—after you see what the others cost. The CASE tools assist in logical data and process modeling as well as physical database and system design. In these tools you will capture the data requirements of the business, many of the business rules, and much of the metadata. Some of these tools have interfaces to extract/transform/ load (ETL) products and to repositories (both to be discussed later). Most modelers can move relatively easily from one modeling tool to the next. Some tools allow conversion from other popular modeling tools but may lose something in the process.

Repository

A repository stores the metadata. It can store information about the data models, the data in the data warehouse, the source files, and the transformation rules used in the extract/transform/load process. The repository can store information about valid values, business data definitions, and much more. Most of the ETL tools claim a repository, but these repositories are geared primarily to support the tool and can incorporate the metadata only from other tools with some effort or special code.

The interfaces to the repository are especially important, as you will want this process to be as clean as possible and without the need for your installation to write interface code. The interfaces from and to the modeling tools, the query tools, and the ETL tools should be evaluated.

Cleansing Tools

These tools analyze the source data for noncompliant data values. Noncompliance would include data that does not match expected data characteristics (character stored as hex), data outside of acceptable ranges, data inconsistent with valid values (domains), data that does not conform to business rules (minimum interest rate is greater than maximum interest rate, no birth dates before 1881), or inconsistent address data (Los Angeles, AL). Most ETL tools have a "lite" cleansing capability, but for serious cleansing, a special tool is required. There are some tools that specialize in name and address cleansing. The name and address cleansing tools are not as useful for most data warehouse activities. Special consideration should be given to the cleansing tool's capability to integrate with the ETL tool, if an ETL tool is to be used.

Extract/Transform/Load (ETL)

These tools are at the heart of the most labor-intensive activities in data warehouse, in both implementation and maintenance. These tools extract selected data from source systems, transform portions of the data (state code 01 is transformed to AL), aggregate data from multiple source files (customer name and address from the customer information file, customer credit history from the customer scoring file), create derived data (precalculated revenue amount), calculate summarized and aggregated data, and load the data to the data warehouse. Most of these tools have a repository storing metadata on the source system characteristics, the transformation rules, the target data models, and the data warehouse characteristics. These tools are generally expensive and require extensive training.

Relational Database Management System (RDBMS)

This software is the physical data store—that is, the place where the data warehouse data resides. There are products that are general and work for both operational systems and data warehouses, whereas others are specific to data warehouses. If your data warehouse is small and of limited function, almost any RDBMS will perform adequately. However, as the data warehouse grows and becomes more complex, the performance and functional limitations of some of the RDBMSs will become apparent. By this time it is too late, as the switch from one RDBMS to another is usually painful.

Another major factor to consider is the support of the RDBMS by the other data warehouse tools you will be using. For example, you will want to know how well your choice of RDBMS works with the ETL tool and the delivery tool you selected. How well will it work on your chosen hardware and operating system platform? You will want to know if your utilities work with the RDBMS or if you have to buy additional ones. There are significant cost differences among the RDBMSs. Your budget may dictate your choice.

You will want to consider the skills you have in place, primarily those skilled people who are available to work on the project. Be aware that design, administration, and tuning are more demanding for some RDBMSs than for others.

Query Tools

These are the tools the users see. They provide access to the data warehouse without the need to write arcane SQL code. Many of the tools have a point and click graphical user interface (GUI), insulating the users from most of the complexities of the data warehouse databases and making the training easier. Some tools are limited in their function and are not able to handle complex queries. Most tools allow you to create libraries where predefined queries can be stored and invoked when needed so that a substantial percentage of the users do not have to write their own queries. Most of these tools have report-writing functions, and most now have Web capability, including the ability to launch a query from a Web site. This is particularly interesting for applications that need remote, on-the-road, and Internet access.

The query tools all have some level of security that, along with the security capability of the RDBMS, protect the data at some level from unauthorized access. The security capability of the query tool may not conform to the organizational standards or may require labor-intensive administration or unacceptable authorization delays. The Web opens a new set of concerns, since both internal and external users may be given access to the data warehouse. The security features of the Web versions must be carefully examined.

Multidimensional Tools

These tools allow the users to analyze the data along multiple dimensions such as time, region, product, and salesperson. They share many of the features of the query tools, plus they provide additional functions such as the ability to slice and dice the data. The multidimensional tools allow analysis and present data in ways that are meaningful to business analysts. They provide for groupings across categories and are very effective for historical and trend analysis. Some of these tools have their own proprietary databases (MOLAP), whereas others allow multidimensional analysis against RDBMSs (ROLAP).

Data Mining

We define data mining as a discovery process of unknown or unsuspected patterns of data. The analysts are not starting off with a hypothesis they want to test; instead, the data mining tool looks in the data for patterns, correlations, and relationships that could be useful. Data mining often uncovers the obvious or the worthless (99 percent of "husbands" are also "men"). Occasionally data mining finds an important relationship that has high value but was not initially obvious (for example, a high percentage of credit card transactions at gas pumps for one dollar or less are done with stolen cards).

Utilities and Miscellaneous Tools

The following is a list of some of the other categories, a brief description of where they fit, and their importance.

- *Performance monitors.* These tools provide the metrics to determine machine and database resources used, response time, and information on who is running the queries and reports. Without this information it is almost impossible to know how to address a performance problem. There invariably will be performance problems with large databases.

- *Data warehouse methodologies.* These tools have a road map with tasks, deliverables, and suggested roles to perform the tasks. They generate a project plan showing task and resource dependencies as well as predecessor tasks, and they identify the critical path that will become important as the project manager negotiates and explains realistic schedules to management.

- *Industry models.* These data models are specific to industries, such as property and casualty insurance, banking, health care, and telephony. While many organizations believe in the uniqueness of their business, most companies can profitably use these models as starting points, even if they do business somewhat differently than the models suggest. The models can shorten the time to develop and can remind the developers of some important aspect of the business they may have forgotten.

7.1.2 Which Categories to Choose

You will not be selecting tools from each of these categories. Many of the products are very expensive, and they usually require knowledge or support from your organization or from an outside contractor. The total costs of a tool may outweigh its benefits. You need to consider the ability of your organization to use the tools effectively. If you don't have the people who can install and use the tools, then these tools have much less value to you (a less desirable alternative to having your own people is to use contractors or consultants from the vendor). Your schedule will also dictate the number of new tools that can be properly absorbed. A short delivery schedule usually suggests not bringing in many (or any) new products.

Focus on the tools that will provide the greatest leverage, improve your productivity, or reduce the risk of failure. At a very minimum, you will need an RDBMS (there may be some isolated applications that use a proprietary database, in which case you may not need an RDBMS), you will want a monitoring tool, a modeling tool, and a query tool or report writer.

7.2 WHERE THE TOOLS FIT IN THE TECHNICAL ARCHITECTURE

The technical architecture describes the primary platforms, interfaces (middleware), and standards by which systems will be implemented. While organizations may have a number of platforms (OS/390, Unix, and NT/Windows 2000), you must decide where the data warehouse will run. You must decide how much of the data and which applications will reside on what tier (primary server, intermediate server, or desktop). These choices will drive many of your other decisions.

Your architecture specifies the existence or absence of an enterprise data warehouse, the existence or absence of an operational data store, and most likely the existence of data marts. The vendors will support these different architectures to varying degrees. Your architecture will help determine which vendor products to choose. The vendors' limitations should not constrain your architectural decisions (Inmon 1997).

The target environment, including volumes of data, number of users, number of queries, types of queries, skills in-house, existing products, and service level agreements for performance and availability, will help to determine the platform choices.

Many tools are platform-specific—for instance, they may run only on Unix, whereas other tools may support more than one platform. When evaluating tools that support more than one platform, investigate whether your platform is the vendors' primary focus. While the vendors may want to support your platform, their in-house expertise may be lacking, they may not have given much thought to the performance implications of running on your platform, and they probably have not tested thoroughly with your platform. They also may have fewer customers using your platform, and as a consequence, that particular version of the product may not have been as extensively exercised in the field.

7.3 PRODUCT REQUIREMENTS

The next step is to determine what functions are needed in the tools you are selecting. You will want to include the functions you need today and the functions you anticipate needing in the future. Be sure to separate what you really need—that is, what is "mandatory"—from what is just "nice to have." As a Rolling Stones' song goes: "You can't always get what you want. . . But if you try sometime, you just might find you get what you need." Your budget will constrain what you will be able to purchase.

Some people use this opportunity to ask for everything that could possibly be in a product, including functions that are still a gleam in the eye of the developers. This approach makes it difficult for the vendors, and it is almost impossible for those who are evaluating the products to know how to score the responses. Don't do it. All the stakeholders should be given the opportunity to provide input, but they need a template that allows them to prioritize their requirements. The Workshop has a suggested process for scoring the selection criteria that differentiates "mandatory," "desired," and "nice to have" requirements. The Workshop also has a process to weight the answers.

An interesting anomaly lurks in the evaluation process. It may be that the key decision maker (the Big Dog) has already decided on the product, or it may be that a highly influential technical person has already decided. In this case, if their decisions will carry the day, there is no reason to waste time in evaluating tools. The only thing left is to be sure that the tool conforms to the architecture and then to declare a winner and compliment the Big Dog on his insightful recommendation.

7.4 VENDOR EVALUATION

Why evaluate the vendor? Why not just look at the product made by the vendor? The financial stability of the vendor, their level of support, and their reputation for integrity and honesty are necessary conditions for a beneficial relationship.

7.4.1 Financial Stability

Some vendors are not financially stable. Even if the product is terrific, the vendor may not be able to support it, and without support, you have nothing. The notion that, even if the vendor fails, the product will be picked up by another vendor is an optimistic notion. While it is true that the new vendor may continue to cash your checks for maintenance, their level of support and continued development may be in question.

7.4.2 Vendor Support

There are a few levels of support available from the vendors, all of which have varying degrees of importance.

- When you have a problem.

  — The code doesn't work as you understand it should.
  — You need an answer to a specific question.
  — You have problems with performance.

- When you need consulting help.

  — You are looking for direction on how to proceed.
  — You don't have enough resources with the necessary skills.

- When you need training.

Vendors will tell you their support is exceptional—they were rated #1 in an independent study (funded by the vendor). However, this is another claim that is discoverable. Tell the vendors you would like to see just how well their Help Desk functions. After all, they told you it was great. Ask to be able to call the Help Desk and pose a question or state a problem. You will need someone in your organization or a consultant who understands the product actually to make the call. From this process you will discover the following:

- How many busy signals you get before establishing a connection.
- How long it took to navigate their phone system and how long you were on hold. Call during prime time. (One vendor suggested using a speaker phone so you could do something productive while you are on hold—because their product is so popular. We suggest some other, less favorable explanations.)
- How knowledgeable their Help Desk is.
- How quickly, clearly, and accurately they were able to answer the question.

Furthermore, the caller can chat with the Help Desk staff, find out how long they have been employed by the vendor, what kind of training they received, and how much experience they have.

7.4.3   Vendor Reputation

Vendors have reputations for integrity and honesty—or a lack thereof. In the pursuit of a sale, marketing representatives have sometimes embellished the capabilities of the product, have confused current capabilities with those of future releases, and have unfairly maligned their competitors.

Vendors will sometimes announce enhancements to their products and then grossly miss their dates, or, when finally delivered, their products are poor reflections of their announced capabilities. Vendors will sometimes make announcements in response to or in anticipation of a competitor's announcement or product capability. Any pronouncements from a vendor with this type of track record should be questioned.

Some vendors have a reputation for buying companies or products, laying off most of the development staff, cutting back on support, and sometimes eventually killing the product. Some vendors are difficult to deal with, are considered unyielding with their contracts and negotiations, and are unbending in their terms and conditions.

7.4.4   Getting the Most from the Vendor

Have a face-to-face meeting with the vendor. Explain your goals and how their product will be an integral part of your success. Tell the vendor what you are doing with their product and how your use of their product can make them more successful. Give them something they can use, such as being willing to be a very good reference or speaking at their conferences. Let them know what you need from them for support of their product. Be clear on what is acceptable and unacceptable support. Hand them an agreement that includes what you expect from them. Ask them to review and initial the agreement.

7.5   RESEARCH

7.5.1   What to Read

Vendors spend considerable sums on printing glossy materials. Since glossies are so expensive to produce and the field is changing so rapidly, vendors are reluctant to incorporate much that may change. For this reason, glossy publications are usually content free; they provide little information you can use. Glossy materials often highlight the ease of use, the incredible productivity benefits, the cost savings, walks down the path to success with vendor and customer hand in hand, and absolutely no problems with the implementation. Disregard these fantasies.

The trade press often has comparisons of products. These are useful, but carefully watch the product release indicated in the articles and disregard anything older than one year—some even suggest anything older than 6 months should not be considered. These comparisons are never able to evaluate all the products in a category. Just because a product is not included in the review, don't eliminate it from your consideration.

Another type of article is the "puff piece," often written by the vendor or their paid lackey. These articles are aglow with the tremendous successes of a customer using the product.

The Web has a wealth of information on the products. The major advantage of the vendors' Web sites is that they can frequently update the information on their products. There are Web sites that provide vendor URLs (TDAN: www.tdan.com).

Some of the major vendors have periodic public seminars. The proceedings of these seminars may contain useful information for later reference.

7.5.2 Consultants

Most companies have relations with research and consulting organizations, such as Gartner, Meta Group, Giga, Forrester, or some other service. These organizations often have on staff or on contract consultants who are familiar with the data warehouse products. There are also a few independent consultants who are experts in evaluating data warehouse tools. These consultants should be used but should not be relied on as the definitive source of information. You still need to do your own analysis.

A final word on consultants: We are all human, we have had different experiences, and we all have biases. Consultants will often steer you to the products they know and the products they can help you with. Naturally, consultants will feel most comfortable using tools that have performed well for them in the past.

7.5.3   Client References

This is by far the most productive way of discovering the true capabilities of the products. You should request and receive a list of client references from the vendors. In addition to those on the list, try to speak with organizations that the vendor did not refer you to. You do not have to visit the reference sites. On-site visits cost too much, take too much time, and may eliminate references that do not want to host you. Client references do not have to be local; they do not even need to be in your industry. Companies in your industry may be reluctant to talk with you for fear of losing their competitive advantage. On the other hand, references in your industry carry great credibility with your management.

If a client reference tells you there were no problems with the installation and everything went perfectly, you know you are talking with the marketing representative's brother-in-law. Unless it is a trivial product, is still sitting on the shelf unwrapped, or is only lightly used, all products have problems. The question is the severity of the problem, whether the type of problem is relevant to you, how well the vendor responded, and how quickly and easily the problem was fixed. You also want to ask the client reference if the problem delayed the implementation and by how long.

Try to give something back to the client reference, such as information you have learned or some publication or article they may find helpful. Ask if they would be interested in staying in touch with you.

Be sure to write up the results of each reference call and distribute them to your other stakeholders. In your document, don't edit out information that may conflict with your preconceived view of the product. If you edit, you will lose credibility with the stakeholders and decision makers. Be sure to include all the relevant information given by the client reference and include verbatim quotes when appropriate.

Appendix 7.A has a suggested list of the types of references you want; Appendix 7.B has a list of the types of questions to ask the references.

7.5.4   Conferences and Seminars

There are a number of conferences on data warehouse, and these conferences often have vendor involvement, including exhibits, presentations, and demonstrations. Attendees are often overwhelmed by the amount of information they receive at these conferences. You should approach these conferences with some idea of what you are looking for. You should at least know the categories of interest and have a start on your evaluation criteria. The demonstrations are useful mostly to get a feel for the graphical user interface of the tool.

Vendors often bring their most attractive personnel to lure customers to their booth. The vendors will also bring a staff member who can answer technical questions, someone who really knows how the product works. When visiting an exhibit booth, search out the people who can answer your questions, not necessarily those who are the most attractive. *A hot tip:* Connect with the guy with the pocket protector.

7.5.5 Vendor Presentations and Demonstrations

When the vendors come to visit, be sure you control their presentations. Speak with the vendors beforehand, and then send them your agenda for the meeting. Let them know what you want to hear and what you don't want to hear. Send them your rules of engagement, so they don't waste your time knocking the competition. Tell them you have no interest in seeing a picture of their sumptuous headquarters. Present them with questions you want answered at the presentation. Send them a profile of your environment—so they know your hardware/software architecture. Tell them what you are expecting their product to do. If vendors want to tell you about their partnerships with other vendors, tell them what you care about in a partnership (you have no interest in marketing relationships). At each presentation, have someone take copious notes. Send a copy of those notes to the vendor with a request asking them to correct any errors you've made by either omission or commission. Then distribute the corrected notes to all those who were in attendance as well as to the stakeholders who were unable to attend.

The vendors will want to give demonstrations of their product. Depending on the category of tool, you are in a position to ask them to show you specific functions and capabilities of their product. Vendors will present capabilities of their product about which you may have questions or concerns. You will want to ask them to demonstrate these capabilities to see just how they work and how much effort to make them work.

7.5.6   The Short List

If you have done a good job with your selection criteria, compiling a short list is relatively easy. Any products that do not meet the mandatory requirements are excluded. Products that meet the mandatory requirements but are consistently low in the overall evaluation can also be excluded. If you have a bad feeling about a product or vendor, you may also want to exclude the product. Trust those feelings, but you will need to document something more objective to support dropping the product.

The short list should have between two and four products. If there are more than four, your selection criteria were not as critical as they should have been. If there is only one product on the list, your mandatory criteria may have been too demanding, and you are in the difficult position of deciding to accept the one or to go back and reassess your selection criteria. If there are none on the list—no products met all the mandatory criteria—you can either relax your mandatories or, in some cases, not use the tool and write the code yourself. This is not feasible for RDBMSs and is foolhardy for CASE and query tools.

7.5.7   Install and Compare—the Bake-off

Some organizations install two or three candidate tools on a trial basis and get hands-on experience with the products. They use this approach to make the final selection from the "short list." This gives them a chance to see if the product really installs flawlessly, if it integrates and runs well with the operating system with their data and with the other tools, whether the users like the tool, and how well it performs. It also allows them to evaluate the vendor support. Often the "technical types" who like to play with new products are the ones who usually sponsor this type of approach.

Despite the benefits to this approach, there are also a few problems.

- It delays the final decision. This is particularly important in the era of immediate user gratification.
- Some vendors will not agree to participate without serious up-front money. This could eliminate an important contender.
- It takes significant effort from skilled people to install the product and make the evaluations, and most organizations are already strapped for skilled resources.

- There is rarely enough time in the bake-off to discover all the warts on the product.
- You will probably not be able to stress the system fully to determine its true scalability.
- Some of the candidate tools may require additional hardware and software that may not be usable to you in the future if you don't buy their product.

While you may find flaws with the tool in your environment, most of what you will learn from this exercise can be more effectively, more cheaply, more quickly, and more thoroughly learned from talking to the client references.

7.6   MAKING THE DECISION

You have gathered all the literature, seen the demonstrations, received input from the stakeholders, weeded out the products that do not conform to your architecture, dropped products that do not meet your "mandatory" requirements, talked to references, possibly executed a bake-off, and eliminated weak or disreputable vendors. Now what? Is there a clear winner?

There are a number of factors to consider.

- Cost of the software. Are there any associated or hidden costs, any additional utilities that need to be purchased as part of the whole package?
- What does it take to implement and support the product? The client references should be able to tell you how many people, what skill level, and what degree of their involvement are necessary for a successful implementation—the vendors are often somewhat optimistic in their suggestions for resources.
- What outside skills, contractors, and consultants are necessary? Are these people even available for hire?
- What buy-in is there from the stakeholders and management? It's important that there is relative unanimity on the decision. An assassin in a high or influential position can cause serious problems.

7.7 SUMMARY

Selecting software is often the primary focus of new data warehouse teams. They are courted by the vendors and are able to perform evaluations similar to those done for operational systems. It is important not to be lulled into a sense of complacency just because you chose the best set of tools.

After you have a sense of your budget, you must choose which categories of tools will give you the greatest benefit. You must know where the tools fit into your organization's standards and architecture. Be sure to have the right people involved in the process, and don't take forever to make the decision; the users are waiting.

THREE CAUTIONARY TALES

Complex Software

The customer did not know what he was buying. He had no idea how difficult the software was to install and maintain. He accepted the vendor's word about the ease of installation. When references were checked, there were no questions asked regarding any difficulties or effort of installation or maintenance. Only later did the customer discover that the product could not be installed or used properly without significant outside help. The software was complex, and the cost for consultants and contractors was three times the cost of the software—the consultants have taken up permanent residence.

Shelfware

The customer bought an expensive ETL tool that is essentially sitting on the shelf. The marketing was excellent. The evaluation team was new to the data warehouse and too accepting of the vendor's promises and representations of ease of use, capabilities of the package, and how well it worked with other installed products. When the tool did not perform as expected, when the learning curve seemed too high (six months!), the ETL team went with what they knew: They wrote COBOL code rather than use the tool.

Vendor Goes Out of Business

The key software vendor had financial trouble and was purchased by a stronger company. The vendor assured the customer that if some other company bought the vendor's software, it would be in the best interests of the purchasing company to enhance and maintain the code. The purchasing company had a competing product, and the vendor's product was no longer being enhanced or even supported. The new company has provided a "migration" path that will require a new installation (of their competing software), new interfaces, new training (of course), conversion to their system and data, and *lots* more money.

7.8   **WORKSHOP**

In these Workshops you will identify the categories of tools you need. You will also develop your own list of criteria for evaluation, and you will apply weighting factors against your selection criteria to match the priorities of your requirements.

7.8.1   Identify Categories of Tools Needed

For the categories (See Section 7.1 for a list of the categories) you are most interested in, complete the following.

For example:

Category of tool_____ ETL Tool _____

_____ Performance Monitoring Tool _____

Now list your own.

Category of tool_____

_____

_____

_____

List the benefits or the mandatory nature of the category.

For example:

1. ETL tool is estimated to shorten code maintenance efforts by 30 percent to 50 percent.

2. A performance monitoring tool will help diagnose performance degradations early and will allow tuning or other intervention before the problem gets out of hand. Primary benefit is to keep users satisfied over a long period of time.

Now list your own.

1. _____

2. _____

3. _____

4. _____

Cost (average) Including the software, additional hardware, and the requisite consulting skills.

For example:

1. ETL tool is estimated to cost $275,000 (including installation and support).
2. Performance monitoring tool is estimated to cost approximately $120,000 (including training, administration, and support).

Now list your own.

1. _____
2. _____
3. _____
4. _____

Cost feasibility of writing and maintaining our own code rather than buying a tool.

For example:

1. ETL process will take six contractors four months to code and test without a tool at a total cost of $170,000.
2. Writing a performance monitoring utility from scratch is not doable.

Now list your own.

1. _____
2. _____
3. _____
4. _____

List problems in doing without this category—for example, not implementing performance monitoring.

For example:

1. Without an ETL tool the project will be delayed by two months at a potential business loss of $400,000.

2. Users may get dissatisfied with the data warehouse if performance problems go unchecked or take a long time to diagnose and resolve.

Now list your own.

1. _____

2. _____

3. _____

4. _____

7.8.2 Criteria for Evaluation

The criteria for evaluation are at the heart of the evaluation process. Take this list as a starter set, and create your own set of criteria for evaluation for a specific category of product (ETL, Query Tool, CASE).

1. Does the product have the following functions? *Note:* This will vary for each category of product.

   • [list of mandatory functions]

   • [list of desirable functions]

   • [list of nice-to-have functions]

2. Does the product run on our chosen platform? (Y/N)—mandatory

3. How well does the product work with others we have already chosen?

4. Is the vendor financially stable? (Y/N)—mandatory

5. What is the cost of the product (include maintenance and required consulting)?

6. What is the administrative effort (number of full-time employees)?

7. What is the learning curve?

8. Issues involving recruiting or training staff (could be very important).

9. If the user will see the product (query tool, report writer, data mining), does the user like the product?—mandatory

10. Is the vendor support good?—mandatory

11. Is the vendor training adequate?

12. What percentage of this market does the product (not the vendor) have?

7.8.3 Weighting Factors and Scoring

Every organization must determine the importance of the criteria in each category and must establish a weighting factor to reflect the importance. A weighting factor is relevant only for criteria that are not mandatory. If a tool does not conform to a "mandatory," it is dropped from consideration.

Including the cost in the weighting is problematic. If the costs of the products are similar—be sure to include all the costs—no weighting for cost is necessary. If one of the products will cause the project to exceed the budget, then "reasonable cost" becomes mandatory, and the high-priced product will be dropped. If the costs are very different, the importance of cost to the organization will determine its weighting.

Evaluate every tool in each category against the established criteria for its category, and rate it on a scale of 0–5, 5 being best. Derive the score for each tool by multiplying the weighting factor by the evaluation rating. Total the scores for each tool. The highest score determines the winner.

For example:

Network Performance Monitoring Tool *A* Criteria for Evaluation	Weighting Factor	Evaluation Rate	Score
Reasonable cost	100	2	200
Minimum administrative effort	60	4	240
Short learning curve	40	3	120
Vendor support	80	1	80
Vendor is financially stable	100	5	500
Comprehensive vendor training	30	3	90
Strong security features	100	4	400
Heterogeneous RDBMS support	50	0	0
Scalability	80	4	320
Distributed console support	10	5	50
Tracking of network utilization	100	5	500
Troubleshooting diagnoses	100	2	200
Total Score for Tool *A*			**2700**

Now assign weighting factors to the criteria for your tool categories, and apply them to your short list.

Tool Name: Criteria for Evaluation	Weighting Factor	Evaluation Rate	Score
Total Score for Tool			

REFERENCES

Inmon, William H. "Does Your Data Mart Vendor Care about Your Architecture?" *Datamation*, March 1997.

CHAPTER EIGHT

Organization and Cultural Issues

As traditional career paths exist today, they are excellent for selecting the wrong kinds of people for tomorrow and, with a great deal of care and at considerable expense, training them to be dinosaurs.

—Bill Sebrell

The technical problems will be solved. What's going to kill us are the unresolved organizational and cultural issues.

This chapter addresses the organizational and cultural issues of a data warehouse and how to keep them from killing your project. The chapter discusses what most enterprises have today and how the current organization could keep the data warehouse from being successful. The chapter deals with the following issues:

- The current situation in most organizations
- The cultural imperatives that address what must be in place for organizational success
- Roles and responsibilities
- Advisory boards
- Recruiting and retention
- The data warehouse team
- Training

The Workshop has a template for assessing your organizational needs and a template for assessing those personnel available to you. Appendix 8.A has sample organizational structures with their related pros and cons, and Appendix 8.B is a salary survey for data warehouse project managers (Foote 1999).

8.1   CURRENT SITUATION

Senior management knows about most of the assets in the organization: money, property, equipment, even people who are now called "human capital" or the new knowledge worker. However, management is just beginning to appreciate the value of data as an asset. Thus an organization is often not prepared to assign or reassign roles and responsibilities related to data management. Organizations also neglect to effect and support the culture shift that has to occur in a managed and shared data environment.

In many enterprises, the people organization—including roles and responsibilities—have not been well defined. On the one hand, there is often overlap in roles, and, on the other hand, some important roles are not being covered at all. Those organizations with well-established data management groups are in a much stronger position to be able to implement a successful data warehouse.

The responsibility for data quality is unclear. As bad data is detected, responsibility for evaluating the problems associated with the bad data and the responsibility for cleansing the data are typically not assigned. The sorry state of the data and its degraded quality have not occurred overnight. We struggle with inherited legacy systems containing suspect data that has accumulated over the years. Data elements that were clear when first generated have degraded into fuzzy, undefined content that we must now attempt to reconcile and understand.

The users often do not understand their data, or put more accurately, they do know their data but are sometimes unsure of the real business definition for each data element and of the actual content stored in the database. Users are often frustrated by inconsistent reports. This frustration extends all the way up to boards of directors. Reports that should have the same numbers often do not. Many hours are spent trying to reconcile these reports. The inconsistencies are often the result of discrepancies in timing of the source data. Most organizations are familiar with the problem of "end of the month." Is it the last business day in the month, or is it the last calendar day of the month? In most situations, we have seen both definitions being used. Different coding schemes as well as different business rules for rejecting a transaction may also contribute to the inconsistencies. And finally, the assigned definitions may be a problem; two columns with the same name are computed differently and have a different business meaning.

Because of these inconsistencies and because of the data quality problems, users often don't trust their reports or the underlying data that produced the reports. This lack of trust forces the users to verify the results, often at great expense and with a time delay. The lack of trust may result in a decision not made or the halfhearted implementation of a decision.

Data is often not shared by users for a number of reasons. The users may genuinely believe that they are the only ones smart enough to receive, validate, and interpret the results of a query or report. Some managers may believe that sharing their departmental data would give their bitter rivals ammunition to criticize the way their department is run. Sharing data may give supervisors the ability to micromanage, which is not appreciated by their staff. Since data is power, by sharing data, managers may—rightly—believe they lose some of their power. And finally, managers may not want to share their data because before it is released, they may want to put their own spin on the numbers or have enough time to be able to justify poor results or actually change the numbers before the results are seen by the rest of the organization.

8.2 CULTURAL IMPERATIVES

For the data warehouse to be successful, it is imperative that the following are in place.

- The users must be able to choose their data. IT cannot make these determinations without input from the users. The users usually know the source files and databases, as well as the initial fields and columns within those files and databases, that they need for their analysis. For those exceptions where the sourcing is not clear, IT must be ready to assist in the hunt.

- The users are the ones to determine the timely requirements of the data. There are two aspects to data timeliness. The first is the frequency with which the data is loaded or refreshed; the second is how soon after a period close (daily, weekly, end of month) the data will be available.
- The data warehouse applications must deliver acceptable performance from the viewpoint of the user. This means the users must have realistic expectations of what is acceptable performance. From experience with online transaction processing systems and with their own personal computers, users may expect response time in seconds. Some data warehouse activities can give this sort of response time, but for those queries accessing a million-row table and joining with other million-row tables, minutes or hours is more likely. At a minimum, users need to have a cursory understanding of what the server will do to process their queries. Armed with this knowledge, they will be able to partner with IT in the intelligent balancing of workloads and in setting runtime priorities.
- Users must also have clear expectations of what functions they will get and what they won't get. They should know the plan and schedule for completion of the project. A schedule can come only after a project manager has established a scope and created a project plan with tasks, deliverables, resources, dependencies, and dates, as described in Chapter 12, "Project Planning." Users should also have clear expectations for the system's availability.
- Users should know their role in the project and what is expected of them. Close involvement in each major phase is imperative, assuring the buy-in of the business community and creating an atmosphere for success.
- Users must trust the results of their queries and reports. This trust requires the underlying data to be accurate and clean, as discussed in Chapter 11, "Data Quality." Without this trust, they are unlikely to act boldly on the information.
- The data warehouse should be cost justified. No project—unless the law or a governmental agency mandates it—should be started if the

benefits do not outweigh the costs. Chapter 6, "Cost Benefit," has a more comprehensive discussion of this topic.

8.3   ORGANIZATION TO SUPPORT THE DATA WAREHOUSE

The most important task for the project manager is recruiting the right team. The people on the team should have a track record for successful implementations within the organization. They should have a reputation with the users for understanding the users' problems, and they should have reasonable understanding of the data that will be in the data warehouse and the business rules governing that data. They should have a good relationship with the users and should be known as "listeners." The ideal team has the business and IT working closely together on all phases of the project.

Not all users are created equal. There is a great variation in how much the users know about computers, how much they know about the data, and how willing they are to use the new tools they are given. Power users are much more likely to write their own queries and more willing to experiment with the tools and go where no other users—or only a few— have gone before. The more timid users are unlikely to write their own queries. The appropriate model for these users is canned, prewritten queries they can launch with just the entry of a few parameters, such as a region number or an amount range. The training for each group of users should be tailored to their needs and their propensity to learn and to try what is new.

Users will have problems. Therefore, user support is critical and must be planned for early in the project. If users are treated with sensitivity, they will be far more likely to ask for support and call the Help Desk. Users' interest and use of the data warehouse should grow as they have successful experiences with the data warehouse.

8.4   DATA WAREHOUSE ROLES

What should people be called? What is written on their business cards? Does it matter? It's not just for a person's self-identity; it's how the rest of the organization views them. Reluctance to assign appropriate titles may be indicative of an organization's lack of commitment to the data warehouse. The right title sends a message to the rest of the organization, indicating the importance placed on the project. In some cases title indicates compensation. Titles should be chosen carefully. They should not overstate the position but should be descriptive of the functions and responsibilities.

You will find some of the roles described in this section to be cumbersome and inappropriate as titles for your organization. Map these roles to the most appropriate titles in your own organization, or create new titles. The important point is that the responsibilities listed for each role are assigned to somebody on the data warehouse team. The following responsibilities are mandatory for a successful project.

8.4.1 Executive Sponsor

The executive sponsor is the person who has the need for the data warehouse. This is usually the line-of-business manager who recognizes the value of the decision support capability of the data warehouse. The executive sponsor will be the primary driver of new requirements and be aware of how these requirements would affect the schedule, the budget, and requirements that have already been accepted. This is the person who provides budget and political support for the project. The executive sponsor assures the availability of business people who can articulate the requirements and provide support throughout the life of the project. Your executive sponsor should also be the champion for the data warehouse project, and he should promote it whenever he has the chance.

8.4.2 User Liaison and User

User liaisons usually come from the business side. They have a very close relationship with the users; they speak their language, are credible, and have the users' trust. Some organizations do not have this role, and so the users perform these tasks. These individuals have a great deal of visibility over the whole business environment. User liaisons help to establish the true definitions of the data and what type of data is needed, what format is needed, and whether the data should be detail or summary or both. They know what security and authorization are needed and on which data.

The user liaison monitors the quality of the data. The user liaison is heavily involved with determining user requirements and helps to set priorities when there are more requests than there are time or resources to accommodate.

Users and user liaisons identify what data they need, how timely it should be, and where the data originates. The users specify what information they will need and in what format. They determine the need for historical data, including the periods and how far back to maintain the history.

With the help of Data Administration, users provide the business definitions. These definitions will be in the terminology of the business, not in IT terminology. These definitions should be stored in a metadata repository and should be available to anyone running a query or receiving a result set or report. Many organizations are putting the definitions on their Intranet, giving accessibility to these definitions throughout the organization. The author of the definition and the last date of update are available along with the definition. Data Administration must keep the definitions current; they perform the mechanics of the updates. The currency of the content is up to the business stewards of the data. They are the first to know of changes or updates to the business.

The users own the data. This means they are responsible for determining who can access the data and at what level of detail. Access may be given for summary data but not for the detail. The owners are responsible for identifying the domains (valid values) of the data.

Users will determine the availability requirements. There are two aspects of availability. The first is the number of hours each day and the number of days each week the data warehouse should be accessible. An example is 18 hours per day, six days per week (18×6). The second is the percentage of time the system should be available during scheduled hours. Availability requirements may vary by both the time of the month and the time of the year. Typically, the data warehouse does not have the same availability requirements as an online transactions processing system. Note that there is disagreement on this point. Some data warehouses have service level agreements of 24 hours per day, 7 days per week. This is appropriate for international systems where the data warehouse is centralized. It is also appropriate in installations where users run queries that run all night or where insomniac users launch queries from home at night and during weekends. A 24/7 system is usually not required, as knowledge workers are rarely on swing and graveyard shifts and only occasionally work into the night. There are exceptions, and some long-running queries often run into the wee hours.

Users may ask for a service level agreement for performance. This rarely makes sense, since response time on queries is highly variable. A query may access ten records or ten million. The response time will be very different (see Chapter 7, "Selecting Software," for a discussion of monitoring tools). Some organizations have established response time service level agreements for known queries or reports as a benchmark to validate the ongoing performance health of the system. User expectations must be set and continually reset so they do not expect subsecond query response time.

Users know if summary data is adequate or if they need to access the detail data. In a number of cases, users have thought a summary would be enough, but once they saw the summary, they realized they needed the detail to understand what made up the summary.

Users are in an excellent position to validate the quality of the data as they review their reports. The Fifth Law of data warehouse is "There will always be data quality problems." These are sometimes uncovered by IT—if IT has a proactive quality program (see Section 8.4.12, Data Quality Analyst). Users should be sensitized to looking for data quality problems and reporting them to IT. It's not enough just to identify the data as "junk." Equivalent to a Neighborhood Watch Program, all suspicious dirty data should be reported. Users should be closely involved in data certification of the initial population of the data warehouse. The certification process will alert IT to data errors, especially as a result of transformation errors. Certification will increase user involvement and buy-in for data quality. We should all know by now, that even if an application program has generated a report, it might still be incorrect. It is up to the users to validate the accuracy of all reports. Users will know what to expect and are well suited to write test cases. If the data is much different than expected, users should be responsible for investigating further.

Users will often be involved in identifying the transformation rules and the cleansing rules in the extract/transform/load process. They will specify code transformations (01/02/00 becomes 01022000), indicate what to do when mandatory fields are blank, determine which records are invalid and should be dropped, and so on.

Depending on the organization's charge-back policies, the users are often responsible for paying the bill. They may be charged for the use of machine resources, for IT personnel, for consultants and contractors, and for data warehouse-related software. The way people are charged will often drive their behavior and interactions. Charge-backs can have a self-regulating effect on how resources are applied, or the charge-backs can cause aberrant and counterproductive behavior. The charge-backs should be tailored to generate the desired user behavior and should not result in unhappy users. Any charge-backs should be carefully considered.

8.4.3   Business Analyst

The business analyst is usually from IT but is very knowledgeable about the business, its processes, and the operational data that supports the business. The business analyst will meet with a broad range of users and will capture their standard, traditional decision support requirements. If the business analyst is very good, the analyst will be able to help the business people identify additional possibilities and "killer" applications that would give the organization a significant boost in revenue, cost reduction, or customer satisfaction. The business analyst will facilitate discussions and help the business people anticipate future needs and opportunities.

The business analyst will organize and run joint application development (JAD) sessions with different groups of users. Together, they will brainstorm, explore options, weigh approaches, and make decisions on which data and which decision support applications would be most beneficial.

8.4.4   User Support

User Support is the first line of defense when the user has problems. They must be customer/client oriented and know that the calls from the users are not just annoyances but their reason for being. They must be knowledgeable about the tools, understand the database structure, know the data, and be familiar with frequently executed queries and reports. They must recognize the users' concerns and problems and be familiar with the frequently asked questions and the answers to them. They must have a profile of the users and recognize the power users and the more casual users. They must be patient and responsive. If time elapses between hearing about and resolving the problem, the users must be informed on how the resolution is progressing. Just as in operational systems, an incident tracking system should be in place.

In some organizations, User Support creates some of the canned queries and reports and administers the libraries that store these queries and reports. Administration includes developing and implementing the standards for admission to the query library and for maintaining the canned queries. Expect periodic changes. Queries and reports submitted to the library must have use beyond that of the submitter, must be well documented, and must be thoroughly tested—including testing any entries that have been subsequently modified. Information on the submission must be communicated to interested parties with an explanation of the purpose of the query, how it can be invoked, expectations of resources used, response time, and what to expect in the report or result set.

Some of the problems that are seen by User Support relate to the update/load process, such as whether it completed on time and if it ran successfully. These processes must be monitored, and any variance in availability or timeliness of the data should be communicated to the users. Other problems relate to performance. User Support must have a feel for performance, monitor performance, report performance degradation to Database Administration, spot poor query techniques that could cause bad performance, and help the users write more efficient queries and reports.

Some organizations assign training to User Support—sometimes to organize training classes and bring in professional trainers and other times to teach the classes themselves.

User Support will create and maintain frequently asked questions (FAQs) that could be accessible through the Internet. User Support should make extensive use of metadata to train, inform, and answer user questions. A large percentage of questions that come to Help Desks involves problems of the users not understanding the meaning of the data, the timeliness of the data, or the source of the data. Most of these questions can be answered with metadata.

8.4.5 Data Administrator

Data Administration got a second wind from the data warehouse. The data warehouse did for Data Administration what *Lady Chatterley's Lover* did for gamekeeping. The roles and benefits of Data Administration were not well understood by most organizations, and the role of Data Administration was relegated to writing documentation that was rarely used. With the advent of the data warehouse, it became apparent that the primary roles of Data Administration are key to a successful data warehouse.

Data administrators model the business data according to the business rules and policies governing the data relationships. They also document and maintain the mapping between the logical data model and the physical database design and between the source data and the data warehouse target data. Data administrators understand the source files and know which are the appropriate source files for extraction. Data Administration establishes and maintains the naming standards. They communicate the availability of data and, when appropriate, suggest that departments share their data. Data Administration is responsible for administering the tool used in data modeling as well as the tool libraries, although in some organizations this is the responsibility of the application development team.

Data Administration is responsible for administering the metadata repository. Metadata will come from a number of sources: the modeling tools, the extract/transform/load tool, the query tools, the reengineering of the source file data definitions, and the direct entry into a metadata repository tool. The metadata repository could potentially be updated, as well as accessed from each of these source systems. Tight controls are necessary to minimize corruption of the metadata. Data Administration is responsible for controlling entry, updates, and deletes.

8.4.6 Application Developer

Application Development is split into two groups with different skill sets.

1. Back-end extract/transform/load (ETL) application developers who need to be hard-core programmers with years of experience in serious programming languages (COBOL, C++, etc.)
2. Front-end delivery application developers who need to know client/server and modern languages (Visual Basic, PowerPlay, Java, etc.), the query tools, report writers, and OLAP tools

The back-end ETL application developers are responsible for the acquisition process that constitutes the major effort for any data warehouse—the extract/transform/load process. It has been estimated that these tasks take 70 percent to 80 percent of the total time and effort to implement a data warehouse.

Extract/transform/load will be performed with an ETL tool, conventional programming, or a combination of both. The back-end ETL application developers will be responsible for the process regardless of which approach is used. Do not assume a tool will eliminate the work or effort involved with this process. The required analysis is still time-consuming, and describing the complicated transformation logic to the ETL tool can be difficult.

The back-end ETL application developers are responsible for tie-outs that are the controls of numbers of records extracted matched to the number of records loaded, controls on dollar totals, on errors, and on the types of errors.

Data cleansing, whether it is done with a cleansing tool, with an ETL product, or with conventional coding, is also the responsibility of the back-end ETL application developers. Neither the data warehouse nor the back-end ETL application developers are responsible for fixing the operational systems that feed the data warehouse.

The ETL process is always time- and resource-consuming, even with a data warehouse of moderate size. Application Development must be aware of the performance implications of their architecture, design, and coding.

The front-end application developers play a critical role in delivering the data from the data warehouse. The front-end application developers are usually heavily involved with the users.

One of the selling points of the data warehouse is to empower users to write their own queries. Power users are capable of writing incredibly complex queries—often to the detriment of performance. However, there are many users who are not capable of writing all the queries they need. In these cases, the front-end application developers will be responsible for writing the queries for them.

8.4.7 Security Officer and Auditor

Security is becoming more and more important as people outside the organization are being given access to reports, results sets, and even the ability to query the organization's data warehouse directly. Access is being given to suppliers in an effort to improve their ability to supply timely quality parts. Access is being given to commercial customers to tie them as closely as possible to the organization's products and services. With access allowed outside the organization, security must be exact and uncompromising.

Many department heads are concerned about anyone looking at their data. If they have the authority to restrict access, the security officer must set up the procedures to implement the restriction and to make the department heads feel comfortable that they have retained control of the access. This type of control is especially important when data has been classified as private, even within the company. Examples are personnel records, sensitive client data, and patient data in the health care industry.

Data can be secured at different levels of granularity. Data may be available at the summary level but not at the atomic or detailed level.

The security officer should work closely with those administering security (Web administrator, DBAs, query tool administrators, repository administrator, CASE tool administrator, and ETL tool administrator) to understand the capabilities of the products and determine the optimal approach to establishing security. This would include exposures, difficulties in administration—we don't want to make this a bureaucratic nightmare—and the productivity of administration.

The primary role of the security officer is the identification of exposures with recommendations and actions to plug security holes. Another important responsibility of the security officer is to understand the interaction of security features between the tools and the RDBMS. There have been some cases reported where the security feature of one tool negated that of another.

8.4.8   Database Administrator

The database administrator (DBA) is responsible for the physical aspects of the data warehouse. This includes physical design, performance, backup, and recovery. Before starting, the DBAs must understand the users' basic requirements and how the data warehouse databases will be accessed. Some changes to the design and configuration of the system are more easily made than others. The more that is known initially, the less disruptive and costly the changes will be.

Data warehouse DBAs are usually more closely involved with the users than are the DBAs responsible for operational (OLTP) systems. Data warehouse DBAs are constantly monitoring and tuning the data warehouse databases, and adding indexes and summary tables. They monitor the SQL generated from the queries to help improve individual query performance.

The DBA will typically use a modeling CASE tool to create the physical database design. The DBA will work closely with the data administrator in designing the database. The same CASE tool should be used for the physical database design that was used for the logical data model. The advantage is that the mapping between the logical and physical data models can be done on the CASE tool and exported to the central repository without having to write additional programs.

Database administrators will then create the data definition language or use the CASE tool to create the data definition language to build the database. Database Administration will always have an eye on performance. Performance will dictate designs and the creation of keys and indexes.

If a distributed database environment is being considered, a good rule of thumb is the three- (or four-) to-one complexity of a distributed database over one that is centralized. This does not mean data marts should not be distributed. There are some excellent reasons for distribution, but their cost, complexity, increased administration, and availability risk must be factored into any distribution decision.

Database Administration is sometimes responsible for capacity planning and always responsible for physical design for good performance, monitoring response time and resources used (CPU, disk I/O), evaluating performance problems, tuning the databases, and reviewing the complicated SQL statements written by both application developers and power users.

8.4.9 Technical Services

Technical Services—sometimes called System Administration—is responsible for establishing the data warehouse technical architecture. This includes decisions about the hardware, the network, the operating system, and the RDBMS, although some of these decisions may fall to the data warehouse architect. Technical Services should develop capacity plans and make plans that would allow the data warehouse to scale to a size that is much bigger than that which was originally planned—Data Warehouse Rule #3: Successful data warehouses always grow much bigger than expected. Technical Services should monitor ETL and query performance at a high level, keeping track of increased resource usage. This will give them time to plan for an upgrade long before performance becomes unacceptable. Technical Services will develop disaster contingency plans in line with the criticality of the data warehouse.

8.4.10 Data Warehouse Architect

The data warehouse architect will develop for the data warehouse the architecture that would include the data warehouse tools and how they work together, and their interfaces and how they feed each other.

The architect will determine whether an enterprise data warehouse is to be used, how and by whom it would be accessed, and how it would feed the data marts. If an operational data store (ODS) is to be used, he will specify how and by whom the ODS would be accessed and how it would feed the enterprise data warehouse or the data marts. The architect is heavily involved in understanding and determining data sources. The architecture will painstakingly detail how the data marts would be integrated and reconciled. The architecture will specify if the data warehouse would be two or three tiers.

The data warehouse architect will establish the standards and procedures for the data warehouse (not for each project). A major part of those standards would address the ETL process and how it should flow, what tools would be used, and where tie-outs have to occur, as well as responsibilities for the process, walkthroughs and inspections, testing procedures, and user sign-off. The standards and procedures would incorporate the use of external data and how it would be incorporated into the ETL process.

8.4.11 Data Warehouse Project Manager

The data warehouse project manager has overall responsibility for a project's successful implementation. The project manager defines, plans, schedules, and controls the project. The project plan must include tasks, deliverables, and resources—the people who will perform the tasks. The manager will monitor and coordinate the activities of the team and will review their deliverables. If contractors and consultants are used, the project manager assigns the tasks, monitors activities and deliverables, and assures that knowledge transfer is indeed taking place.

The project manager will estimate the cost of the project and monitor conformance to the cost estimates. The manager will also project the benefits, measure the effectiveness of the data warehouse, and report on the benefits and costs based on the analysis described in Chapter 6, "Cost Benefit."

The most important task for the manager is recruiting the right people, people who have the requisite skills and who work well with the users and each other. Getting the right people will require an understanding from management on the importance of the project and their cooperation in the recruiting process. The problem is that the good people are already taken, and a smart manager outside of the data warehouse area is loath to give up an outstanding performer. Hiring people from the outside has its own risks and time delays. An outside hire will need some time to become familiar with the organization, to learn how things are done, to understand the minefields, and to learn about the source data.

8.4.12 Data Quality Analyst

Don't assume that just because there is a data quality analyst, no one else has responsibility for quality in the data warehouse. Data quality is everyone's job, but it is the only focus of the data quality analyst. Although information about data quality problems often originate in IT, it most often comes from the users. The data quality analyst is responsible for finding and reporting problems relating to data quality, tracking these problems, and assuring that the resolution is assigned to a responsible party. Some of the discovered problems must be reported to Data Administration, where the data exceptions can be properly incorporated into the logical data model. The data quality analyst can be involved in writing the programming specifications for the transformation logic that needs to occur during the ETL process.

Not all problems can be resolved, nor should they be. It might cost more to fix the problem than it's worth. The data quality analyst along with other interested parties, including the business unit, should determine the criticality of the problem. Analytical requirements could determine the quality requirements. The cost to fix the problem should be estimated, and the priority would then be assigned. The data quality analyst should be proactive in trying to find problems before they surface. Data quality analysis tools or simple queries could identify many of the problems.

The most important role for the data quality analyst will be evaluating and improving the processes in the data warehouse, specifically the ETL process. By improving the processes, the quality of data is likely to improve. The data quality analyst might also seek out cleaner sources of data to replace those that have proven troublesome.

8.4.13 Query Tool Administrator

The query tool administrator has responsibility for dealing with the tool vendor, assuring excellent support, and getting answers to questions. The query tool administrator deals with problems associated with the tool, including queries that produce incorrect results and queries that perform badly. The query tool administrator has responsibility for assigning passwords and, along with the security office, making sure the query tool environment is properly protected. The query tool administrator has responsibility for new releases.

8.4.14 Web Administrator

The Web administrator has the responsibility to establish an environment where result sets can be distributed on the Web, where reports can be made available on the Web, and where queries can be launched from the Web. The Web administrator will work on the Web implementation of the query tool and will be responsible for securing the Web server from unauthorized access.

8.4.15 Consultants and Contractors

Consultants and contractors are often brought in to help the organization get started, to develop an architecture, produce standards, and provide missing skills. Contractors are often retained to support a complex piece of software or to train the IT staff and the users on the use of a tool.

Consultants and contractors are expensive, and it's up to the organization to use them effectively. Consultants should be used as mentors. They posses knowledge and experience that the organization is lacking. Contractors should be used if the organization is short on resources with a particular skill.

Should contractors do the whole job—that is, should you outsource the development effort? The project may be completed more quickly—and perhaps better. The downside is that the organization becomes dependent on the contractors for maintenance and for implementing changes and enhancements. This brings up Data Warehouse Rule #7: With the data warehouse there will be more maintenance, more changes, and more enhancements than with an operational system. So, unless you want to marry the contractors, have a plan in place to transfer their knowledge to your team. This means having the people in place to receive the knowledge and allowing time for this type of training to occur. Make the knowledge transfer part of the contractor's scope, including it on the project plan, and making their payment dependent on it help to ensure it happens. Be wary of the contractor's excuse that there is not enough time to train your people and still make the scheduled deadline. Doing the work themselves and not transferring knowledge should not be an option. If your employees have not been significantly involved with the development, they will be much less interested in maintaining something that others implemented.

Documentation is usually the last task to be accomplished and, in many cases, is not completed adequately. Documentation from contractors who are expected to be leaving is especially important. Each of the contractors' deliverables must be documented to the point where an employee can support the work developed by the contractors.

8.5 ADVISORY BOARDS

Advisory boards or steering committees will make the critical decisions on the direction of the data warehouse. The absence of such boards usually means there is no high-level management commitment, little budget, and minimal support from management for the data warehouse. This almost always means the data warehouse will fail. The data warehouse is not a one-time effort; it is ongoing, and the advisory boards should also meet on an ongoing basis.

8.5.1 Technical Advisory Board

The Technical Advisory Board coordinates and authorizes IT resources. The good people are going to be hard to get, and this board will make the difficult choices about allocating those good people. There will always be changes in schedules and budgets. The Technical Advisory Board will consider and approve these changes. There will always be issues to be resolved among the IT groups, and there will always be projects such as implementation of standards, conflicting projects, redundant projects, access to certain data, security issues, and machine and personnel availability.

The Technical Advisory Board will approve the data warehouse architecture including key hardware and software components, infrastructure, and standards.

8.5.2 Business Advisory Board

The most important role for this board is the prioritization of projects. There will always be more candidates for data warehouse projects than resources to implement them. There are some projects that are mandatory, such as those directed by governmental agencies or by law. Most of the data warehouse projects are not mandatory but are cost justified, provide a competitive edge, or the CEO's pet project. The Business Advisory

Board must weigh the costs, benefits, and political significance of each project.

The Business Advisory Board will help establish, or at least approve, the data warehouse objectives and the critical measures of success. They will approve budgets, review high-level project agreements and changes to those agreements, and review the major milestones and key deliverables of the projects.

8.6   RECRUITING AND RETENTION

The data warehouse project manager must be creative to recruit and retain a good team. The manager has to position the data warehouse project as a desirable assignment. This means realistic schedules—no "death marches" here as described by Ed Yourdon (Yourdon 1997). The data warehouse can be exciting, and it should be sold as such. The team has the opportunity to work in new areas, to work with new tools, and to make a significant contribution to the business. (To make sure that the project has real value, read Chapter 6, "Cost Benefit.")

If you outsource a portion of the data warehouse to contractors and consultants, be sure that your employees have the opportunity to work on the interesting parts of the project and are not just relegated to the more mundane work. Employees often complain that the "overpaid outsiders" have all the new and exciting assignments.

How do you retain good people? The most common reason for leaving an IT job is not money but dissatisfaction with management, specifically, the immediate boss. The project manager must be seen as having power in the organization, both with IT and with the users, must be reasonable in making requests, and must be able to make good decisions. Good people like to work with other good people. (See Section 4.3 on how to keep your good workers from being hurt by having to work with the Poison People.) A strong, cohesive team is a major contributor to employee retention. Retention also means giving employees "ownership" of their work, as well as a flexible work environment. Organizations now spend considerable money on training, conferences, educational materials, and leadership development to help them retain employees.

Other retention approaches, such as family-friendly environments (day care, well-mannered dogs allowed in the workplace), telecommuting, and flexible schedules should also be considered. Bonuses should be considered and given at major milestones and at the completion of a successful project. It is important that bonuses be given to the entire team; if they are awarded only to the stars, there will be resentment.

8.7   THE DATA WAREHOUSE TEAM

Individual members working independently cannot complete a data warehouse project. *It takes a team to raise a warehouse.* The team must have the right composition of skills and experience, but there are other key factors that make it a team. There must be common goals. Creating a model or designing a star schema database is not enough. Everyone on the team must be successful in his work and must be able to incorporate his work into the whole project. A major part of that success is how the team works together and strives for the common goal of a successful project.

We recommend a two-tier team structure: the core team and the extended team (see Figure 8.1). All team members have the responsibility

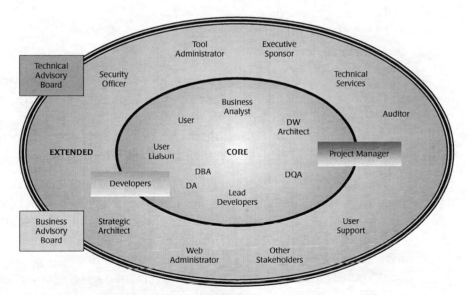

Figure 8.1: Core Team and Extended Team

for the project's success. The following roles are represented by members of the core team:

- User and user liaison
- Project manager
- Business analyst
- Data administrator (DA)
- Data quality analyst (DQA)
- Database administrator (DBA)
- Lead back-end ETL application developer
- Lead front-end application developer
- Data warehouse architect

Members of the extended team will participate in all project reviews. They will also be called into the core team to participate in activities and decisions that pertain to their specific expertise. The following roles are represented by members on this team:

- Technical services
- User support
- Security officer and auditor
- Tool and Web administrators
- Executive sponsor
- Other stakeholders
- Additional developers

The project manager will be wise to select people who work well together. Dissension on the team or philosophical differences usually result in many hours of complaining about the other members and in lack of communication. If you don't like or respect the other members, you are less likely to give them some important information.

There will still, however, be disagreements. There needs to be an atmosphere where disagreements are aired and everyone's point of view is considered. The person responsible can make most of the decisions in their area of expertise. For example, the DBAs will decide on the best physical design, and the users will choose the appropriate business definitions. There will be times when the disagreement overlaps into more than one area of responsibility. After all voices have been heard, the project manager should make the decision, and the decision should be accepted by all, even those whose positions were not chosen.

Don't involve negative forces in the project. A data warehouse team needs customer-focused people—not people who have attitudes, who hate their jobs, or who think they are smarter than anyone else. The project team should consist of open-minded business and technical individuals who will work well as a team (Rehm 1998).

The data warehouse team needs to have its own "war room." This should be a dedicated working room large enough to accommodate meetings. It should be equipped with several white boards and flip charts and have plenty of wall space to hang important documents, such as models, issues, project agreement, and so forth. The core team may work in this room and will convene for days at a time when difficult problems have to be solved or challenging decisions have to be made.

This room may also be used for regular weekly reviews with the extended team. At least at the beginning of the project, a two-hour time slot should be scheduled each week for every member of the core and extended teams. Items to be reviewed include status of activities, deliverables, problems, and proposed solutions.

8.8 TRAINING

In spite of what some query tool vendors tell you, training is absolutely necessary. Training should include the use of the tool, the data, standards for use, and the canned query libraries.

If possible, students with similar skills should be scheduled in the same training sessions. Otherwise, the questions coming from power users are likely to intimidate the casual users. A compromise pace will satisfy neither category. A slow pace will bore the power users, and a fast pace will lose the casual users.

8.8.1 Just-in-Time Training

Training on the tool should complete just before the users are given access to the tool. The more time that elapses between the class and the first use of the tool, the more likely the student will be to use the tool ineffectively. Some students will not use the tool at all because they will have forgotten most of what they had learned in class.

8.8.2   The Users' Data

Standard classes have for the workshops sample data that have little or no relevance for the students. Some students are able to see beyond the sample data and visualize how the tool would work with their data. However, these students are the exception. The difference between using sample data and data from the students' departments can be seen by their sitting posture. In the case of the sample data, students are slouched in their chairs. When using their own data, they sit on the front of their chairs and can't wait to see how to manipulate their data. It's not necessary to have an entire database loaded; a sample of their data is sufficient. Use only a sample and not the full database, otherwise the students might be tempted to focus on solving a real-life analysis question, thereby missing important content being covered in the class. Having just a subset of the data will keep them from doing any real analysis in the class. This "workshop" data is maintained on a separate database that should be refreshed each time a class begins, giving a clean and consistent set of test data.

8.8.3   Mentors

Most students will have some problems in their workshops. Depending on the size of the class, the students may have to wait for the instructor to get around to them. Some organizations have used mentors from IT who already know the tool to help the users with their problems. With mentors, the students become less frustrated because their problem gets solved sooner and they are able to finish more of the class exercises. This mentoring also helps bond IT and the users.

8.8.4   Monitoring Effectiveness of the Class

The class will not be a one-time occurrence; it will be given a number of times to different groups of users. By monitoring the effectiveness of the class, you will be able to improve it constantly. You will want to know (1) what worked and what didn't, (2) what modules the students found irrelevant, and (3) which topics should have been covered or should have been covered in more detail. You will want to know about the pace of the class, whether it was too slow or too fast. An evaluation at the conclusion of the class is fairly standard. For a more comprehensive evaluation of the content, you will want to ask about the effectiveness of the class one or two months after the students began using the tool.

8.8.5 Curriculum

Training should go beyond just the capabilities of the tool. It should include a module on the data, standards, procedures, and guidelines for the use of the tool. The class should make the students aware of the canned query library, when it is appropriate to use it, and how to use it. There may be certain functions in the tool that the organization chooses not to use for performance or security reasons. Some functions are extremely slow and resource intensive. If functions are not to be used, they should not be included in the training. This is especially important if the training is being given by an outside organization that usually has a standard curriculum and needs to be aware of the material to be eliminated.

For the power users, there should be a module on performance, showing the students the impact of certain expensive functions and how to get better response time and pay less for an operation.

The students should be exposed to using the metadata repository to give them a complete understanding of the meaning of the data and the reports. The metadata can tell them the source of the data, when it was last updated, who owns it, what it means, how it was transformed, and how reliable the data values are.

In some training classes, the underlying data models are described and given to the students. This gives them an appreciation of the relationships in the data, that each data element is not disjointed but rather fits into an overall picture.

The curriculum should include information on security, why it is important, and how it is administered. This module should include an appreciation of the value of data as an asset to the organization and why it must be protected.

The class should also address User Support, how to contact them, their role in supporting the users, how to get questions answered, familiarity with any help facilities, and, if it's in place, an introduction to frequently asked questions (FAQs). Students should also be given a form to request data that may not already be in the data warehouse. The simple requests will not require the formal prioritization, but the more complex or resource-intensive requests will go through the normal prioritization process.

8.8.6 Vendor Training

Vendors usually provide training on their product and sometimes offer training that goes beyond their product. Classes may be scheduled on-site for the customer, or they may be public classes. On-site classes may be tailored (at a cost) but will be more effective than public classes. Vendors sometimes use the classes as a selling tool for additional products or priced features. These portions of the class should be excluded, as they provide little benefit to the students.

8.9 SUMMARY

There are some who think that if they select the right tools, success is guaranteed—they are wrong. Almost all data warehouse failures can be attributed to failures in organizing properly or in not recognizing and dealing with the cultural issues.

The roadblocks to a successful data warehouse are a lack of management commitment and a lack of vision (it's not clear what the organization is planning to do with data warehouse). Without a clear vision and a strategic plan, individual projects may succeed, but there will never be an integrated view of the enterprise, and the organization will have failed to achieve one of the primary goals of the data warehouse.

The most important activity for a data warehouse project manager is assembling a team with the right skills, assigning the correct tasks to the team, and closely monitoring the execution of the tasks and their associated deliverables. While not all the team members will report to the project manager, their assigned tasks are critical to the success of the project.

The advisory boards will play critical roles in establishing priorities and finding the requisite resources to make the project successful.

Training of both IT and the users is necessary so both groups will know how to use the rich tools and understand the data that is part of the data warehouse.

 A CAUTIONARY TALE

Loss of Key Personnel

Critical members of the team became disheartened and were lured away by other companies to build their data warehouses. Nothing was documented, and there was no one left who knew the software, the system, or why decisions were made. The data warehouse could not be maintained, and, as we have learned, an unmaintained data warehouse will soon be a dead data warehouse.

8.10   WORKSHOP

8.10.1   Your Organization

Describe your organization in terms of the existing defined roles and responsibilities, the number of people in each area, full-time vs part-time, matrix vs line responsibility, and where they report.

Skills and capabilities will be categorized as follows:

5–Knowledgeable and experienced in data warehouse

4–Trained and knowledgeable but with limited experience

3–Some knowledge but training and mentoring definitely required

2–Very little knowledge but trainable

1–The CIO's fraternity brother

Indicate gaps in both assigned personnel and skill level, as well as any organization issues that could result in problems.

For example:

Existing Organization

Role	Number	Skill Level	Reporting	Reports to
DBA	5–full time	3, 4	Direct	DBA Manager
Delivery Applications Developer	12–full time	2–4	Direct	Applications Development Managers

Required Organization

Role	Number	Skill Level	Reporting	Reports to
DBA	1—full time	4	Matrix	Data Warehouse Project Manager
Delivery Applications Developer	3—full time	4, 5	Direct	Data Warehouse Project Manager
DA	1—full time	4, 5	Matrix	Data Warehouse Project Manager

Use this matrix to justify your need for resources, skills, and training. Be sure to include the time you will need to bring in, train, and familiarize these new people with your project and the data.

Existing Organization

Role	Number	Skill Level	Reporting	Reports to
DBA				
ETL Developer				
Delivery Applications Developer				
DA				
Data Quality Analyst				
DW Architect				
User Liaison				
Technical Services				
Security/Audit				
Web Administrator				
Query Tool Administrator				

Be sure to include the time you will need to bring in, train, and familiarize these new people with your project and the data.

Required Organization

Role	Number	Skill Level	Reporting	Reports to
DBA				
ETL Developer				
Delivery Applications Developer				
DA				
Data Quality Analyst				
DW Architect				
User Liaison				
Technical Services				
Security/Audit				
Web Administrator				
Query Tool Administrator				

REFERENCES

Foote, David. "IT Salary Survey Data and Job Descriptions." Foote Research Group, New Canaan, Conn., 1999.

Rehm, Clay. "Warehouse Dos and Don'ts," *IDWA Navigator*, Fall 1998.

Yourdon, Edward. *Death March: The Complete Software Developer's Guide to Surviving "Mission Impossible" Projects.* Upper Saddle River, N.J.: Prentice Hall, 1997.

CHAPTER NINE

Methodology

Every organization has a software development methodology. Many just don't know what it is.

—*Watts Humphrey*

You just have to spend time discovering the right thing to do—it's not enough to do things the right way.

—*Earl Hoskins*

Most companies use the "Sinatra Methodology," where everyone does it "their way."

Developing any automated system without a formal methodology is about as smart as playing Russian roulette with a fully loaded gun. Data warehouses are no exception. In this chapter we explore the iterative nature of data warehouse development and explain a different development approach for these types of projects. This chapter covers the following topics:

- The back-end extract/transform/load process
- The front-end data delivery process
- The repository navigation process
- The technical infrastructure process
- Major development steps with tasks and deliverables
- Postimplementation reviews

In the Workshop you will itemize the infrastructure components that you will need for your project, you will draft a project agreement, and you will select tasks and deliverables appropriate for your project. Appendix 9.A describes some service level agreement (SLA) standards.

9.1 DATA WAREHOUSE ITERATIONS

A data warehouse cannot and should not be built in one "big bang." Instead, a data warehouse is an evolving system that must be built in iterations—small iterations—that evolve over time into a robust, well-defined, quality-oriented data warehouse. Although this concept is easy to understand and appreciate, it is difficult to apply.

Users have been conditioned over the past few decades to ask for all they can during their initial identification of requirements because they may never get a second chance. With this "If I don't ask for everything under the sun now, it will take years before I'll get it" philosophy, they do the following:

- Ask for *everything* (usually at transaction level detail).
- Ask to keep everything *forever*.
- Ask to have it all *immediately* (which usually translates into deliverables of 90 to 120 days or less because all the vendor hype makes this seem reasonable)
- Expect that *everything, forever* and *immediately* will instantly be clean and integrated—as if by magic

This doesn't work. It doesn't work for a number of reasons.

9.1.1 Reasons for Big Bang Failures

First of all, in a decision support environment, the requirements are never as stable nor as well understood as in an operational system. Moreover, in a data warehouse environment, where users can "play" with their data as never before, they are constantly discovering new requirements, and they are changing or dropping some of their old ones. This means that the underlying system would constantly have to change as well. The larger the system, the longer it takes to change it.

Second, *everything* and *immediately* have never been able to live in the same sentence, not in an operational environment and especially not in data warehousing. *Everything* in data warehousing means data from many operational systems, data that has never been cleansed or integrated. It also means data from external sources and sources completely new to the business and to the developers. The time and effort required for all that dirty and disparate data to be cleansed and integrated definitely will not fit the category of *immediately*.

Third, since *everything* implies a colossal scope and *immediately* implies a minuscule amount of time, all the vendor hype in the world won't change the laws of physics. There is great merit in asking for immediate delivery so that the organization can quickly gain from added value to its business. However, since it is not possible to deliver everything quickly, let alone *immediately*, there must be a strategy in place to deliver small increments over time.

Finally, the larger the scope, the harder it is to manage and the higher the risk for failure. Adding to this formula the probability that the requirements are unstable and subject to change, any Big Bang data warehouse project would be heading straight for disaster, as it is guaranteed to miss target dates and budgets and, most important, fail any user expectations. It is difficult to recover from these outcomes.

9.1.2 Considerations for First Data Warehouse Project

The first data warehouse iteration is the most crucial one and should be kept restrained in scope, both functional scope and data scope. Users, especially those who still panic about IT's past nonresponsive track record, will resist this, and it will be up to you to explain the reasons for this approach.

Huge Learning Curve

The staff may have attended training seminars for the new tools, they may have gone to data warehouse conferences, they may even have a mentor aboard who will help overcome hurdles. There will still be a tremendous learning curve for everyone on the IT as well as the user side because training is in no way a substitute for experience. There is only one way to gain experience, and that is through the school of hard knocks.

New Technology

Besides all the adjustments the team members will have to make, coming up to speed with new technology will be a challenge. This will be especially true for those whose first exposure to the client/server or Web environment is the data warehouse project. The Web especially adds an additional layer of complexity to building, testing, maintaining, and operating the data warehouse. In addition to learning new technology components, such as new development tools (ETL) and new delivery tools (OLAP), the team members will have to learn to navigate the new environment. That means learning a new operating system, how to manipulate files, new languages and their compilers, new testing tools, and new utilities. It also means learning on their workstation about operational features that they never had to worry about before, such as the network setup, library management, file backup, and recovery.

Cultural Adjustment

As described in Chapter 8, "Organization and Cultural Issues," roles and responsibilities will have shifted, and the team members may be struggling with their new roles. Some may not have the skills or the confidence to carry out their new responsibilities. Some may not be used to working in a core team group where brainstorming on issues, reaching consensus decisions, and occasionally challenging old work habits are the norm of the day.

Lack of Infrastructure

When speaking of infrastructure, we must divide this topic into two sections: the technical infrastructure and the nontechnical infrastructure.

Although most organizations already have a technical infrastructure in place, some new technical infrastructure pieces, such as new hardware, network components, a new RDBMS to be used, as well as new utilities and tools, as outlined in Chapter 7, "Selecting Software," may have to be added. This is not a trivial effort, and it must take into account future data warehouse iterations in order to be scalable.

As involved as the technical infrastructure components are, the nontechnical infrastructure components often take more time to implement. Standards have to be established. A methodology for data warehouse projects has to be purchased or developed. As part of that methodology, roles and responsibilities have to be established, change control procedures have to be written, and an issues log has to be created. Security considerations for hardware, network, database access, Web access, tool usage, and sensitive corporate data have to be documented. Procedures for enforcing security measures also have to be set up and published. In addition, a help facility along with personnel to assist users must be established.

Lack of Standards

Many organizations are very lax in enforcing their standards, if they have any at all. Since operational systems and traditional decision support systems have always been separate and nonintegrated, the lack of standards might have been tolerable, although never advisable. In an integrated data warehouse environment, lack of standards will contribute to a chaotic development environment and will result in noncohesive data delivery to the users. When developing standards, the following categories have to be considered.

Prioritization. Users may be in disagreement of whose requirements should be the first or the next data warehouse deliverable. If a procedure for prioritization is not in place, IT will be caught in a political fight that it cannot resolve without causing bad feelings among users and possibly losing some future data warehouse users. Guidelines for resolving governance issues are discussed in Chapter 8, "Organization and Cultural Issues."

Data naming (including synonyms and aliases). Both the business names and the technical names should follow some standards. A common standard for creating business names is to base it on its concise business definition, to eliminate articles, prepositions, conjunctions, and excess words, and to classify the remaining words as a prime word, a qualifier, or a class word. A business name is typically made up of one prime word, one or more qualifiers, and one class word at the end. Examples of prime words are *customer, account, order, product,* and *loan.* Examples of qualifiers are *checking, savings, medical, prospective,* and *pending.* Examples of class words are *date, code, name, amount, percent,* and *number.*

Abbreviations. Technical data names should always use abbreviations. This requires that an approved abbreviation list be compiled and published. A rule of thumb for creating these abbreviations is to eliminate the vowels and double consonants of a word. A common standard for creating a technical name is to use the approved abbreviation of each component of the business name. If the resulting technical name is still too long, one or more qualifiers are eliminated. Under no circumstances should an approved abbreviation be further abbreviated.

Metadata capture and usage. Metadata provides the navigation through a data warehouse. It is imperative that metadata is complete and accurate. Therefore, procedures must be set up with clearly assigned responsibilities and authorization to capture and maintain the metadata, as well as how and when to use it. There are two types of metadata: business metadata and technical metadata. Business metadata serves the users and provides clarification on a daily basis for data they access and use. Technical metadata assists both users and IT staff in navigating the labyrinth of tables, columns, and programs which are used for defining and maintaining the data warehouse and its associated processes. These two sets of metadata have very different focuses and purposes. Appropriate individuals should be assigned the task of capturing and maintaining their metadata in the most complete and timely method possible. Metadata is also discussed in Chapter 7, "Selecting Software," and Chapter 8, "Organization and Cultural Issues."

Data quality measures. Since a main objective of every data warehouse is to improve data quality to some degree, standards and procedures on how to accomplish that should be established. These standards and procedures should include a process for determining what level of quality is required of the data warehouse data and for assessing the data quality of the feeding source systems. Refer to Chapter 11, "Data Quality," for an in-depth discussion. The standards and procedures should also include guidelines for determining the severity of the problem and for performing a cost benefit analysis for the data cleansing effort. Finally, the standards and procedures should also outline a program for periodically monitoring and measuring the quality of the data within the data warehouse.

Testing. Just because we deliver data and functionality for a data warehouse incrementally does not mean "Skip testing! We'll fix it in the next iteration." There may not be a next iteration if the quality of the deliverable does not meet the stated user requirements and their expectations. Testing standards for each development track should include guidelines for developing test scripts, writing test cases, documenting expected test results, logging actual results, as well as having a process in place for test reruns.

Security. Similar to testing, just because data warehousing is a decision support environment does not mean "ignore security." Security standards should include procedures for defining the security requirements for each data element and for identifying data ownership responsible for assigning access privileges to the data. The standards should include rules for reviewing the current security features in the operational environment so that the requested security features for the same data in the data warehouse environment can be better evaluated. The standards also should have guidelines for identifying approaches to implement the security requirements and for assigning security responsibilities to the appropriate staff members. Security may be set by group or by individual and may be controlled at the data access tool, the database, or both. If the data warehouse application is going to be Web-enabled, additional security exposures must be identified and addressed. Firewalls must be tested by someone who is looking for ways to break through and not by someone who is attempting to prove the invulnerability of the firewall.

Service level agreements. Most likely your organization already has some standards in place regarding service level agreements (SLA). These standards need to be adapted to data warehouse projects. If these standards do not exist, they must be created, and the guidelines for the SLA categories should be described. SLA categories are typically the following:

- *Response Time:* A commitment on how fast a report will run or a table be refreshed. Note that response time for ad hoc queries are impossible to estimate.
- *Availability:* A commitment to the percentage of time the data warehouse will be available during scheduled hours.
- *Timeliness:* A commitment to the currency of the data.

- *Data Quality:* A commitment to the reliability of data. An indication of how many records or what percentage of records have accurate values.
- *Ongoing Support:* A commitment on how quickly response will be given to problems.

9.1.3   Guidelines for First Data Warehouse Project

You should consider the following guidelines when planning your first data warehouse project.

Small in Size

What constitutes *small* in size? This is very difficult to judge because we cannot give a guideline in terms of gigabytes, the number of new reports, or even the number of users. In fact, the meaning of *small* is directly related and balanced against the time it will take to implement or at least to consider all the other guidelines in this section. Small in size is defined as follows:

> Whatever is doable, in terms of functionality and amount of data, in the amount of time given to this project, considering the cleanliness of the data, or lack thereof, the number of new tools, the current skill set of resources, the number of standards in place or the standards yet to be established, and the availability of the users.

Few Legacy Source Files and Few Data Elements

It is not difficult to judge the number of source files to include, as it purely depends on the effort involved to (1) cleanse and transform the data elements of each file and (2) integrate the data from the files based on the business rules of the logical data model. Availability of the source files must also be taken into consideration and whether they are internal files or externally generated files.

We have measured the time it typically takes to process a data element from the time it is identified as a requirement to writing the transformation and cleansing programming specifications for it. The average was two to three data elements per day, although some clients averaged only one per day.

Fairly Clean Data

Never base your assessment of the source data on simply asking the users or the IT staff the question "How clean do you think the data is?" The answer will always be "Oh, pretty good" because the person answering will think only of typographical or programming errors. There are ten different dirty data categories described in Chapter 11, "Data Quality." These need to be dealt with, and without a thorough analysis of the candidate source files, there is no way to estimate how long the effort for cleansing and transforming will take. When a source file is an externally generated file, it may be very difficult to obtain it in advance in order to assess it. In that case, generous estimates and a contingency plan must be developed for any portion of the data warehouse that relies on the external file.

Value-Added Data, Yet Not Mission Critical

Although the first deliverable will be small in size, it is nevertheless important that it provides some value-added functionality and new ways for the users to view the data. This could be the integration of two disparate source files or the collection of all customer data into one customer table or some derived data whose calculation is very complex and often misused or misinterpreted by users. This value-added functionality or data, however, should not be so mission critical that it will harm the business operation if not delivered on time or as promised.

Few New Tools Required

This is another category that can be somewhat controlled. You have to build in a learning curve for every new piece of technology. The more new tools, the longer the learning curve, the smaller the size of the deliverable has to be. Leveraging technology that already exists in the work environment where feasible is the most prudent approach. When new technology is introduced to IT or users, be sure there is adequate and timely training, as well as time allocated to become familiar with the tool following the training.

Standards to Be Defined

The status of your standards will be the biggest influencing factor on all of the guidelines described in this section. The fewer standards that exist, the more that will have to be established, and the smaller the first deliverable can be. This is not to say that the project has to come to a screeching halt until all standards are in place. Like all other aspects of data warehousing, the standards will develop in an iterative fashion. A lot will be learned during the first project, and the standards will have to be adjusted. It is crucial that the standards be documented as they are being developed, or they will be postponed indefinitely, much to the detriment of subsequent projects.

Strong and Supportive User Sponsor

This is the most critical ingredient to any data warehouse project, especially your first. Many companies claim they have strong sponsorship for their data warehouse project, but when the challenges start to appear, these strong sponsorships turn out to be nothing but lip service. The sponsor should have a record for being supportive on other projects and should have a reputation for removing roadblocks for the team. Unfortunately, many data warehouse teams don't know enough about their sponsors and find out about their strength and supportiveness only when something goes wrong. If, when faced with a critical decision, the sponsor's immediate reaction is to threaten to cancel the project, voice doubts in the project manager's ability to manage the project, or express concerns about the competency of the staff, you do not have real support. Instead, you have an additional problem that must be resolved. If, on the other hand, the sponsor's reactions are a willingness to explore all possibilities for correction, an offer to get involved and run interference, or supportive pep talk, you probably have a competent and caring sponsor.

Experienced Project Manager

Data warehouse projects are not for rookie managers. The development environment is much too dynamic to be controlled by an inexperienced project manager. Development activities for the back-end developers run at a different speed than those for the front-end developers. Roadblocks abound, and adjustments have to be made frequently. Managing these projects with a tighter change control procedure than usual is the only recipe for not losing control. Prior experience with a data warehouse project would be very helpful, and at a minimum, the project manager must be educated on data warehousing through seminars, conferences, or books and articles. This, coupled with strong management and communication skills, will contribute much to the project's success.

Users Involved in All Development Steps

Data warehouse projects cannot be developed without full-time user participation. In this dynamic environment, unanticipated problems come up constantly, the impact of those problems has to be evaluated immediately, and decisions for correction have to be negotiated. This is not a process the IT project manager can or should take upon himself. These decisions have a business impact and should be made jointly by the IT project manager and the business project manager after taking all the technical and business related repercussions into account.

Implemented as a Pilot

After all is said and done, and all the testing has been performed, all the data and queries have been validated against the requirements, it may still be wise not to rush into the production environment. Experience shows that during the first month or two in production, users create a laundry list of changes. This list might include anything from minor adjustments to major changes of the original requirements. IT often scrambles to apply the minor adjustments to the production tables. Since the production libraries reside in a tightly controlled environment, their scramble often proves time-consuming and painful. Delay moving the tables and programs into the frozen production environment until these adjustments have been identified and applied.

9.2 PROTOTYPING AS A DEVELOPMENT APPROACH

Prototyping has traditionally had two meanings:

1. Throwaway proof of concept. This is usually not a full-function database but merely a mockup of a proposed system. This type of prototype is never meant to be used for anything other than demonstration purposes, and the users and management understand that it will be discarded.
2. Salvageable pilot to be completed or rewritten into a "real system." This type of pilot is more than a throwaway demo but less than a full-function system. It often uses real data and is distributed on a limited

basis to a small number of users to test. Once approved, another project is launched to turn the pilot into a real production system.

We would like to introduce a third meaning: prototyping as a methodology, where the pilot *is* the real system without having to be completed or rewritten. We suggest a modified version of the rapid application development (RAD) approach, which is commonly used for prototyping, as the development method to produce the data warehouse deliverables. This is not a quick-and-dirty approach where tasks, documentation, and testing are skipped and where the price to be paid later will be in rewrites and fixes.

9.2.1 What Is RAD?

To start with, RAD is not hacking away at an application until it works—that is, the word *rapid* in RAD does not mean taking the requirements over the phone and coding them the same day in a trial-and-error fashion, skipping over tasks, and ignoring documentation. On the other hand, it also does not mean finishing the requirements definition before proceeding with analysis or finishing the analysis before starting design. Due to the dynamic environment, much experimenting occurs, from nailing down the requirements and establishing scope to proving new technology components. In this type of environment, whatever is thought to be finished one day will have to be reworked the next day. Therefore, the word *rapid* in RAD means performing each task in as much detail as is known and feasible at the time with the expectation to come back to it and refine it. We refer to these refinements as *looping* activities. New and looping activities continue to occur in an iterative fashion until the prototype becomes the defined data warehouse pilot project.

9.2.2 Prototyping Success Spiral vs. Death Spiral

Many prototyping projects fail because there is no clear problem definition, the scope keeps changing from day to day, the clients are not participating, the team bites off more than they can chew, and no flexible tools are available. The final twist on the prototyping death spiral, however, can usually be attributed to the fact that the development activities are neither managed nor controlled. These projects generally show a timeline of several weeks for each prototype iteration without specific tasks assigned to specific people, without anyone assigned to track and report daily and weekly activities, without change control procedures or issues logs, and without anyone monitoring the activities. Everyone is busy, but nobody knows where he is, what he's done, or when he'll get to wherever he's going. Often he doesn't even know where he's going.

To turn a death spiral into a success spiral, all activities must be immediately time-boxed. That means that each week should be planned, managed, and controlled like a small project. For each week, the scope and the deliverables are clearly defined, tasks (including those for looping activities) are assigned to the resources at hand, all problems are recorded on the issues log, and all changes are subject to the change control procedure. These activities and deliverables are managed by the core team members and are controlled and reported on by the project manager. If severe roadblocks that cannot easily be resolved within the week are encountered, an impact analysis is performed, and the results are negotiated between IT and users against the whole project plan. In some cases the roadblocks will force some major redirection of the project, which requires the approval of the executive sponsor.

9.3   PARALLEL DEVELOPMENT TRACKS

Another typical aspect to data warehouse development is the three, sometimes four, parallel development processes, or tracks, occurring at the same time. It is true that some parallel work is done on traditional projects as well, such as building interfaces to downstream and upstream systems, but these activities are usually peripheral to the main project development work. On data warehouse projects, the main development activities, such as building the target databases, developing the applications, and creating the metadata repository, are divided into multiple major parallel tracks. The project manager now has to manage the team for each track and coordinate among them.

9.3.1 Back-end ETL Track

The back-end ETL team is responsible for creating and populating the data warehouse databases. This group must be staffed with senior hardcore developers who have several years of structured programming experience. The ETL process is the most involved and the most complicated of all processes in a data warehouse. This process will consume from 70 percent to 80 percent of the development time. It is here where the extraction, sorting, merging, integrating, cleansing, and transformation of the source data take place. It is this process that produces source-to-target reconciliation totals and prepares the load files for the data warehouse target databases. Since the ETL process must be centrally controlled, the process flow from source to target will adjust and expand continuously with each data warehouse iteration. Over time, this process becomes very complicated. This complication is responsible for the extensive amount of time required for regression testing on each new data warehouse project. Regression testing means that all programs in the ETL process flow, from extracting source data to creating load files, must be retested every time a change is made to any portion of that process.

9.3.2   Front-end Data Delivery Track

The front-end data delivery team generally does not concern themselves with the quality and consistency of the data in the data warehouse target databases, as that is the responsibility of the back-end team. However, they will assist in the entire data quality and data delivery certification process. The delivery team concentrates on presenting the data to the users through a variety of tools. The developers on this team must be intimately familiar with the client/server environment as well as the Web and with all the chosen data warehouse tools, from report writers to OLAP query tools to Web-enabled access. They must also understand multidimensional database design because more often than not, they will be required to manipulate the summary databases and help users with drill-down and roll-up functionality.

9.3.3   Repository Navigation Track

There often is a group on the data warehouse team that deals with metadata delivery. If your organization has installed a repository with good reporting capabilities and a graphic user interface (GUI) front-end, or even a Web interface, there may not be a need for this team. However, if a metadata repository is being developed from scratch or if a metadata delivery application is being developed, this team would be responsible for those development activities. This team would also create a help function, preferably context sensitive, to assist users in navigating through the data warehouse databases. The content of such a help facility is often packaged and used in conjunction with training materials.

9.3.4 Technical Infrastructure Track

The development teams are supported by another group, the technical infrastructure team. These are the people who are responsible for installing and testing all the technical infrastructure components, such as the network, the hardware, the software, the tools, and the utilities. Members of the technical infrastructure team are usually matrixed into the data warehouse project and operate under the direction of the data warehouse IT project manager. For details on organizational placement of this team, refer to Appendix 8.A.

9.4 MAJOR DEVELOPMENT STEPS

Although some data warehouse methodologies still group development activities into *phases*, we prefer to call these groupings *major development steps* because the word *phase* implies a conventional waterfall approach. Traditionally, activities and deliverables of one phase have to be completed and signed off by the user before another phase can begin. For example, Requirements Definition has to be completed before Analysis can begin, and Analysis has to be completed before Design can begin, and so on. In data warehousing, activities and deliverables, which traditionally would fall into one specific phase, are guaranteed to be repeated in subsequent phases and can therefore not be considered completed.

A major development step, on the other hand, usually spans over multiple traditional phases and includes looping activities. Like a traditional phase, a major development step also denotes a completed segment of work, which is tracked as a milestone. However, the definition of a data warehouse segment of work is not Planning, Requirements Definition, Analysis, and so on, but is instead aligned with a major deliverable for a development track, such as Build the Target Databases, Produce Canned Queries, and so forth.

9.4.1 Project Agreement Step

The main objective of this development step is to produce the Project Agreement document, which is a detailed roadmap for the data warehouse project. Sometimes the Project Agreement document is also known as a Project Charter, Document of Understanding, Scope Agreement, or Statement of Work. It should contain the following sections.

Data Warehouse Goals and Objectives

As mentioned in Chapter 2, "Goals and Objectives," it is important that the data warehouse goals and objectives are in line with the organization's strategic goals and objectives. Both the data warehouse goals and objectives and the strategic goals and objectives should be captured in this section.

Specific Business Requirements and Their Solution

The data warehouse is a complex decision support environment with different types of databases designed to solve different types of business problems. This section should have a clear statement describing the nature of the broad-based requirements and categorizing them as operational reporting requirements or as tactical or strategic business analysis requirements. A high-level architecture diagram should pictorially represent the proposed solution, showing the number of target databases and their type (Operational Data Store, Enterprise Data Warehouse, Data Mart), the potential source files, and the proposed source-to-target ETL flow.

Cost/Benefit Analysis

The business requirements and their solution, as described in the previous paragraph, should have a detailed cost/benefit analysis showing the expected return on investment (ROI) and the time frame during which it is estimated that ROI will be achieved. Although some organizations launch their data warehouse projects based on an edict from upper management without performing a cost/benefit analysis, we believe it is a prudent business practice to determine the return on any significant investment. For a comprehensive discussion of ROI, read Chapter 6, "Cost Benefit."

High-Level Functional Scope

Once the business problem and the proposed solution alternatives have been stated, it is important to consider the scope of the project, keeping in mind that a big bang development approach to solve a business problem is not a viable option. It may be necessary to go through several iterations of analysis before the functional scope and actual solution alternatives can be totally realized. How much functionality can be delivered will depend on a number of factors:

- How much data must be captured from the source files
- How much effort will go into the data cleansing and transformation process
- How many source files have to be integrated
- Availability of external source files
- How much new technology has to be evaluated, installed, and learned
- Current skill set of the team
- Anticipated budget and delivery date

High-Level Data Model of Target Subject Area

An excellent technique to use during the scoping of a project is logical data modeling. A conceptual data model showing the subject area(s) under consideration is a premier method for the following functions:

- Identifying data elements that must be subject to source data analysis
- Capturing business rules as well as process rules relating to the data
- Showing data dependencies and data integration points
- Collecting business metadata

Furthermore, a conceptual data model can be built on and refined during the more detailed analysis activities. It can serve as a starting point for physical design if your data warehouse target database is a two-dimensional database structure, as would be appropriate for an ODS or EDW, or for designing conforming dimensions of a multidimensional database structure.

Infrastructures

The only deliverables users see for their data warehouse iteration is the data and the functionality made available to them. But from a project development perspective, the data warehouse deliverables must rest on an infrastructure. There are two types of infrastructures: the technical infrastructure and the development infrastructure. Technical infrastructure deliverables on a project may include a new processor, a new database management system, new development tools, new data delivery tools, and a purchased or developed metadata repository. Development infrastructure deliverables on a project may include a purchased or developed methodology, new or changed standards, new staff roles and responsibilities, and establishment of technical and business advisory boards. These infrastructure deliverables must be carefully considered and planned. Review the technical and the development infrastructure components that do not yet exist at your organization but are necessary for a successful data warehouse environment. Since the entire infrastructure does not have to be built all at once, negotiate for those infrastructure components that are critical to your project.

History Requirements

Most users want to have historical data from the time their data warehouse is implemented, rather than waiting for it to accumulate over time. If history has to be loaded, it will add another layer of complexity. Some record layouts change frequently, and it is entirely probable that the historical source files will be structured differently from the current files. It also means that another set of programs, albeit similar to the initial load programs, will have to be written and tested. This must be balanced against all other components of the Project Agreement document so that expectations remain reasonable.

Number of Source Files

It may not be possible to determine the final selection of source files at this stage in the project, but the users and the team members usually have a good idea of how many and which possible source files they may need to analyze.

Quality Assessment of Source Data

Once the candidate source files have been identified, it is advisable to look at the data values as they are identified on the logical data model to find data errors, business rule exceptions, redefined fields, and encoded values on the source files. The number of exceptions found and their severity will be an indication of the necessary effort for data cleansing and transformation. Refer to Chapter 11, "Data Quality," for details on assessing the quality of your source data.

User Responsibilities

Users are accustomed to graciously granting some interview hours to the IT analyst to convey their requirements and then waiting for the system to be delivered. Since that approach won't work in data warehousing, users must learn about their new role and their new responsibilities. Users are unaccustomed and unprepared for their new role, and much groundwork must be laid in terms of educating them on the key issues of data warehousing and on the necessity for their full-time availability and participation. The Project Agreement document is an excellent place to capture this information. A detailed accounting of user roles and responsibilities is given in Chapter 8, "Organization and Cultural Issues."

Availability Requirements

Similar to operational systems, users have a need to access their data warehouse at certain times of the day. However, since this is a decision support environment, availability requirements of 24 hours a day, 7 days a week should be questioned. There are exceptions to every rule. For example, an organization that is international with offices around the globe and that has a centralized data warehouse may need to be up and running 24 hours a day, 7 days a week. However, in most other cases, much shorter availability requirements will suffice, as long as there is sufficient time allowed to cover the required time zones and the scheduled jobs have enough time to complete. It is not unreasonable to allow weekly downtime for essential database backups, database loads, and other maintenance functions.

Security Requirements

It is erroneous to assume that because a data warehouse is a decision support system you do not need to be concerned with security requirements as you would for an operational system. This is a dangerous assumption, especially if delivery of the data includes the Web and if users of the data have the ability to drill down into more detailed records. Security requirements should be specified for the database, the tools, any particularly sensitive data, and the environment as a whole. In addition, the granularity of access should be defined. Some users may have access to summarized data but may not have the need, or the authority, to go to the detail records from which the summaries were created. For example, summary salary totals by department may be accessible to everyone, but authority to drill down to individual salaries may be inhibited or given to only a select few.

Report/Query Libraries

Most data warehouses provide prewritten and parameterized reports and queries. Those need to be stored and their versions managed in a query library. Many query tools provide such libraries. The Project Agreement document should define the implementation of a library and should also identify the person or group responsible for populating and maintaining it.

Access Tools for Data Delivery

With hundreds of tools on the market, it is wise to narrow the scope for purchasing, installing, and using such tools as early in the project as possible. This section of the document should contain the categories of tools to be evaluated, the criteria for evaluation and selection of a tool, a methodology or procedure for tool selection, and a list of people or groups who will be participating in the evaluation process. If tools have already been chosen, they should be identified.

DW Project Team Roles and Responsibilities

In Chapter 8, "Organization and Cultural Issues," we described the shifted roles and responsibilities of project team members. The Project Agreement document should list the roles and responsibilities and assign them to team members as soon as they are identified.

High-Level Project Plan

Of course, no Project Agreement would be complete without a high-level project plan. Be sure to show the various parallel development processes with their individual milestones on the project plan. Assign administrative support responsibility for expanding and maintaining the consolidated plan, as each development leader will have input for those activities specifically assigned to him. Use this high-level project plan in the review meetings to gauge the progress against the overall initial schedule, to examine issues, to adjust tasks, or to renegotiate the schedule as required. Appendix 12.B contains a sample project plan.

What Is Not in Scope

Has this ever happened to you? After several long meetings, you success-fully negotiate a feasible scope only to discover halfway through the project that the users expect to get a function that had been discussed but later discarded during the negotiation meetings. That's Life's Lesson #37: Different people remember different things! If something was discussed and discarded, document that as well.

Assumptions and Known Constraints

Naturally, you won't have all the answers at the beginning of a project. All of the components in this Project Agreement document are based on assumptions and known constraints at the time. Be sure to document them, and expect them to change. An example of an assumption is that the production server will be up and running by no later than April 2. In reality, the date may turn out to be April 24, but given adequate lead time, this delay can be addressed and dealt with without necessarily impacting the balance of the project schedule.

Change Management Procedure Outline

We dislike and discourage change on traditional projects. On data ware-house projects, change comes with the territory. Change by itself is not destructive, but failing to assess and control change can kill the project. Outline a change management procedure for the project from its incep-tion in this section of the Project Agreement document. Focus on impacts to major tasks and milestones, as opposed to minor subtasks, or you will become lost in the weeds of minutia.

Risk Scenario Document

On data warehouse projects, risk also comes with the territory. No matter how much you've planned and analyzed and feel you've covered all your bases, there will still be risk. Like change, risk must be evaluated and controlled. In this section of the Project Agreement document, list all the possible known risks that might apply to your project, as well as the likelihood of their occurrence, their impact, and most important, your contingency plans. Then be ready for the unknown! We discuss risks and failures in Chapter 4, "Risks."

Preliminary Service Level Agreements (SLA)

Users like service level agreements because they are tools for measurement. The first item users like to commit to is usually performance. In data warehousing, an SLA on performance should be last because there are too many factors involved in monitoring database access and tuning for performance to make a strong commitment early in the project. Agreeing to preliminary response time numbers and fine-tuning them as the project progresses, including after it has gone into production, is a compromise approach. Remember that an SLA for ad hoc query performance does not make sense because it is not possible to predict what types of queries users will write. Some may be extraordinarily complicated, and some may not be written very efficiently.

To be able to produce a detailed Project Agreement document with all of the components listed earlier, it is necessary to go beyond the traditional high-level requirements and planning activities. You and your user must perform some data analysis on the source files, be aware of candidate tools, establish a framework for standardization and infrastructure, address roles and responsibilities, and manage expectations. The Project Agreement must be a jointly developed and negotiated document between IT and user. It must be presumed and accepted that the contents of the document will change during the project. These changes will have to be controlled by both IT and user through a change management procedure.

During the Project Agreement step, the following major activities and deliverables lead up to producing the Project Agreement document.

Activity	*Deliverable*
Prepare the project.	Strategic business goals and objectives
	Data warehouse goals and objectives
	Project Agreement outline
	Project plan outline
	Memos to advisory boards
Define business requirements.	Business requirements document
Model the data within the scope.	High-level logical data model
	Significant attributes in scope
	Business metadata (see Chapter 10, "Data Models")
Identify data sources.	Data quality exceptions document
	Draft of data transformation specifications
Determine technology architecture.	Technology model (see Chapter 7, "Selecting Software")
	High-level architecture diagram
Determine distribution architecture.	Data distribution matrix
	DW distribution model

Source: MapXpert Methodology™, Xpert Corporation.

9.4.2 Establish Technology Platform Step

The purpose of this development step is to review and analyze the proposed technology platform components identified during the Project Agreement step and to determine the most appropriate technology platform for the data warehouse, which may include the following:

- Central processing unit (CPU)
- Direct access storage device (DASD)
- Relational database management system (RDBMS)
- Extract, transform, and load (ETL) tool
- Cleansing tool

- Reporting and querying tools
- Web-enabled tools
- Test tool
- Computer-aided Software Engineering (CASE) tool
- Repository
- Utilities

Some of these components may already be in place, others may have to be purchased, and others may not even be needed.

The business requirements document from the previous step, the high-level solution alternatives, and the desired access tools must be analyzed and compared to the available technology components already in house as well as those on the market. Tool selection criteria must be developed in preparation for evaluating tools and vendors and for narrowing the choices to a short list. This topic is elaborated in Chapter 7, "Selecting Software."

Once the tools are selected, they must be installed and all of the tools' capabilities must be thoroughly tested in your environment. Besides testing the tools' advertised capabilities, be sure to include testing of interfaces to other tools, such as Web delivery tools. The testing must also include the tools' performance under your operating system. Tools that are designed for a specific operating system—for example, Unix—and are later adapted to other popular operating systems—for example, Windows NT/Windows 2000—do not always perform equally well on each operating system.

The following common activities and deliverables occur during the establish technology platform step.

Activity	Deliverable
Define selection criteria.	Selection criteria document
	Selection methodology/procedure
	Vendor candidate list
	Vendor short list
	Request for proposal (RFP)—optional
Select vendor/product.	Final selection list
	Questions for references
	Reference interview notes
	Contract/Purchase Order
Install/test/prototype product.	Prepared facilities
	Installed product
	Test log with documented test results
	Trained tool administrators

Source: MapXpert Methodology, Xpert Corporation.

9.4.3 Database and Extract/Transform/Load (ETL) Development Step

While some project team members are establishing the technology platform, others are concentrating on the back-end ETL process. The business requirements document from the Project Agreement step must be analyzed and updated if necessary. The logical data model is fully attributed during this step, and the gathering of business metadata is completed. While the logical data model is being attributed, the source files are rigorously analyzed for each defined attribute. All data exceptions are reported back to the data modeling team, which models any new attributes discovered during the source analysis process. During this step, the source to target data transformation programming specifications are also completed and given to the ETL developers, who code the ETL programs either with the help of an ETL tool or in native code.

As soon as the logical data model becomes stable and the ETL programming specifications are being developed, the access patterns are identified from the business requirements document, and database structures are designed. If the target database is either an Operational Data Store (ODS) or an Enterprise Data Warehouse database (EDW), the database design will most likely be two-dimensional. In the case of an ODS, the structure should closely represent the operational view, which is two-dimensional. In the case of an EDW, which will serve all current and future users and their requirements, the only way to accommodate these numerous contradicting requirements in one database is to keep it in a two-dimensional design.

If the target database is a data mart and the requirements are mostly summaries, the database design will most likely be a multidimensional star schema or other multidimensional database schema, although occasionally a two-dimensional database with standalone summary tables may be used. On the other hand, if the target database is a data mart and the requirements are unstable or maximum flexibility is a priority, the database design will most likely remain two-dimensional, as opposed to multidimensional. For details on database design options, refer to Chapter 10, "Data Models."

The major activities and deliverables for the database and ETL development step can be summarized as follows:

Activity	Deliverable
Complete analysis activities.	Updated business requirements document
	Fully attributed logical data model
	Updated business metadata
Identify access patterns.	Data access requirements document
Design and develop databases.	Denormalized physical data model(s)
	Data definition language (DDL)
	Physical database structures
	Technical metadata (see Chapter 10, "Data Models")

continued

Activity	Deliverable
Finalize data ETL specifications.	Updated data transformation specifications
	Updated technical metadata
	ETL process flow diagram
	Test plan, test script, test cases, test log
Design and code ETL programs.	Coded transformation programs
	Reconciliation totals
	Tested transformation programs
	Updated test plan, test results
Conduct acceptance test.	Tie-out reports
	Reconciliation totals (reports)
	Record rejection counts (reports)
	Updated programs
Prepare for implementation.	Production database structures
	Production program libraries
	Operational procedures

Source: MapXpert Methodology, Xpert Corporation.

9.4.4 Query and Reporting Development Step

While the database and ETL design and development processes are taking place, the front-end data delivery team is designing and prototyping the reports and queries and other data delivery mechanisms, including delivery of metadata. By this time, the technology platform should have been established, and new tools should have been installed and tested.

Using the business requirements document from the Project Agreement step and the data access requirements being identified during the parallel database and ETL step, a complete set of specifications is developed for data delivery. This set includes report layouts, canned query illustrations, sample ad hoc queries, screen displays, and Web pages, if applicable.

During this development step, another set of activities that establishes the data warehouse support infrastructure is performed. This includes delivery of metadata, establishing a Help Desk facility, producing training manuals, and actually training some users during the prototyping activities. For metadata delivery, the specifications could include standard help files, reports of data definitions, and a design of help function screens. The content of delivered metadata should extend beyond data definitions to transformation specifications, aggregation algorithms for derived data, and summarization algorithms used in queries and reports.

Another activity performed during this development step is creating a procedure for proactive performance monitoring and tuning in order to avoid sudden and unexpected degradation of response time.

It is possible that during this step of prototyping the data delivery functions, technical issues, or design problems that affect the database design being developed by the ETL team or might even challenge the feasibility of the scope as specified in the Project Agreement might surface. It is quite conceivable that original decisions may have to be adjusted or reversed during this step. Therefore the project plan must reflect this possibility by including looping activities back to the Project Agreement step as well as all subsequent steps.

The major activities and deliverables during the query and reporting development step are as follows:

Activity	Deliverable
Prototype queries and reports.	Query scripts
	Report programs
	Working prototypes
	Updated business metadata
	Updated technical metadata
	Test scripts, test cases, test log, test results

continued

Activity	Deliverable
Establish support infrastructure.	Metadata delivery mechanism
	DW usage monitoring plan
	DW performance measurement plan
	Updated policies and standards
	Implementation plan
	Updated operating procedures
	User Help Desk Instructions
Review/revise Project Agreement (or subsequent steps).	Updated Project Agreement document
	Updated logical data model
	Updated physical data model(s)
	Updated data definition language (DDL)
	Updated physical database structures
	Updated technical metadata
Provide training.	Training manuals
	Trained Help Desk staff
	Trained users
Conduct acceptance test.	Query results
	Reports
	Exceptions document
	Updated programs
	Test results
Prepare for implementation.	Updated analysis documents
	Updated design documents
	Updated training manuals
	Updated business metadata
	Updated technical metadata
	Production program libraries
	Production query libraries

Source: MapXpert Methodology, Xpert Corporation.

9.4.5 Implementation Step

This final development step requires the data warehouse project deliverable to be in a stable condition as it moves into the frozen production environment where scheduled operational processes will take over. It is advisable not to rush into this step until users have had a chance to use the database and run their queries and reports for a month or two on the development machine. The main reason for this lag is that, inevitably, user requirements for how they want to view the data will change, and this period gives them the chance to make those decisions in a more flexible setting. If you have the opportunity, you should load several months of history into the development databases to simulate a production environment. Then be prepared to loop one more time through some or all of the development steps. We all know that it is much easier to make changes in a development environment than in a tightly controlled and protected production environment.

The high-level activities and deliverables should reflect the IT department's standard internal turnover procedures.

Activity	Deliverable
Move ETL and report programs to production libraries.	Executable code ETL Procedures
Populate production databases.	Loaded databases
Train operations personnel.	Trained operators
Close the project.	Updated documentation Updated metadata Signed-off project close report

Source: MapXpert Methodology, Xpert Corporation.

9.4.6 Postimplementation Review Step

Although the data warehouse project is done and in production, there is one more development step to plan for and execute: the postimplementation review step. Since a data warehouse is an evolving system, the next iteration is probably already in the planning stages. It would be foolish to proceed without reviewing and learning from past experience. There will be some things that worked very well, and others that did not work at all. As an example, the change control procedures may have turned out to be invaluable, but the overall development approach slowed down the project. Before starting the next iteration, adjustments to the development approach should be made.

The proper time frame to schedule this review is around two months after implementation. Everyone on the core team, the extended team, and all stakeholders should be invited. This should be a formal and facilitated review. An agenda should be published at least one week ahead of time to encourage attendance. Any documents to be reviewed and discussed should be sent out with the agenda. We suggest you include the following topics on your agenda.

Scheduling. How close to the scheduled completion date was the data warehouse actually completed? What did you learn about scheduling that will help on the next project?

Budget. How close to the budget was the final data warehouse cost? Which areas exceeded the budget, and which areas were below the budget? What did you learn about budgeting that will help on the next project?

Scope. Upon completion, did the data warehouse meet client access needs without additional work? If additional work was required or the scope had to be adjusted, discuss the situation and brainstorm on corrective procedures.

Requirements Definition. What did you learn about defining access needs that will help on the next project? Were access patterns defined early enough in the life cycle? Were they documented in an effective format? Were users able to devote enough of their time?

Dirty Data. How much dirty data was discovered unexpectedly, and what implications does that have for the next project? Is that indicative of other source files? Were triaging procedures in place, and did they work? If not, should some be developed before starting the next project? (Triaging dirty data is discussed in Chapter 11, "Data Quality.")

Staffing. What did you learn about staffing and required skill sets that can be applied to the next project? Were consultants or contractors used?

Which consultants were the most effective and valuable, and why? How can consultants and contractors be used more effectively on the next project?

Project Management. What did you learn about tracking status? Do adjustments have to be made for the next project? Were the number of looping activities overestimated or underestimated? Were there other unanticipated and unplanned activities or problems? How did they affect the project schedule?

Technology. What technological advances were made on this project? Were the products as easy to install as expected? Did the users have any trouble using the products? Were the vendors responsive?

9.5 SUMMARY

A data warehouse is an evolving environment that cannot be built with a Big Bang approach. It expands and changes over time with project iterations that either add to existing databases or create new ones. The most appropriate methodology is one that uses a rapid application development (RAD) and a prototyping approach to achieve the goal.

Each project, or data warehouse iteration, will have three or four parallel development tracks: the back-end ETL track, the front-end data delivery track, the repository navigation track, and the technical infrastructure track. The projects are organized by major development steps, which denote completed segments of work. The different development teams are aligned with different development steps and perform their work in parallel.

After all data warehouse components have been moved into the production environment, it is advisable to schedule a formal postimplementation review. During this review all participants and stakeholders should have a chance to express their opinion on what worked well on the project and what didn't. This information should be used to make any necessary adjustments to staffing, methodology, tools, techniques, standards, budgeting, scheduling, or project management before the next project starts.

A CAUTIONARY TALE

Building the Data Warehouse Using a "Waterfall Methodology"

The data warehouse was new to the organization. The team had no experience developing a data warehouse, but they did have experience with operational systems and their well-defined system life cycle development methodology—a waterfall methodology. This methodology had been purchased years ago, and the team was trained on it. The investment in it was significant. Not realizing that this project would be different, the project manager applied the waterfall methodology to the data warehouse project. The force-fit of the traditional phases was difficult and in many instances made no sense. The front-end team members kept making discoveries that affected the back-end team members. Some team members were growing angry over the constant changes and rework required after a phase had been "completed" and signed off by the user. The project manager discovered that there were a number of activities required for the data warehouse project that were not part of the waterfall methodology and therefore not on his project plan. The users were getting frustrated and refused to renegotiate the schedule. The team's workdays were growing longer and their weekends shorter. They discovered the hard way that they were using the wrong methodology—that the waterfall approach was not working on data warehouse projects.

9.6   WORKSHOP

In these Workshops you will identify the nontechnical infrastructure components to be included as a deliverable of your data warehouse project. You will also develop the outline for your Project Agreement document, and you will select the high-level activities and deliverables for your project plan.

9.6.1 Nontechnical Infrastructure

Select all of the infrastructure components that will need to be worked on during your project from the following list, and add new ones where applicable. Describe the deliverable for each of the components.

Example:

Abbreviations   Create a list of abbreviations for all of the name components within the scope of this project. Send the abbreviations list for approval to the following individuals: _____

Now identify your own.

Nontechnical infrastructure components

  Methodology _____

  Modeling techniques _____

  Change control procedures _____

  Testing procedures _____

Standards for:

  Governance _____

  Data naming _____

  Abbreviations _____

  Metadata capture and usage _____

  Data quality measures _____

  Security _____

  Service level agreements _____

9.6.2 Project Agreement Document

Start filling in the sections of the Project Agreement.

1. Executive overview
2. Data warehouse goals and objectives
3. Business problem and problem categorization
4. Solution alternatives
5. Cost/benefit analysis
6. Functional scope
7. Target subject area(s)
8. Infrastructure (from previous exercise)
9. History requirements
10. Number of source files
11. Condition of source data (give examples and counts)
12. User responsibilities
13. Availability requirements
14. Security requirements
15. Report/query libraries
16. Access tools
17. DW project team roles and responsibilities
18. Project plan
19. Not in scope
20. Assumptions and constraints
21. Change management procedures
22. Risk scenario section
23. Service level agreements

9.6.3 Activities and Deliverables

Now review Section 9.4, and select the activities and deliverables applicable to your project. Elaborate where necessary by referring back to your own methodology.

Example:

Activities	Deliverables
Create high-level data model.	E-R diagram with entity definitions, primary keys but no attributes
Schedule facilitated sessions.	Scheduled room
Communicate meeting time to team.	Memo/e-mail to: _____
Set up room with flipcharts, pens, and movable whiteboards.	Delivered room accessories

Now identify your own.

Activities	Deliverables

REFERENCES

MapXpert™, *A Methodology for Data Warehouse Projects*. Newport Beach, Ca.: Xpert Corporation, 1996.

CHAPTER TEN

Data Models

The majority of software development errors occur during design and analysis, not coding.

—*Carl Fink*

Seventy-five percent of delays in implementation of new applications are due not to coding or related problems but to misunderstanding of requirements which result from inadequate user involvement.

—*Jayne Hogan*

Building a data warehouse without a data model is like building a house without blueprints.

Data modeling is a technique that has existed for over two decades. Its popularity rises and falls with the development of new technology and new applications. In data warehousing the term *data model* has been used in different ways, which has led to some confusion and even to disagreements. Some people use the term to mean a logical data model or *conceptual data representation*, whereas others use the term to mean a physical data model or *logical database design*. This chapter presents both types of data models through the following topics:

- Purpose of a logical data model
- Data integration

- Understanding the business
- Data analysis and the need for it
- Controlling modeling scope creep
- Concepts of a logical data model
- How to use a logical data model in database design
- Purpose of a physical data model
- Concepts of a physical data model
- Denormalization
- Two-dimensional design schema
- Multidimensional design schema

As always, you will have a chance to practice what you have learned in the Workshop at the end of the chapter.

10.1 LOGICAL DATA MODEL

There have been a lot of heated discussions among the experts about the most appropriate data model for the data warehouse. Should it be an entity-relationship model, which is two dimensional, or a star schema model, which is multidimensional? This has created a lot of confusion, especially for data administrators and data modelers.

It is clear that the term *data model* is not fully understood because in the context of these discussions it is obvious that the experts are discussing only database design alternatives and not business analysis and data integration. Data models, however, address all three of those topics. The term *data model* simply means it is a diagram, typically stored on a Computer Aided Software Engineering (CASE) tool and printed out on paper, representing some type of data architecture.

The traditional term for a business data architecture is *logical data model*. It is called logical data model because it is the basic blueprint of business objects and their data contents as they *logically* relate to each other according to business policies and business rules. It represents what an organization actually is in terms of its business data and what an organization does in terms of its business actions, business rules, and business policies. It does *not* represent how data is physically stored in a database or how data is accessed and displayed on screens or reports.

Every organization already has a business data architecture, even though it may not be documented as a logical data model, because every organization has customers, every organization has products or services, and every organization has employees. In every organization all of these business objects are related to each other based on some business action between the objects and according to some rules. For example, an employee performs a service for a customer if the customer guarantees payment with a credit card.

The most significant characteristic of a logical data model is that it is completely process *in*dependent. That means the model is database independent, access path independent, tool independent, program independent, query independent, language independent, and platform independent.

10.1.1 Purpose of a Logical Data Model

The purpose of a logical data model is to document the existing business data architecture of an organization. One way of documenting all the components of a business data architecture is simply to write about it. Start with naming the business objects, the data elements that make up the objects, the relationships, the business rules, and so on. For each component write a short definition, capture allowable values for data elements and business rules, and gather other informative facts about each component. This process of "writing about it" is called creating metadata, specifically business metadata as opposed to technical metadata, because only business names and business definitions are captured at this point.

You can document the entire business data architecture as textual business metadata, but it would not be easy to grasp at a glance what an organization is all about without manually tracing through the text to find all the relationships between the business objects. Therefore, since a picture is worth a thousand words, we supplement the metadata with a diagram, specifically an entity-relationship diagram (ERD), as illustrated in Figure 10.1 [Legend: 1 = one occurrence; M = many occurrences; -O- = subtypes].

Now we can see at a glance how all the objects are connected. We see what the organization is about and what it does. In other words, we see

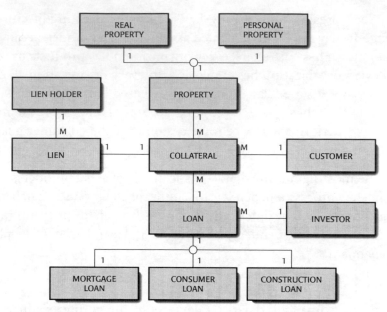

Figure 10.1: Example of a Logical Data Model

the integrated business data architecture of an organization. This is the blueprint, or foundation, from which to start the database design.

There are a number of reasons why it is important to create this baseline architecture first. The reasons are to achieve data integration, to understand the business, and to uncover hidden data.

10.1.2 Data Integration

First and foremost, the business data architecture is the ultimate integrated view of the business. It is a representation of how all the business objects of an organization are tied together in real life. Because a logical data model is completely process *in*dependent, this is an extremely stable model. Unless the business of the organization itself changes, which is rare, or the business policies and business rules change, which does happen occasionally, this model will not change. In contrast, a physical data model that is process dependent will change when the underlying technology changes or when users want to see their data in a different way or when a new tool cannot access the old database structures or when a new database design schema is invented.

10.1.3   Understanding the Business

Time and time again, we hear users complain about not understanding or misunderstanding their own data. Different users may call the same thing by different names. At the same time, different users may call different things by the same name. Sometimes users put their own spin on data values without documenting what they have changed. Other times users in one department don't even know or understand what occurs in other departments, or how they affect other departments. Occasionally one user's business rules for a data element is diametrically opposed to another user's business rules for the same data element. Many times no one knows who is responsible for the data and who the authoritative source is over any set of data. No one seems to see the whole picture, because no one has had the need to see it.

During the process of logical data modeling, "the whole picture" is put together over time in a diagram with supporting metadata, much as you would put together a jigsaw puzzle. Consensus on data definition and meaning is reached among users, and anomalies are resolved in this process.

10.1.4   Data Analysis

Logical data modeling is an excellent technique for business data analysis. The process of identifying business objects and their relationships and the process of assigning data elements to these objects according to the rules of normalization will uncover new business objects, new relationships, and new data elements that have always existed in the business but were not commonly known before. The few users who did know about the "hidden" data developed elaborate programs to decipher and translate the data but never shared that knowledge with the rest of the organization. On many occasions, users discovered during modeling sessions that other departments had data that they never knew was available but could have used had they known it existed.

All organizations have data and report inconsistencies; some are known to the users and others are not, but they exist. The advantage of creating a logical data model over just gathering business metadata alone is that by following the strict rules of logical data modeling (Simsion 1994), these inconsistencies become very obvious. When adhering to data modeling rules, it is not possible to model inconsistencies, but it is possible to miss inconsistencies when documenting the rules as text.

10.1.5 The Need for Data Analysis

By now you are probably thinking that this type of analysis will take more time because it takes more thought and more research than just coming up with a database design with a limited set of requirements for a particular user. Yes, it does. You may also be thinking that you might have to put your data warehouse project "on hold" until all these inconsistencies in your data and your reports have been analyzed and resolved. No, you do not. We do not recommend that you model your entire enterprise for a data warehouse project, but we do recommend that you model the data within the scope of your project when you are building a data warehouse.

You need to perform this analysis for the following reasons:

- You want to integrate your data.
- Nowhere else do you have a complete picture of your organization's business data architecture that will tell you what you need to know for correct and complete integration.
- You want to separate embedded logic from data so that it will be easier for all users in the organization to navigate through the data warehouse.
- You want to understand all the significant relationships between the business objects that exist in the organization because they may be potential access paths to the data.
- Sooner or later users will ask to see the data based on any or all of these relationships.
- Users deserve nothing less than the best quality data IT can provide for them, and this is the best technique to address data quality.

This type of data analysis is not the same as analyzing user requirements for a set of reports or queries or for a set of summary tables while designing those reports and tables. It is not the same because analyzing reporting requirements for the purpose of design gives us information only about how a particular user wants to see a particular set of data, which is a process-dependent view that can change when presented to the next user. In addition, when we are designing, our deliverable is a well-tuned and well-designed database for those particular requirements. A design deliverable is not a stable, process-independent, integrated, and expandable logical view of the business data architecture. Design activities are obviously an equally important part of development, but they are not to be confused with business analysis activities.

10.1.6 Controlling Modeling Scope Creep

A question frequently asked is "How can I control the scope and duration of logical data modeling activities?" This question is sometimes rephrased as an exclamation: "My data modelers don't know when to quit!" The answers are simple, but their enforcement is not.

First, use the business requirements of each project, the objectives to be met, and the set of reports and queries to set the scope for logical data modeling activities on a project. This way each project would produce only a few pieces of the entire business data architecture jigsaw puzzle. The risk of the pieces not fitting together is minimal if the data modelers are experienced, communicate with each other as a unit, and adhere to the strict guidelines of logical data modeling.

Second, be sure an experienced data modeler is facilitating and leading the data modeling activities. The data modeler should have led data modeling activities on more than one major project and should have successfully resisted the temptation to pursue the "hooks" on the logical data model. The "hooks" are those business objects at the rim of the project scope; they have relationships to other objects that are clearly outside the scope. Having users in the modeling sessions who understand those relationships makes it tempting to capture their knowledge right then and there, thereby expanding the scope of the project and possibly jeopardizing the project schedule.

Third, don't mix analysis activities with design activities. They require different thought processes and are usually performed by different people. Good business analysts do not need to be very technical, but they do need to have in-depth business knowledge, have an inquisitive mind, be detail oriented, have above average communication skills, and be trained in logical data modeling. Database designers, on the other hand, must be very technical, have an in-depth knowledge of the database management system and the tools they use, and must understand how to create and fine-tune physical database structures based on the access requirements.

10.1.7 Concepts of a Logical Data Model

It is not the purpose of this book to teach the technique of logical data modeling, but it is important to understand its basic concepts and what functions they serve. This understanding is important later when we compare logical data modeling to physical data modeling.

Subject-oriented

The main function of a logical data model is to group data in a subject-oriented way, not in a process-oriented or departmentally oriented way. Subject oriented means that all data elements, which describe a business object, are grouped under that business object. For example: All customer-related data found in the Customer Master file, the Customer Credit file, the Product Sales file, the Shipment file, and the Account file would be stored in one, and only one, business object or *entity* named CUSTOMER. A business object is called an "entity" in a logical data model.

Process-independent

Data organized in a subject-oriented way is process-*in*dependent. That means that all programs that process transactions for updating customer information, checking a customer's credit, recording a product sale, making a shipment, or posting a payment to a customer account would access CUSTOMER to write or retrieve customer-related data for those transactions. Those programs would also write or retrieve product-related data from PRODUCT, sale-related data from SALE, account-related data from ACCOUNT, and so forth.

Process-oriented means that all data elements, which are used for a particular process, are grouped in one data store. If another process needs some of the same data elements, these data elements would be duplicated in another data store grouped with other data needed for that process. The design of flat files was based on this concept because the notion of shared and cross-functional data was foreign to data processing at that time and because the power of the relational database had not been unleashed. It is not unusual to find customer-related data in hundreds of files. Unfortunately, many IT professionals who used to work with flat files continue this process-oriented way of grouping data when working with hierarchical, network, and relational databases, so that we still find customer-related data in hundreds of databases as well.

From a logical business perspective there is only *one* business object called CUSTOMER. Sure, there may be different categories of customers, who in turn may have different data relationships and different data elements or *attributes*. A data element is called an "attribute" in a logical data model. It is vitally important to model all these differences about CUSTOMER into a CUSTOMER *subject area*, where all customer-related data elements would be regrouped in a subject-oriented way. The result of this regrouping is that all information known to the business about CUSTOMER is defined and documented in a cohesive and consistent manner.

One Fact in One Place

Another important concept of logical data modeling is to put one fact into one, and only one, place. The term *fact* is not to be confused with facts in a multidimensional FACT table. "Fact" refers to one *attribute*, and "place" refers to one *entity*. The meaning of this concept is that a data element in the real world describes one, and only one, business object. For example, a "Customer Name" cannot describe a customer and an account at the same time. An "Account Name" would describe the account. The purpose of this concept is to eliminate redundancy in order to show pure logical data integration. Pure logical integration of data can best be achieved in a CASE tool in a logical data model. This is the reason we call this the blueprint for all subsequent development activities.

While technological limitations affect physical database designs, they do not impact the logical data model. Therefore, in most cases, a logical data model cannot and should not be used as a database design AS-IS. This pure logical integration of data usually cannot be achieved in a physical environment without incurring severe performance penalties. There are very few exceptions where database engines are specially designed for executing efficient JOINS on a large number of tables.

Normalization

A fourth concept of logical data modeling is normalization, which is the process of decomposing entities according to a set of rules applied to the entities' attributes. Very simply stated, the rules require that all attributes, which are not part of the entity's key, are dependent on the entire key of the entity. For example, an entity called STUDENT GRADE has two attributes comprising its key: Student Number and Seminar Number. Other nonkey attributes in this entity are Student Name and Letter Grade. Applying the rules of normalization, in this case second normal form, we see that Student Name is dependent only on Student Number and not on Seminar Number. In other words, the student's name does not change for every seminar he attends. Student Name should be removed from this entity, otherwise it would be repeated over and over for each seminar. On the other hand, Letter Grade depends on both the Student Number and the Seminar Number because the grade letter can be different for each seminar the student takes. The purpose of normalization is to eliminate redundancy, achieve placement of one fact in one place, and support the ultimate goal of data groupings in a subject-oriented way—all of which, again, translates into pure logical data integration.

10.1.8 How to Use a Logical Data Model in Database Design

We have already stated that most of today's database management systems, with very few exceptions, do not allow us to implement a fully normalized and fully integrated business data architecture. If we tried to implement it, and some have tried, we would have a poorly performing system. The reason is that the data has been decomposed and separated into its most logical business components in order to "see the whole integrated data picture" as it really exists for an organization. However, users don't usually need data from only one business object at a time. Since they need to see data from different related business objects together, any process, any query, any report would have to access multiple entities to produce the requested report or query result. That is not efficient. Grouping data in an access-oriented way, which is process-oriented, is much more efficient. However, we do not want to end up again with uncontrolled redundancy, with no data sharing, and without a clue on how the data should be integrated. What do we do?

Some people throw out the entire concept of logical data modeling. By throwing out the logical data model, they throw away the knowledge they would have gained about the data of the business, how it needs to be integrated, how data relates in a business context, and, therefore, how users may want to access it in the future. They also throw away any possibility of detecting and resolving dirty data, deciphering embedded logic in the data, finding and fixing the inconsistencies in data, and uncovering and solving other ailments that exist in the current environment. In other words, they throw out the business analysis activity and go straight for the database design. We do not recommend this approach. *Throwing out business analysis activities just because they don't produce a well-tuned database design is as absurd as throwing out database design activities because they don't produce a fully functioning application!*

We recommend that business analysis activities are executed in the same accelerated and *looping* fashion as all other development activities as described in Chapter 9, "Methodology," and Chapter 12, "Project Planning." Data modelers, who usually have the title of data administrators, should work closely with database designers, who usually have the title of database administrators, during both logical data modeling and physical data modeling. Of course, the lead role would switch from the data administrator during business analysis to the database administrator during database design. When database designers understand the business rules behind the normalized logical data model, they are less likely to overlook requirements during the denormalization process.

Denormalization is the process of collapsing several entities into one table in order to enhance performance. The price for denormalizing is data redundancy, but the resulting performance gains often far outweigh the cost. Denormalizing entities into tables for database design does not mean starting to create a new model from scratch. On the contrary, entities become tables, and attributes become columns, just not one-for-one as some CASE tool vendors would want you to believe.

10.2 PHYSICAL DATA MODEL

While the logical data model is process-*in*dependent, physical data models are process dependent. Where only *one* logical data model evolves for the organization, several physical data models are created, typically one for each database. A physical data model is a representation of actual database structures to be built, such as the tables, the columns, and the relationships between tables, which are to be implemented through foreign keys and referential integrity rules. To create an efficient database, the database designer must consider how the data will be accessed and how many tables will have to be joined for how many queries and in what way. The designer must also consider how many people will access the database at the same time and during what times of the day.

10.2.1 Purpose of a Physical Data Model

The main purpose of a physical data model, also called logical database design or database architecture, is to document the actual database structures that are about to be implemented. Like the business data architecture, the database architecture can be documented by simply "writing about it," which is the process of creating metadata, in this case technical metadata. Technical metadata consists of the physical table names, column names, data type and length of a column, domains or allowable values, stored procedure calls, and so on. As before, it would take some tracing through the text of technical metadata to understand the conceptual layout of the whole database. To see the layout at a glance, we supplement the technical metadata with a diagram, in this case a *physical* data model because we are drawing a picture of our physical database structures.

It is noteworthy to review the disagreements about the "best data model" for a data warehouse and to clarify once again that these disagreements are about *physical* data models and not *logical* data models.

Just because a diagram is printed on a piece of paper does not make it a "logical" data model. What determines whether a model is logical or physical is whether it is process-independent and normalized or process dependent and denormalized. Database design schemas must be process dependent to be efficient. Therefore, when printed out as a diagram on a piece of paper, database design schemas—also known as logical database designs—are physical data models.

It is also noteworthy to review the claims of CASE tool vendors that profess to produce logical as well as physical data models. Some CASE tools do, but some don't. Just because there are notations on a diagram that are typically used on a logical data model, such as crow's feet, does not make the diagram a *logical data model*. And replacing the logical notations on a diagram with notations that are typically used on a physical data model does not automatically make it a *physical data model*. Again, what determines whether a data model is logical or physical is whether its data is grouped in a process-*in*dependent or process-dependent way, not what type of notation is used.

Note: The *logical data model* and the *physical data model* should never map one-for-one! The only exception to this rule would be if you deliberately plan to implement a fully normalized data architecture physically, which most of you will not be doing.

There are many less expensive CASE tools that do map the logical and physical data models one-for-one. These are not very sophisticated tools, because they do not have built-in intelligence about the target RDBMS optimizer and they do not have an intelligent "forward-engineering" function. Hence, the data modeler is required to maintain two different data models manually. These CASE tools do, however, provide the graphics capabilities needed by a data modeler to produce a logical data model, and they also provide different graphics capabilities needed by a database designer to produce a physical data model. Other than changing notations, these tools simply translate each entity to a table and each attribute to a column, one-for-one.

The more sophisticated CASE tools first ask the designer to answer detailed process-related and platform-related questions. Then these tools automatically produce a first-cut denormalized physical data model, and they automatically map the physical data model back to the preserved logical data model. These CASE tools were designed with the understanding that a logical data model is a normalized process-*in*dependent model and a physical data model is a denormalized process-dependent model and they therefore should never map one-for-one. These CASE tools keep the different models separate but synchronized and mapped to each other.

10.2.2 Concepts of a Physical Data Model

Theoretically, the best design for a relational database is a fully normalized logical data model because the concept behind relational databases is to store the data in a process-*in*dependent, or subject-oriented, way. The whole idea is to enable any and all processes to access the same data in any way necessary, thereby giving the users total flexibility and unrestricted access to all of the data in the organization, *theoretically.* Practically, of course, this rarely works because of intolerable performance due to excessive numbers of JOINs and because this design is difficult for the casual user to understand and to navigate. Something must be done to the grouping of data from the logical data model to make it usable and efficient. This process is called database design.

During database design we concentrate on "streamlining" the logical data model into a workable physical data model. We may even decide to build two databases, in which case we would spawn two physical data models from the one logical data model. The process of streamlining is called denormalization, a regrouping of data that often involves collapsing two or more entities into one table. In order to know how to denormalize our logical data model, we have to know how it will be accessed, and we have to make it process dependent.

As different users have different data needs and different, sometimes conflicting, access requirements, we are faced with the difficult question of whose requirements to use for denormalization. What gets collapsed for one set of requirements will adversely affect all the other sets of requirements. There are two choices:

1. Keep the denormalization to a minimum so as to retain a high degree of flexibility, but be aware that performance will be degraded for everybody.
2. Design and build separate databases for different patterns of access path requirements. These multiple databases could then individually be denormalized to a great extent because they support only a limited number of applications and users. The databases would still be logically integrated through the logical data model because the multiple physical data models would be mapped back to and reconciled against the one logical data model.

In the data warehouse environment we have another challenge. A very high percentage of users, maybe as high as 90 percent, want to see all of the data summarized in various ways. We have three choices to satisfy this common requirement:

1. Denormalize as little as possible so that all users can summarize any data they want, any way they want, and suffer terrible performance.
2. Create summary tables for each of the summary patterns, and keep creating more summary tables for every new pattern. Very soon there may be dozens, if not hundreds, of summary tables to maintain. Since a summary table is nothing more than a flat file in a table, most of the data is duplicated from table to table.
3. Create separate schemas for each summary pattern using the star-schema method. If the logical data model is used as a guide, it will be easy to connect these schemas through shared, or conforming, dimensions, (Kimball et al. 1998) which are the basic business objects, or kernel entities, from the logical data model. If the OLAP product used with the data warehouse does not allow sharing dimensions, the different schemas could be implemented as different databases. Integration of data is still achieved through mapping the physical data models, in this case star schemas, into the logical data model.

Keep your users involved in all of the design decisions by explaining the impact of the various alternatives to them. Most users certainly are not technical enough to understand all the aspects of database design, but they do appreciate having the pros and cons of design alternatives explained to them in layman's terms, especially as it relates to their usage of the database. Some of your power users may have enough technical background to participate actively in the database design activities. In that case be sure that roles and responsibilities are clearly defined. As stated in Chapter 8, "Organization and Cultural Issues," it is the database administrator who plays the lead role during database design.

Although it is not the purpose of this book to teach database design, it is important to understand the three design principles we have introduced in this section: denormalization, two-dimensional design schema, and multidimensional design schema.

10.2.3 Denormalization

As previously stated, denormalization is a procedure of regrouping normalized data for a specific set of processes in order to make those processes more efficient. A high-level description of the steps for denormalizing a logical data model is as follows: First, the access paths are determined from the requirements and are traced through the logical data model to determine the number of table joins necessary for each path. Second, the number of users and their physical locations are identified, and the size and width of the tables are determined. The subsequent design steps take all of these process-related factors into consideration and determine the best way to regroup the data without violating the business rules stated on the logical data model. The designer has many choices. Here are a few examples.

- If several entities are always accessed together, the designer can collapse two or three of the entities into one table, thereby reducing the number of joins necessary.
- If two tables are always accessed together to pick up only one or two columns from the second table, the designer can duplicate those columns in the first table to avoid the join.
- If some calculations are performed frequently, the designer can create new columns to store the precalculated results to avoid repeated lengthy SQL runs.
- If different users use different rows of data, the designer can split the rows among multiple tables to separate the access paths.
- If different users use different columns, the designer can further group the columns into different tables. This process is called over-normalization.
- If those users who use different columns also reside at different locations, the designer can go even further and physically separate the new table into a new database and place it on a new server.

There are many complicated aspects to denormalizing, and the process of creating an efficient physical data model for the target RDBMS must be left to a trained database administrator. However, since we want to contrast the traditional two-dimensional design schema with the new multidimensional star schema, we need to discuss some basic concepts for those two schemas.

10.2.4 Two-dimensional Design Schema

A two-dimensional design schema resembles the logical data model. Because it is based on the logical data model, the resulting design, or physical data model, resembles an entity-relationship diagram, only with fewer tables and fewer relationships. The remaining relationships between the tables on the physical data model should be similar to the ones on the logical data model. Maybe some relationships had to be moved during the denormalization process, and maybe some additional relationships had to be introduced in order to reduce the number of joins between tables, but overall the diagrams look similar.

As shown in Figure 10.2 [Legend: 1 = one occurrence; M = many occurrences], in a two-dimensional design schema, *all* of the attributes from one entity are collapsed into the adjacent entity with which it has a relationship. LIEN was collapsed into COLLATERAL, which also moved the relationship from LIEN HOLDER to COLLATERAL; REAL PROPERTY and PERSONAL PROPERTY were collapsed into PROPERTY, and so on. This means that in a two-dimensional design schema, all the data remains grouped in a subject-oriented way, where the principle of one

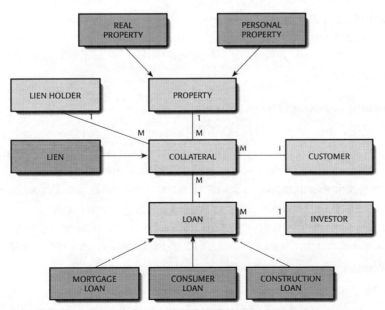

Figure 10.2: Example of a Two-dimensional Physical Data Model

fact in one place and the rules of normalization are preserved as much as possible during the denormalization process. The reason for this preservation is to achieve a balance between performance and flexibility. Usually, the more a database structure is denormalized, the better its performance but the less flexible it becomes. It is less flexible because data relationships, which are potential access paths, are removed.

If you are building one database for many users with many different and often opposing and changing requirements, as is frequently the case in an ODS or an EDW, you have little choice but to preserve some degree of flexibility. If you don't, there will soon come a time when some users will not be able to use the database at all because their requirements don't fit into your highly denormalized database design schema.

The two-dimensional design schema is also appropriate for those users whose requirement is maximum flexibility to detailed data no matter what the performance. Granted, these users rarely exceed 5 percent to 10 percent of the organization's population, but they do exist. These are usually financial analysts or power users who frequently devise new ways of analyzing organizational data. Their access requirements change from day to day. They do not access the data in repeatable patterns. They are used to response times measured in days, if not weeks, because that is how long it currently takes them to extract data from different sources, manipulate that data, and get the final results. These types of users are elated with a response time of 24 to 48 hours, while most other users wouldn't be.

10.2.5 Multidimensional Design Schema

To address the requirements of the majority of users, especially if those requirements include repeatable reporting patterns, summarization, rollups, and drill-downs, the multidimensional design schema should be considered. A multidimensional database can be constructed by using a proprietary DBMS, which is usually referred to as a cube, because it is often based on a construct of multiple layers of nested arrays. A multidimensional database can also be designed for a common RDBMS using a star schema.

At first glance, a multidimensional physical data model, or star schema, does not have any resemblance to a logical data model because all of the relationships have changed. The relationships now surround a new table, called a FACT table, like points on a star.

However, upon closer examination of Figure 10.3 [Legend: 1 = one occurrence; M = many occurrences], we recognize some parts of our logical data model again, namely the dimension tables.

Denormalizing into a star schema follows different rules than denormalizing into a relational schema. Instead of preserving the flexibility of our logical data model, to be able to ask any question in any way at any time, we want to maximize data access performance for a common, or similar, set of access patterns. Think of a set of access patterns as a set of reports, which have similar columns, such as Loan Commitment Amount, Loan Balance, Number of Loans Originated, and Number of Loans Closed. One report may subtotal these columns by Lien Holder, by Property, by Month, by Quarter. Another set of reports may subtotal the same columns plus an additional column, Sold Loan Amount by Investor, by Property, by Quarter, by Year. These two reports display a similar pattern. A star schema could therefore be designed and tuned for such a report pattern or query pattern.

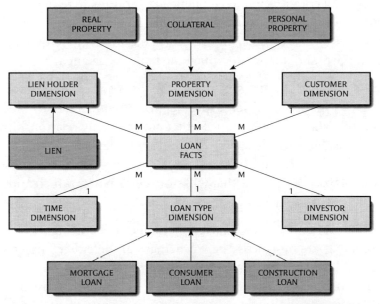

Figure 10.3: Example of a Multidimensional Physical Data Model

Although flexibility is traded for performance, by no means is a star schema restricted to satisfying only the predefined reports or queries, especially if the regrouping of data into a star schema started with the logical data model. The dimension tables on the physical data model should be more or less the same as the kernel entities on the logical data model. Maybe two or three entities had to be collapsed into one dimension table or maybe some columns of one entity were overnormalized, or further decomposed, into a new dimension table. However, overall, the dimension tables resemble the entities because the grouping of data for dimensions remains subject-oriented and can be directly mapped into the logical data model, with one exception. The Time dimension, which appears on virtually all star schema models, usually does not exist on a logical data model.

The "odd" table in the middle of a star schema is the FACT table. This is a fabricated table that does not map into any entity on the logical data model. However, most columns in this fact table do map into various attributes in various entities on the logical data model. The physical columns that don't map directly one-for-one into logical attributes are calculated or derived columns. However, the logical attributes used in the calculations, as well as the calculation itself, can be mapped to the derived columns. All columns in the fact table are grouped together in a process-oriented way. Precalculated and summarized attributes from different entities are stored together in one fact table to facilitate quick access by those reports and queries for which the table is designed.

The purpose of a star schema is to focus on a set of common reporting or querying patterns for a specific group requiring that information, not on the whole organization. To that end, the only relationships shown on a star schema are those between the fact table and the specific dimension tables that are used by that fact table. Think of it as representing a report database, a database that will store certain data which appears on a set of reports and queries.

Since every organization has more than one reporting pattern, several star schemas are designed. These schemas can be either implemented as separate databases or connected through the dimension tables. If a dimension table is used by a second fact table, then that dimension table would have an additional relationship to the second fact table and would appear on the second star schema diagram, and so on. Since a star schema basically represents a reporting pattern, a multidimensional physical data model that links multiple star schemas together represents a joined view of multiple reporting patterns. It does not represent, and it should not be confused with, an integrated view of the business data independent of any reporting patterns. That representation would be the logical data model.

Multidimensional database design is not a trivial activity, and it must be studied as a separate topic. The goal of this chapter is merely to introduce the basic concepts of multidimensional database design in order to contrast it with the basic concepts of two-dimensional database design. All types of models have their place and their purpose.

10.3 SUMMARY

There have been many discussions among experts about the "best data model" for a data warehouse, specifically whether it should be an entity-relationship-based model or a star schema–based model. These discussions are confusing because they revolve only around database design, whereas data models are also used for business analysis and data integration. Therefore any discussions about whether a star schema model is "better" than an entity-relationship model is equivalent to arguing over whether database design is "better" than business analysis. It is not a matter of choosing one over the other; it is a matter of doing both.

A logical data model documents a business data architecture that already exists in every organization, even though it may not be documented. There is only one logical data model for an organization because there is only one business data architecture in an organization. The logical data model is created as a result of business analysis activities, and it focuses on normalization to show the pure logical integration of business data.

A physical data model documents the proposed database architectures. There are several physical data models, typically one for each database. The physical data models are created as a result of database design activities, and they focus on denormalization to enhance performance. A physical data model can be either a two-dimensional design schema or a multidimensional star schema.

A CAUTIONARY TALE

Jumping from Requirements to Design

The emphasis was on technology. Development tools were purchased for seemingly every task, from CASE tool to ETL tool to OLAP tools. The team had 90 days to build a data mart. They met with the users, gathered their reporting requirements, reviewed a few existing reports, and immediately got to work designing the database. Since "slicing and dicing" was a desired feature requested by the users, the database they designed was multidimensional. They looked for the best source data to populate the new target database and found that their ETL tool could handle all data type and length transformations except for one flat file, which they had to preprocess and temporarily load into a relational table. They proudly finished the project within the 90 days. Then the phone started to ring. Users asked for new queries that did not fit into the design pattern. Users complained about query and report results, even though the SQL for the query checked out but the data content was dirty. Users started to look for new data relationships that were never built but that existed in the business. Nobody had bothered to do any business analysis or data analysis, during which all of these additional requirements and data value discrepancies would have surfaced.

10.4 WORKSHOP

In these Workshops you will create a high-level logical data model and popu-late it with some key and nonkey attributes. You will also create two physical data models, one using the two-dimensional design schema and the other using a multidimensional star schema.

10.4.1 High-level Logical Data Model

If you don't have any experience in logical data modeling, you may want to solicit help from a data modeler, probably your data administrator, since we did not fully explain the techniques of logical data modeling beyond some of its basic concepts.

1. Look at the scope and the requirements of your project, and write down a list of possible business objects, or entities, for which you will need to store data.

2. With the data modeler, review the list of entities and their possible relation-ships to each other, and create a high-level entity-relationship diagram.

3. Write business metadata for every entity and every relationship (name, definition, etc.).

4. Identify the attributes that make up the key of each entity.

5. Identify some of the nonkey attributes for each entity.

6. Write business metadata for every key and every nonkey attribute (name, definition, allowable values, etc.).

7. Apply the normalization rules to validate your model.

If you used real data from your project and if you spent some time doing this exercise with your trained data modeler, the logical data model produced from this exercise may just be good enough to be used as a straw-man data model to kick off the facilitated modeling sessions. A straw-man data model is a first-cut skeleton data model.

10.4.2 Two-dimensional Physical Data Model

If you don't have any experience with relational database design, you may want to solicit help from a relational database designer, probably your data-base administrator, since we did not fully explain the techniques of denormal-izing for a two-dimensional relational database design beyond some of its basic concepts.

1. Look at the reports and the query requirements of your project, and trace through the logical data model until you find all of the columns to satisfy the reports and queries.

2. With the database designer, discuss the access paths for every report and query, and start the denormalizing process.

3. Collapse those entities that are always accessed together.

4. Draw new and redundant relationships to create "shortcuts" between tables to minimize the number of tables that need to be joined

5. Duplicate columns into other tables if that would avoid a join between multiple tables. Never duplicate more than one or two columns. If there are more columns at stake, the tables need to be denormalized differently.

6. Write technical metadata for the tables and columns (name, type, length, etc.).

7. Map each table into the entity from which it originated and each column into the attribute from which it originated.

10.4.3 Multidimensional Physical Data Model

If you don't have any experience in multidimensional database design, you may want to solicit help from a star schema designer since we did not fully explain the techniques of denormalizing for a star schema design beyond some of its basic concepts.

1. Look at the reports and the query requirements of your project again, but this time from a multidimensional perspective, and identify what columns get reported and by what dimensions.

2. With the star schema designer, discuss the columns to be reported, find them on the logical data model, and group them into the FACT table.

3. Find the entities that represent the dimensions on the logical data model, and create the DIMENSION tables.

4. Review the key structures with the star schema designer, and discuss the pros and cons of generating artificial keys.

5. Review the historical requirements for the dimension tables, and discuss the design alternatives for those requirements.

6. Write technical metadata for the tables and columns (name, type, length, etc.).

7. Map each dimension table into the entity from which it originated and each column into the attribute from which it originated.

References

Kimball, Ralph, Laura Reeves, Margy Ross, and Warren Thornthwaite; *The Data Warehouse Lifecycle Toolkit*, New York, N.Y.: John Wiley & Sons, 1998.

Simsion, Graeme C. *Data Modeling Essentials*, Boston, Mass., International Thomson Computer Press, 1994.

CHAPTER ELEVEN

Data Quality

*The quality of decisions by management is directly related to
the quality and availability of data.*

—GUIDE GRP-153 Repository Data
Model Strategy Paper, *September 1986*

*Few things are less productive than duplication of effort and
the resulting need for reconciliation of inconsistent data.*

—GUIDE GRP-153 Repository Data
Model Strategy Paper, *September 1986*

*Many organizations are going to find, unfortunately, that their
underlying data may not be sufficiently clean to help the organization move forward.*

—Mark Atkins

Never underestimate the creativity of data entry.

—Mark Atkins

"Dirty data" is such a pervasive problem in every
company, in every industry. We have lived with
dirty data for decades, so why is it such a problem *now?*
It's a problem because we promise to deliver data warehouses with "clean, integrated, historical data in a
short time frame for low cost," but we are unable to
deal with the preponderance of dirty data within the
framework of this promise. Some data warehouses are
failing because the promised "clean, integrated, historical" data could not be delivered in a "short time frame
for low cost." This chapter covers the following:

- Data management and data delivery
- Defining data quality for the data warehouse
- Cost of data chaos
- Data cleansing categories
- Triaging data cleansing activities

In the Workshop you will inventory your source data, choose some source files, and determine the quality of the source data. You will identify the dirty data categories, the cost to cleanse data in those categories, and the cost to the business for not cleansing it. Finally, you will have a chance to practice triaging your cleansing activities. If you are purchasing external data, there are questions to ask of the vendor in Appendix 11.A.

11.1 DATA MANAGEMENT AND DATA DELIVERY

Every data warehouse project should have two components: data management and data delivery. Too often organizations concentrate on the fancy new data delivery tools and not enough on data quality. If the data warehouse is populated with dirty data, it will quickly turn off some users. They will see the data warehouse as unreliable, and they will not use it. Then it will be nearly impossible to make them satisfied users again.

11.1.1 Data Management

The primary pupose of data warehousing is taming the data chaos (Bracket 1996) that exists in most organizations, not to display the chaos on a new platform with a new tool. A data warehouse should also provide a new data delivery mechanism that is more functional, more powerful, easier to use, and easier to administer than the old data delivery mechanism. However, keep in mind that regardless of how different the data delivery mechanism is, without cleansing the data first, you are still in GIGO mode (garbage in, garbage out).

To tame your existing data chaos, you must first understand what creates the chaos; then you need to put into action a plan that will correct the situation. Let's examine why organizations have a multitude of duplicate data and so many wrong, inconsistent, and missing data values.

During the industrial age the most efficient way to manufacture a product or offer a service was by division of labor. The assembly of a product or the delivery of a service was divided into small self-contained pieces of work and assigned to people who were highly trained for that particular portion of the work. An assembly line is the most striking example of this concept (thank you, Henry Ford). But it is not just an assembly line that is organized in this way. Our organizations reflect that same division of labor concept in their organizational hierarchy structure.

Most organizations have divided their companies into two camps: the business side and the technology side. The business side is further divided into various self-contained lines of businesses, such as departments or divisions, which are further subdivided into smaller business units, and so on. The technology side is similarly divided into various departments or divisions, which are further subdivided into smaller IT units. There is nothing inherently wrong with this type of organizational hierarchy— until we examine how computer systems are built.

Each business unit at any level in the organizational hierarchy is supported by one or more technology units, and each technology unit may support one or more business units. When a business user has a requirement for new information, the designated support person on the IT side is contacted. After some formality, the designated staff on the IT side gathers the requirements and designs and builds the system. Other business users contact their designated IT staff, which in turn builds separate systems for them. The result is an all-too-familiar spaghetti chart of disparate systems.

Having more than one system or more than one database is not the problem, but having uncontrolled data redundancy in thousands of files and databases and uncontrolled program redundancy in hundreds of systems *is* the problem. Since every IT group gathers and manipulates data based solely on the narrow requirements of their immediate users, the results have been duplicate data with customized data values, leading to inconsistency, inaccuracy, and incomplete information.

It is obvious that the cure for this situation in the long run will have to be a different approach to system development, namely one that is based on cross-organizational coordination. However, that is a topic for another book. At the moment, most organizations are not ready to reevaluate, much less change their organization or their approach to systems development. They are willing, however, to improve the quality of their source data just enough to be able to deliver more reliable information to company executives.

To achieve improved data quality, two techniques must be deployed on every project. One technique is to create a logical data model for each project and to integrate these models and their common data definitions into one enterprise view over time, as discussed in Chapter 10, "Data Models." The second technique is to establish one staging area with a centrally managed and controlled extract/transform/load (ETL) process, as discussed in Chapter 9, "Methodology." In the next few sections we will explore the transformations that need to occur in the ETL process.

11.1.2 Data Delivery

We said that the second reason for data warehousing is to have a more sophisticated data delivery mechanism. This new data delivery mechanism is provided by vendors of online analytical processing (OLAP) product, because most of the OLAP products include some Web capabilities. These new tools are able to present information to a variety of users with different backgrounds, different IT skills, and different requirements. The tools display the information in an intuitive way and also provide users with some powerful capabilities to manipulate the information further in ways never before possible.

For many decades IT has barely kept up with the decision support requirements pouring in. Every time a user wants to see a new column on a report, or a new subtotal, or have the subtotals roll up in a different way, it means writing another program. With the new multidimensional tools, most new decision support requirements can be satisfied by the users themselves.

11.2 THE COST OF DATA CHAOS

Does your organization have source data problems today? Of course it does, unless it is a very young company that has applied data management principles to all of its operational systems from the start. In that case your organization would have developed its operational systems around subject areas, mapped each system into an integrated logical data model, ensured that no inconsistencies or uncontrolled redundancy existed, clearly defined all of its data, and rigorously applied consistent primary keys to all subjects in all databases. In that situation it would be very easy to build a data warehouse with the cross-organizational development approach.

Although there are some companies that fit into a data managed environment, most of these companies are in Europe or Australia. In the United States, we have consistently favored speed to market over quality of product. That choice comes with consequences—some very expensive consequences.

11.2.1 The Need for Pagers

We have gotten so used to being on call 24 hours a day, that we don't even question the need for sleeping with pagers under our pillows anymore. Why do we need to be on call? Usually the reason is something like *just in case* a program abends with a data exception, *just in case* a database does not load because of referential integrity problems, *just in case* two reports don't reconcile, or *just in case* a program encounters a condition for which there was no time to test.

Consider the cost of these just-in-case conditions. Obviously they have happened often enough to have developed a rotating on-call procedure. The person being called at all hours of the day must be compensated, either with overtime pay or more likely with compensatory time off. The work must be redone—the program corrected and retested, the files reloaded, and whatever else is necessary, which is costing additional money in terms of lost computer time for other processes and lost productivity of the people involved in the rework.

11.2.2 Reconciliation of Files and Reports

Although users don't usually get called in the middle of the night, their productivity is severely affected during the day. Instead of relying on and using the reports generated overnight, they spend countless hours reconciling reports, looking up data on source files, researching suspect values, trying to reconcile between reports, and manually consolidating information from multiple reports into one spreadsheet. All this time is totally wasted and could be spent on more productive activities. One of our clients had to employ two financial analysts to compile reliable month-end figures. It took him three weeks, with two and a half weeks of that time spent on reconciliation and research. Using the fully burdened cost for both senior financial analysts, the wasted time amounted to as much as $100,000 wasted per year. Keep in mind that this loss was only for one business unit in one department in a large organization.

11.2.3 Bad Business Decisions and Lost Opportunities

One reason to rush our products and services to market is competition. The threat from the competition is a serious matter. If your competitor can advertise his products to your general customer base, the probability is high that you will lose some customers. For your competitors to be able to know your customer base, they need to know about your products as well as your customers' buying preferences and buying patterns. These facts are easily obtained from outside sources. If you cannot extrapolate the same information from your operational data, you are at a severe disadvantage, and in the long run your business may be in jeopardy.

If the data extracted from your operational systems is unreliable and you know about it, you have an opportunity to correct the most significant and strategic data elements before loading the data warehouse. On the other hand, if you think your data is reliable, but it isn't, and you use it for making important business decisions, you are risking making a financially detrimental decision for your company, from which you may never recover. For example, a company had to pay a stiff fine after an audit uncovered noncompliance with government regulations. The company was not aware of any irregularities because their data was wrong.

11.2.4 Bad Public Relations

Not all costs that result from dirty data are as obvious as the previous examples. In some cases organizations lose customers without realizing that the cause was bad public relations. Losing customers is becoming more evident in e-commerce, where customers choose their suppliers without personal contact. If they hear of a quicker, cheaper, or more reliable service, they simply switch without any explanation or confrontation. In addition, the loss seldom stops with one customer. E-mails sent within minutes to colleagues and friends often result in sympathetic reaction from some of them who also choose to switch. If organizations want to find out why they lost these customers, then some costly options are mailings or telephone surveys, and they still have to hope customers will bother to take the time to fill out the questionnaires or answer questions on the telephone (most won't).

For decades, resolving dirty data problems has been accepted as "overhead" for automated systems. Both users and IT have grown so accustomed to the constant scrap and rework that we do not question our habits. Few people realize the staggering cost of our existing data chaos. Studies have estimated this cost to be up to 25 percent of the annual operating budget (English 1999) in some organizations. It makes you wonder how such waste is cost justified year after year, while data cleansing initiatives are rejected.

11.3 DEFINING DATA QUALITY FOR THE DATA WAREHOUSE

The first thing people think about when asked to define data quality is error-free data entry. In other words, they think of edit checks embedded in the data entry programs that ensure that all the fields accept only valid data values. However, data quality goes far beyond that.

11.3.1 Data Is Correct

For data to be correct, its values must adhere to its domain. For example, a State Code may be one of 50 predefined postal state abbreviations (AL, AK, AZ, . . . WY). If the data value for the column State Code is "AZ," it would be correct because it maps into its domain, which contains the 50 predefined codes. Correctness of data values can often be enforced through edit checking in programs and through the use of domain lookup tables. Note that data correctness is not the same as data accuracy.

11.3.2 Data Is Accurate

A data value can be correct without being accurate. For example, a State Code "AZ" for a City Name "Juneau" would be wrong, since the city of Juneau is in the state of Alaska, and the accurate data value for Alaska is "AK." Accuracy of data values cannot be enforced through simple edit checks. However, sometimes it is possible to check against values in other fields or to use external data, such as a geographic tape from the United States Postal Service to determine if a data value is accurate in the context in which it is used.

11.3.3 Data Follows the Business Rules

A variation of inaccurate data values is those that do not follow the defined business rules. For example, a person's Date of Birth should precede his Date of Death, not the other way around. Another example of a business rule violation may be real property, which is defined in one data field as a single family residence, but another data field shows that it is composed of 12 rental units.

11.3.4 Data Is Consistent

Since every organization is plagued with redundant data, more often than not you will find that the data value for a column in one file will not match the data value for the same column in another file. For example, the customer name associated with his checking account is "Joseph M. Branden," the name on his savings account is "Joe Branden," and his name on a downstream Customer-Account decision support system is "Joseph Branden." A Customer Relationship Management system used as the single point of entry for customer data could solve these inconsistencies.

11.3.5 Data Is Complete

In our current approach to develop systems where the focus is on one user's or one department's narrow data requirements, we often ignore the data elements that are not pertinent to that user's operation. For example, the most important data elements for the Mortgage Loan Origination department of a bank revolve around dollars, such as Requested Loan Amount, Gross Annual Income Amount, Monthly Expense Amount, Property Appraisal Amount, and so forth. Data elements, which are important to downstream user departments like marketing, are either not entered into the system or entered haphazardly. For example, the operations users are not too concerned if they don't capture Gender, Number of Dependents, or Referring Source (what brought the customer to the bank). Yet these are the most important data elements for marketing.

11.3.6 Data Is Integrated

We have already established that most organizations have their data distributed redundantly and inconsistently across many systems and files. These systems and files were never designed to be used together in an integrated fashion; therefore, the primary keys often don't match, and in some very old flat files keys don't even exist. To make things worse, sometimes these systems and files are outsourced to outside companies for processing. These companies do not call each other to find out if the same customer appears in all of their systems. For example, if a customer is a direct investor and has a retirement fund, he would exist on two outsourced systems under different customer numbers, most likely with a different spelling of his name and possibly even with a different phone number and mailing address. Matching this customer across multiple external source files is difficult at best.

11.4 DATA CLEANSING CATEGORIES

Questions that beg to be asked are, How could we, the conscientious IT professionals, have allowed "dirty data" to happen in the first place? How could the users, being the owners of the data, have allowed it to happen? Or are there maybe legitimate, sometimes even justifiable reasons for the existence of "dirty data" in our legacy systems? And what do we do with it now? (Moss 1998)

11.4.1 Dummy Default Values

How many times have you seen dummy values entered, such as a Social Security Number of 999-99-9999, or a Zip Code as 99999? Some organizations capture Customer Age at time of transaction (instead of Date of Birth) and end up with values of 999. The main reason for using defaults was because either the data entry program or the data entry staff was forced to make up values where none was known. There was not much choice in the old days with old file structures because the concept of a NULL was not known. Another reason for using defaults was to speed up data entry because the staff was rewarded for quantity and not quality. Additional reasons include insufficient or lack of quality assurance procedures or lack of training or simply because it is accepted in the culture of the organization.

These dummy default values are easy to detect, but what about some of the more creative solutions to get around mandatory fields? What if the data entry person always used his own social security number or age or zip code?

In some instances we find dummy values that actually have meaning—for example, a Social Security Number of 888-88-8888 to indicate a nonresident alien status of a customer, or a Monthly Income of $99,999.99 to indicate that the customer is an employee.

Data Warehouse Impact

If we moved the dirty data into the data warehouse without any corrections, the users could not rely on their data unless very little of their data was dirty or the dirtiness did not impact their queries. Users could not use social security numbers for selecting customers. Users might end up sending marketing material that was targeted for new customers 62 years and older to 20-year-old college students because their age was entered as 999. Marketing could not use zip codes in their geographic analysis, and any functions summing up or averaging the monthly income of customers would produce an incorrect result.

Transformation

Amounts, such as Monthly Income Amount, and counts, such as Customer Age, should be set to NULL if unknown so any calculations performed on those columns produce the correct results. Columns containing numbers that are not used as keys and are never used in calculations but are only descriptive in nature—for example, Plat Map Book Number—do not need to be set to NULL and could be left with default values.

Any embedded information must be extracted into its own new attributes and transformed into an appropriate value. This would mean creating a new attribute called Nonresident Alien Indicator with values of "YES" and "NO." The ETL program would transform social security numbers of 888-88-8888 to NULL and set the Nonresident Alien Indicator to "YES." For all other valid social security numbers, the ETL program would leave the number and set the Nonresident Alien Indicator to "NO." It would also mean creating a new attribute, Customer Type Code, with predefined values, one of them being EMP (for Employee). Source records with a monthly income of $99,999.99 would be transformed to NULL, and the Customer Type Code would be set to the code "EMP." During this analysis, additional transformation logic would have to be defined for the other values of this new code.

11.4.2 Missing Values

One common reason for "dirty data" is the absence of data. This is not always attributable to lazy data entry habits. Different business units may have different needs for the existence of certain data values in order to run their operations. For example, the department that originates mortgage loans may have a federal reporting requirement to capture the gender and ethnicity of a customer, whereas the department that originates consumer loans does not. We must remember that the primary purpose for operational systems has always been to enable the day-to-day operation of the business, not to provide information for decision support purposes.

Some typical examples of informational data are gender, age, ethnicity, area code and phone number, number of dependents, and referring source. None of this data is needed to open an account, sell a product, or post a payment. However, marketing lives on it, especially referring source, which indicates how the company got that customer and whether it was through direct marketing, TV ads, or the customer is the cousin of an employee.

Data Warehouse Impact

Missing values will skew all queries that count and group customers by this incomplete data. The business unit impacted the most is marketing, as they will not be able to analyze customer demographics and customer buying profiles accurately, nor will they be able to judge reliably which of their marketing channels brings in most of the customers. This will impact marketing's decisions for future marketing campaigns.

Transformation

Correcting missing values is not easy and may not be worth the effort. In some cases it may even be impossible to fill in missing values. The transformation logic would have to read several other fields on either the same source file or other source files and use rather complicated evaluation and comparison logic to determine what the most appropriate values may be. It is not unusual to see specifications of such transformations run into multiple pages of code for one field.

11.4.3 Multipurpose Fields

A very popular and insidious programming construct used to be redefining fields. In the old file structures you will find fields that are used for multiple purposes, where the same field is defined to mean many different things, depending on what record is read. Data groups or even entire records can be redefined and redefined and redefined again, as often as 20 or 30 times, with no documentation left to trace the history of the redefinitions. The content of such records can be anything from a string of dates, redefined as a string of amounts, redefined as a mixture of text and numbers, redefined as any other combination of data types the programmer needed at the time. How were these records initialized? With Low Values or with Spaces. Once you are dealing with up to 20 or 30 redefines, many of the original data values are no longer applicable, and in many cases no one is left even to remember what was meant at one time or who knows what to do with them now.

Data Warehouse Impact

The impact is multifold. First, to move a field that has been redefined several times with incompatible data types into a relational database is not even possible because relational data structures strongly enforce data typing. Second, if the redefines were within the same data type—that is, one text field redefined into two text fields—you would be mixing apples with oranges in what is called an overloaded column because each redefined field has its own unique meaning and domain. This means that users would have to know all the meanings and domains of every overloaded column in order to navigate and use the data in the data warehouse correctly.

Transformation

Writing the transformation logic for redefined fields is not always that difficult as long as the various meanings and domains are well documented. To be sure, every single redefined meaning of every field is a separate attribute. For example, if a data group consists of 6 fields and the entire data group was redefined 10 times, that means there are 60 separate and distinct attributes. The next step is to determine if the user needs all 60 attributes or only a subset of them. The transformation logic will then have to mimic the current documentation, program rules, and extract rules to separate these attributes correctly and populate them with appropriate values.

The necessity of separating redefined fields into separate and distinct attributes creates the problem that for every source record only one value exists for one of the many meanings of a data element. For example, if one field has three meanings, the value for one meaning is known, but the value of the other two meanings is not known. If a source field called Appraisal Amount is redefined as a Listed Amount and is again redefined as a Sold Amount, the amount value on one record can represent only one of those three meanings of the field. The other two are unknown. In other words, correcting multipurpose fields creates missing values.

11.4.4 Cryptic Data

Another version of multipurpose fields is the reuse of a field without a formal redefinition of it. These "kitchen sink" fields, also known as code fields with "domain schizophrenia" (English 1999), are often one-byte alphanumeric fields used for any and all purposes. Their data values are cryptic and beyond intuitive recognition, and they are often not mutually exclusive. For example, the values A, B, C may represent Customer Type Codes "CORP," "SOLE," and "PRSN," and the values K, L, M may represent Sales Type Code "DIRECT," "CATLOG," and "INTNET." In the real world, both meanings of the field exist. There is a certain type of customer who participates in a certain type of sale. Yet the source system has the capacity to capture only one of those meanings. The older these fields are, the worse the conglomeration of incompatible uses of the field. In some cases the problem is compounded by redefining such a field multiple times.

Data Warehouse Impact

A "kitchen sink" field in the data warehouse will make it difficult for the users to write their queries. First, they have to refer back to their code translation manuals to determine what cryptic values to ask for. If they include or exclude a value by mistake, their query results will be wrong, and they won't even know that the results are wrong. Second, users will have to remember the exclusion logic they must currently apply. For example, if the users want to extract all customers and sort them by customer type code, they must remember to exclude values K, L, and M. The example here is fairly uncomplicated, but real world conditions are not this simple. Navigating through the logic embedded in the data may require a procedural program to be written because SQL by itself is not sophisticated enough to let users jump through the required hoops. There are very few users who know how to imbed SQL in a procedural language. They should not have to know.

Transformation

As with multipurpose fields, each different meaning for a group of codes must be transformed into separate and unique attributes. In our example, you would create a Customer Type Code attribute as well as a Sales Type Code attribute and populate each with an intuitive mnemonic instead of the original cryptic code. This necessary correction produces the same problem of creating missing values, since the data value in one field can represent only one meaning at a time, leaving the others unknown.

11.4.5 Contradicting Data Values

The data values in some fields may have to complement, supplement, or synchronize with certain data values in other fields within the record. Sometimes these interdependent fields have contradicting values. For example, a property address in New York, NY, showing a Texas zip code or a woman having prostate surgery.

Data Warehouse Impact

If a user writes a report summarizing on State Code, the dollars associated with our example would be added to New York. If another user writes a similar report summarizing on Zip Code, the same dollars associated with our example would be added to Texas. These two reports will now be inconsistent because the same dollars were summarized into two different states based on whether State Code or Zip Code was used in their queries. The impact of the contradicting rental units on a single family residence is more significant because income property is appraised and funded differently than a single family residence. In addition, mortgage loans for income properties are also sold under different terms to investors, and their profitability is calculated differently.

Transformation

Contradicting values must be synchronized. Evaluating and comparing various other fields on the same source file or other files and correcting the contradicting value that is determined to be wrong are imperative for accurate and consistent reporting.

11.4.6 Violation of Business Rules

This condition exists when the data values do not support the stated business rules. For example, an adjustable rate mortgage loan has two caps: a ceiling interest rate cap and a floor interest rate cap. The ceiling indicates the maximum interest rate, and the floor indicates the minimum interest rate the loan can ever have. A violation of this business rule would be on loans where the floor interest rate is *higher* than the ceiling interest rate. Another example might be that fixed rate mortgage loans have no caps, since their interest rates do not fluctuate. A violation of this business rule would be on fixed rate loans where *multiple* interest rates are captured for the life of the loan. Other examples of violated business rules might be where an expiration date *precedes* an effective date.

Data Warehouse Impact

Data values that violate the business rules are fairly useless if not potentially dangerous because they do not reflect what happens in reality and can therefore lead to incorrect decisions. For example, it is not possible to judge the performance of a product or the profitability of a customer accurately as long as the interest rates are wrong.

Transformation

All efforts should be made to correct inaccurate and illogical data values that blatantly violate the business rules. One option is to evaluate and compare other fields on the same source file or other files to determine what the accurate values really are. If that is not possible, maybe an algorithm can be devised to estimate the most likely values, which would be closer to reality than the existing inaccurate values. In some cases the easiest solution may be to find another source file for the same data element. The probability of finding the same data on another source file is high in the current IT environments where data is stored redundantly dozens of times.

11.4.7   Inappropriate Use of Address Lines

Another popular feature in our old file structures is freeform address lines, such as address line1, line 2, line 3, and line 4. Surely, address line 1 was originally intended to be used for first, middle, and last name or a company name; address line 2 for street number, direction, and street name; address line 3 for suite or apartment number; and address line 4 for city, state, and zip code. In some organizations, however, "freeform" means anything goes. For example:

Address line 1:	ROSENTAL, LEVITZ, AT
Address line 2:	TORNEYS
Address line 3:	10 MARKET, SAN FRANC
Address line 4:	ISCO, CA 95111

In this example, there appears to be a pattern of wrapping text between address line 1 and line 2, and between address line 3 and line 4, which could be parsed fairly easily into separate attributes. However, we have encountered address lines that followed no discernable pattern and had everything from people's birthdays to personal reminders on various lines.

Data Warehouse Impact

Freeform address lines may be acceptable for printing mailing labels, but they are useless for analysis. If these address lines are not converted into structured address components, the users, looking for cities or states, will not be able to write SQL queries against them since SQL has no parsing or substringing capabilities. A programmer would have to write procedural code to report on these fields.

Transformation

Assuming that some pattern was followed, the transformation logic should parse each address line into its distinct and separate address columns. If no pattern was followed, another source file should be substituted.

11.4.8   Reused Primary Keys

One of the most critical "dirty data" issues the data warehouse developers encounter is with primary keys. Since operational systems rarely store history beyond 90 or 180 days, primary key values are often reused. For example, banks reassign branch numbers regularly and therefore have difficulty tracking branch performance over time. Let us assume that branch 84 is located in an affluent area and has originated and serviced 100 mortgage loans totaling $80,000,000. Now branch 84 closes and transfers the servicing of these loans to branch 207. After one year branch 84 is reassigned to a new branch that is located in a less affluent area and is starting to experience a high rate of foreclosures on its originated loans. Since the operational system cared only about the ongoing servicing of the loans and not where the loans originated, it reassigned only the servicing branch, and not the originating branch. This means that the 100 loans for $80,000,000 that were originated by the first, now-closed branch 84 are falsely credited to the performance of the new branch 84. At first glance and without further detailed analysis, it is not evident that the new branch 84 is unprofitable.

Data Warehouse Impact

If primary keys are reassigned, it is not possible to perform any kind of trend analysis because the same key value points to different objects at different times. Even with detailed metadata and cross-reference tables on branch numbers with their effective and expiration dates, it would require IT to write programs to produce trend analysis reports. The reporting problem in our example was worsened because the two different branches with the same primary key rolled up into different regions and areas of the country.

Transformation

It is imperative that primary keys are unique to a specific object and remain with that object for life. If this condition does not exist in the source files, it must be forced to exist in the data warehouse. The transformation logic will have to create and assign a unique key either by concatenating other attributes to the original key value, such as effective date or expiration date, or by creating a surrogate key. A surrogate key is a randomly generated unique number, and it is the cleaner of the two solutions. When implementing multidimensional databases, it is imperative to enforce unique keys through the use of conforming dimensions where possible, as explained in Chapter 10, "Data Models."

11.4.9 No Unique Identifiers

Another interesting problem exists when one object is identified by several primary keys. For example, a branch located at 10 Main Street may be identified as branch number 65 on the loan system and the investor system but as branch number 389 on the checking system and the savings system. Another example would be an employee who has ten different employee numbers because the employee has worked in ten different departments and was assigned a new number with each transfer. Since the old employee number became "available," it was promptly reassigned to a different employee joining the old department.

Data Warehouse Impact

As with other primary key problems, performing any kind of trend analysis on objects that do not have one unique identifier is impossible. In the example of the employee with ten different primary keys, tracking that person's salary, benefits, and performance appraisals over time would require IT to write programs that would navigate through many employee transfer cross-reference records to establish the movement of this person.

Transformation

As previously stated, it is imperative that each occurrence of an object be assigned its own unique identifier for life. The transformation program must create and maintain one unique primary key for each employee or customer or whatever the object. If necessary, the translation table or cross-reference files, which are used by the transformation logic, can be made available to users to help them find the records under the known business keys. The important part to remember here is that primary keys must remain intact and cannot be replaced or refreshed with every load process because many reporting tools reference primary keys, which make up their answer sets. Not keeping the primary keys intact may cause severe problems down the road.

11.4.10 Data Integration Problems

Integration problems come in two flavors:

1. Data that should be related but cannot be because there are no primary keys to relate two objects and there is no easy way to build this

relationship from other fields. A common example of this is found in banks. All banks assign a unique account number to each new account. However, only very few banks assign a unique customer number to each customer. For decades the accounts had to be related back to their customers through a customer name field on the account record. There were different spellings or abbreviations of the same customer name; sometimes the customer was recorded under an alias or a maiden name. Occasionally when two or three customers had a joint account, all of their names were squeezed into one name field. Unless all this information was tracked in some automated fashion, or even manually, which it seldom was, it was very difficult to build the appropriate relationships.

2. Data that is inadvertently related but should not be. This happens most frequently when fields are being reused for multiple purposes. For example, banks customarily buy mortgage loans from other banks, and banks sell their own mortgage loans to various investors. At one bank, two systems used only one operational loan file, recording both loan purchases and loan sales. Both systems had a separate set of programs, each creating the primary keys for either the loan sellers or the loan purchasers. However, since both systems wrote to the same physical file, different loan sellers and loan purchasers ended up with the same primary key values.

Data Warehouse Impact

In the case of not being able to build a relationship between two objects, users will not be able to ask questions against both objects as they interrelate in the real world. In the case of intermingling two objects, like loan sellers with loan purchasers who share the same key values, it would not be possible to load both into the same table, as the duplicate keys would reject. Even if the primary key feature on the database were turned off, users would have to interrogate other fields to determine if they are looking at loan sellers or loan purchasers.

Transformation

If a relationship cannot be built between two objects, there may be a way to indicate through a separate column that a possible association or extension exists. This association would then have to be traced manually by the users. In the case of intermingled objects, the transformation program must separate them into different tables, using the rules from the users and other fields in the source file to determine how to separate them.

Best practice: Whatever cleansing decisions and transformation logic you choose, be sure to document your solutions in the repository as metadata. In addition, include the degree of expected cleanliness for each data element so the users can decide how much to trust the information on their reports. Also, be sure to have a procedure in place to measure the cleanliness of each data element periodically and to update the results in the metadata repository. "Dirty data" does not remain static.

11.5   TRIAGING DATA CLEANSING ACTIVITIES

Many people would like to clean up the whole data mess all at once, but that is not realistic. Some of the data is impossible to clean, and some of it is not cost effective to clean. Therefore data cleansing priorities must be set.

11.5.1   To Cleanse or Not to Cleanse

That is the million dollar question. But the first question to ask is *Can* the data be cleansed at all? The answer is often no. There truly are situations where data no longer exists and cannot be recreated regardless of the amount of manual or automated effort. Sometimes values are so convoluted or are found in so many disparate places with different and opposing meanings to the same fact that any attempt to decipher such data may produce even more errors. In that case it may be best just to leave the data alone, but be sure to inform the users that the data was not cleansed.

The next question is more difficult: *Should* it be cleansed? Here, too, the answer is often no. For most die-hard data managers, this answer smacks of heresy. What purpose would it serve to suck "dirty data" out of the operational systems and plunk it into a data warehouse *as is?* Obviously, none! Clearly, *some* data cleansing must occur. However, everyone has to face the business reality of today, and the business expectations to deliver value-added information in a relatively short time frame for a low cost. By now it should be obvious that fixing some of these decades-old problems will neither be quick nor low cost.

Once you decide which data should be cleansed, the question is *Where* do you cleanse it? Do you clean up operational data on the operational systems? Do you perform the cleansing transformations in the extract and load process for the data warehouse? Usually, the first reaction is to clean up the operational systems, and in some cases that can and should be done. However, all too often those users who are using the operational systems for operational purposes do not need the data any cleaner than it is, and they resist any attempts to change their processes. In other cases it is the IT staff who refuses to clean up the operational systems because it is too complicated to do. It may legitimately be too labor intensive, not cost effective, or simply impossible to do, and so the burden of cleansing falls on the extract, transform and load processes for the data warehouse.

The final question, of course, is *How* do we cleanse what can reasonably be cleansed? Can the data cleansing products on the market today handle a lot of the common data quality problems shared by most organizations? The answer is yes. Are the ETL tools on the market capable of resolving *all* of these very complicated and very customized "dirty data" situations? The answer is no. If you are truly serious about creating value-added information out of the dirty data, you will probably have to write some procedural code to supplement the ETL tool.

11.5.2 Steps for Data Cleansing

What is the right solution for your organization? How do you decide which "dirty data" to cleanse and why? Who makes these decisions? Let's start with more fundamental questions and see if the solutions become apparent.

Why are we building a data warehouse in the first place? What specific business questions are we trying to answer? Why are we not able to answer these business questions today? The answers to these fundamental questions must come from the users, not from IT. Certainly, the expertise and involvement of the IT staff will help the users identify, quantify, document, and analyze their business needs, but it is the users who decide if a data warehouse should be built, not IT.

The next step is for the users, with the help of IT, to define the goals and objectives for the data warehouse (see Chapter 2, "Goals and Objectives"). Once it is clearly understood *what* business questions cannot be answered today and *why*, it is IT's responsibility to analyze the existing operational files and to locate, document, and report the discovered "dirty data" to the users.

The next step is the painful task of determining where to get the "biggest bang for the buck." Users and IT together must evaluate the tangible and intangible benefits for each business question, which cannot be answered today but which will be answered by a data warehouse. Together, you must understand how each "dirty data" case would prevent these business questions from being answered, and you must understand the effort involved to cleanse it.

Now the compromising begins. If the benefits outweigh the costs of the effort, the data should definitely be considered for cleansing. However, there may not be enough resources to cleanse all the data under consideration, and priorities must be set by the users. The most strategically critical data should receive the highest cleansing priority.

The next decision to be made is whether to make the necessary changes to the operational systems to (a) clean up the existing data and (b) prevent future "dirty data" from being entered. Efforts should be made to persuade the owners of the operational systems to improve their systems, unless the effort would be unreasonably high or simply could not be done because the original data sources no longer exist. The reality is that more often than not the majority of cleansing ends up being done in the ETL process.

If the costs of the effort outweigh the benefits, another painful decision must be made: Should the "dirty data" go into the data warehouse *as-is,* or should it be left out? Again, users and IT together must weigh the pros and cons for including the data *as-is.* There may be some possible benefits from including this data, dirty as it is, compared to not having it available at all. On the other hand, including the data *as-is,* may skew results for important trend analysis, rendering it useless or, worse, providing incorrect information that leads to bad business decisions.

There may be instances where a data warehouse should not be built at all because there is too much dirty data to make it useful and because the cost to cleanse the data far exceeds the benefits gained from it.

A reminder: Be sure to document all your cleansing decisions and your measures as metadata in the repository.

11.6 SUMMARY

Every data warehouse project should deal with two major issues: data management and data delivery. Although data management is a subject much larger than data warehousing, certain aspects of source data quality must be addressed. Data going into the data warehouse should be not only correct but accurate. The data should follow established business rules. It should be consistent and as complete as possible. All data from heterogeneous as well as homogeneous sources should be integrated.

Cost for nonquality data is frequently underestimated or not recognized at all. The issue is not "How much will it cost to clean it up?" but "How much is it costing by not cleaning it up?"

Data cleansing goes far beyond data entry and program-induced errors to include the following categories of our old file structures:

- Dummy default values
- Missing values
- Multipurpose fields
- Cryptic data
- Contradicting data values
- Violation of business rules
- Inappropriate use of address lines
- Reused primary keys
- No unique identifiers
- Data integration problems

To cleanse or not to cleanse, what and where to cleanse—those are difficult questions. Cleansing all the data on all the operational systems is not realistic and should not be part of a data warehouse effort. Triaging the cleansing activities in the transformation process in order of criticality *is* the answer.

A CAUTIONARY TALE

Dirty Data Delays the Data Warehouse by Six Months

It was a well-trained and highly motivated project team. Although it was their first data warehouse project, the team members recognized the complexity of their project early on. They prepared their project plan and diligently followed a modified version of their methodology. Work progressed as planned. They negotiated the scope down to a doable size, and they established various standards and worked on some infrastructure pieces. They created a logical data model and designed two target databases: one two-dimensional ODS and one multidimensional data mart. They even finished writing the transformation specifications for the ETL back-end programmers. And then all hell broke loose. The ETL programs were abending left and right with data exceptions. The analysts quickly examined the source files and found to their horror that 90 percent of the source data needed some cleansing and transforming. Two analysts worked ful-time for six additional months, analyzing each source data field and rewriting the transformation specs.

11.7 WORKSHOP

In these Workshops you will identify the data management issues you need to address on your data warehouse project.

11.7.1 Inventory Your Source Data

Review your data requirements and identify all of the potential source files that contain that data on the operational side. Create a matrix similar to this example.

Requested Data	Potential Source File	Potential Field Name
Customer Name	Customer Master	Cust-Name
	Daily Tran File	Customer-First-Name
		Customer-Last-Name
	Account Master	Account-Name
Account Open Date	Account Master	Open-Date or
		Account-Date
Commitment Amount	Account Master	Loan-Amount
	Borrower File	Requested-Loan-Amount

Use the following matrix for your exercise.

Requested Data	Potential Source File	Potential Field Name

11.7.2 Determine Source Data Quality

For each identified data source, print out a subset of records, and review the data values in terms of correctness, accuracy, adherence to business rules, consistency, and completeness. Rate them on a scale of 1 to 5, 5 being always clean, 1 being rarely clean.

Requested Data	Potential Source File	Potential Field Name	cor	acc	rul	cns	cmp
Customer Name	Customer Master	Cust-Name	5	5	5	3	4
	Daily Tran File	Customer-First-Name	4	3	2	2	1
		Customer-Last-Name	4	3	2	2	1
	Account Master	Account-Name	2	3	4	2	3
Account Open Date	Account Master	Open-Date or	4	5	4	2	5
		Account-Date	3	3	3	2	4
Commitment Amount	Account Master	Loan-Amount	5	5	5	4	4
	Borrower File	Requested-Loan-Amount	4	4	5	2	2

Legend: cor   correctness
             acc   accuracy
             rul   adherence to business rules
             cns   consistency
             cmp complete

Use the following matrix for your exercise.

Requested Data	Potential Source File	Potential Field Name	cor	acc	rul	cns	cmp

Legend: cor correctness
acc accuracy
rul adherence to business rules
cns consistency
cmp complete

11.7.3 Choose the Best Source Files

Review your quality evaluation matrix, and choose the best source file for each requested data element.

11.7.4 Cost for Nonquality Data

For each source file and/or each redundant data element, use the following questions to help you determine the cost of maintaining the redundancy and the cost of constant scrap and rework (English 1999).

Source File Name: _____

How many IT programmers and analysts are involved with each source file? _____

How often are any of them called in on an emergency per month? _____

How many hours per month do they spend fixing a problem on the source file? _____

How many files per month need reconciliation? _____

How many reports per month need reconciliation? _____

How many users are involved in verification and reconciliation activities per month? _____

How many hours do users spend on reconciliation activities per month? _____

How many bad decisions are made per month because of dirty data? _____

How many business opportunities are lost per month because of dirty data? _____

How many customer complaints are received per month regarding data in that source file? _____

How long does it take to resolve a customer complaint? _____

How many people have to get involved on a customer complaint? _____

11.7.5   Data Cleansing Categories

Analyze each data element on the chosen source file, and determine what data cleansing categories apply to it. At a high level, define what the transformation logic needs to be. For example:

Requested Data	Chosen Source File	Field Name	Category	Transformation
Customer Name	Customer Master	Cust-Name	Inappropriate use of the name field	Parse Cust-Name into separate name components using spaces as the delimiter.
Account Open Date	Account Master	Open-Date (primary) Account-Date (second)	Missing Values	Use Open-Date when available, otherwise use Account-Date.
Commitment Amount	Account Master Borrower File	Loan-Amount Requested-Loan-Amount	Missing Values	Use Loan-Amount when available, otherwise use Requested-Loan-Amount from the Borrower file.

Use the following matrix for your exercise.

Requested Data	Chosen Source File	Field Name	Category	Transformation

11.7.6 Data Cleansing Costs

For each requested data element, examine the high-level transformation logic, and estimate the number of people required to perform the detailed analysis, the coding, and the testing for the proposed solution. Then estimate the number of effort hours it would take.

For example:

Requested Data	Chosen Source File	Field Name	Total # Hours
Customer Name	Customer Master	Cust-Name	360
Account Open Date	Account Master	Open-Date (primary) Account-Date (second)	70
Commitment Amount	Account Master Borrower File	Loan-Amount Requested-Loan- Amount	150

Use the following matrix for your exercise.

Requested Data	Chosen Source File	Field Name	Total # Hours

11.7.7 Triage the Data Cleansing Activities

After reviewing the cleansing cost matrix with the user, prioritize the cleansing activities on a scale of 1 to 5, 5 being highest. Also indicate where the data will be corrected and whether it will be on the operational side or during the ETL process. For data that is to be cleansed on the operational system, be sure to include a written cleansing agreement from the operational system owner.

If the cleansing of the operational system is to be concurrent with the data warehouse project, be sure to include the operational activities in your status reports.

For example:

Requested Data	Chosen Source File	Field Name	Priority	Location
Customer Name	Customer Master	Cust-Name	5	ETL
Account Open Date	Account Master	Open-Date (primary)	4	ETL (now)
		Account-Date (second)	2	OPER SYS (future)
Commitment Amount	Account Master	Loan-Amount	5	OPER SYS
	Borrower File	Requested-Loan-Amount	2	OPER SYS (future)

Use the following matrix for your exercise.

Requested Data	Chosen Source File	Field Name	Priority	Location

REFERENCES

Brackett, Michael H. *The Data Warehouse Challenge, Taming Data Chaos.* New York, N.Y.: John Wiley & Sons, 1996.

English, Larry P. *Improving Data Warehouse and Business Information Quality,* New York, N.Y.: John Wiley & Sons 1999.

Moss, Larissa T. "Data Cleansing: A Dichotomy of Data Warehousing?" *DM Review,* Volume 8, Number 2, February 1998.

CHAPTER TWELVE

Project Planning

Many IS organizations are so busy meeting deadlines and putting out fires that they don't have much time to think about policies and the development process.

—*Watts Humphrey*

In the time it would take us to create a project plan, we could have implemented a pilot.

Having discussed the key issues that will affect you while managing a data warehouse project, we would like to bring these issues together for you with the guidelines for planning and controlling your project. This chapter covers the following:

- The need for project planning
- Developing a project plan
- Estimating work durations and schedules
- Controlling the project
- First project choice
- Communication

Appendix 12.A is a project plan task template. Appendix 12.B is a sample project plan. Appendix 12.C has examples of data warehouse disasters with references to the chapters that tell you how to avoid those disasters.

12.1 NEED FOR PROJECT PLANNING

Data warehouse projects that have started without a project plan often end up short on required resources and are typically late and over budget. The deliverables all too often are of poor quality, interim products (deliverables) are not clearly defined or are nonexistent, and, most important, the users do not get what they want or expect.

While project management is critical for projects involving operational systems, it is especially critical for data warehouse projects because there is usually little in-house expertise in this rapidly growing area. The data warehouse project manager must embrace new tasks and deliverables, develop a different working relationship with the users, and work in an environment that is far less defined, less predictable, and less stable than a traditional operational environment.

Why do you plan? You plan to control user expectations, you plan to prevent unpleasant surprises, and you plan to minimize the chances that you have left something out. A plan is the basis for monitoring progress; you have something to compare against when you assess the status of your project. It helps you with identifying problems as early as possible. The plan gives you a tool for resisting unreasonable target dates; it helps minimize uncertainty and risk. It helps you make more efficient use of the resources that are available to you. By sharing your plans, you facilitate communication with all the people who are involved with the project. It helps other departments plan as you make demands of their resources. A project plan gives senior management a more comfortable feeling that the project is under control. And finally, a plan gives you a vehicle for constantly improving the process of implementing data warehouse projects. You learn, you benchmark, you evaluate, and you improve.

Without a project plan, the project manager is taking a very high risk because there will be no basis for requesting resources when they are needed or even for identifying which resources are necessary. The project manager is vulnerable to the unrealistic imposition of an arbitrary deadline and a schedule that is beyond his ability to control. Without a project plan, milestones and project deliverables are indeterminate, and the quality of the deliverables has no basis for comparison. Without a project plan, slipped schedules cannot be detected until it is too late. Without a project plan, assigning responsibility is difficult, and dependencies and predecessors cannot be easily determined. Embarking on a data warehouse project without a project plan is development by the seat of your pants and a formula for failure.

12.2 THE PROJECT PLAN

A good project plan lists the tasks that must be performed and when each task should be started and completed. It identifies who is to perform the task, describes deliverables associated with the task, and identifies milestones for measuring progress. While small or simple projects do not require a list of all the tasks and deliverables that are needed in the large or complex projects, it takes experience to know which tasks are required and which tasks can be skipped.

In the discipline of project management there are many similarities between a data warehouse and an operational system, but many tasks and deliverables are specific and unique to data warehouse. MapXpert for Data Warehouse™ is a data warehouse methodology and project planning tool. It identifies some of these unique tasks as follows:

- Define data warehouse objectives—if you do not define your objectives, you will have no way of knowing if you are successful. Without defined objectives, you will not be able to define or control the project's scope.
- Define query libraries—since operational systems typically do not have general-purpose query capabilities, there is usually no need for query libraries in an operational environment.
- Integrate metadata—you would expect metadata to be shared across the enterprise. Since each data warehouse project should not be a standalone system, its metadata must be integrated with the existing repository content.
- Develop a refresh and load strategy—operational systems have updates in place, whereas data warehouse databases are either refreshed or loaded with data for the next period.
- Define data warehouse product selection criteria—there are many new technology components for data warehouses that are not applicable to an operational environment.

- Prepare extract/transform/load (ETL) specifications—ETL programs must be reconciled to each other, and redundancy among them should be removed as appropriate.
- Develop query usage monitoring—queries tend to be susceptible to poor performance, and since queries often use significant resources and data warehouses are not as static as operational systems, monitoring usage for day-to-day volume and resource usage in order to anticipate performance problems is a vital task.

12.2.1 Work Breakdown Structure

A fundamental principal of project management is breaking down a large work effort into smaller pieces that can be easily monitored and controlled. Choose only those tasks and deliverables that make sense for the project at hand. Do not produce useless deliverables or define tasks that represent only "busy work." Conversely, do not hesitate to "invent" a task/deliverable if it is required for the project (Carstens 1996).

A work breakdown structure allows you to divide large tasks such as the extract, transform, and load process into manageable pieces that can be readily assigned, monitored, and controlled. In the example of extract, transform, and load, each program would probably be a separate task that could even require subtasks. A good rule of thumb is if the task involves more than 40 hours of effort, it should be subdivided. Any breakdown of tasks taking less than one day is probably too granular a division. If a task has more than one person who would have primary responsibility, the task should be divided into subtasks so that only one person has the primary responsibility.

12.2.2 Tasks

A task is simply a decomposed, lowest-level activity that must be performed. It is usually measured in hours or days. It often has a predecessor—another task that must be completed before this task can begin. This would indicate a task dependency. An example might be coding that must be completed before system testing can begin. Also a task usually has a successor—another task that follows the one in question, such as testing following coding. The output of one task may be the input to its successor, building a sequential chain of tasks and their associated dependencies into your project plan. By understanding predecessors and successors, you are able to focus on the activities that are critical to implementing on time and establishing a critical path of activities and tasks.

12.2.3 Milestones

A milestone is a development step, an activity, a task or deliverable, the completion of which can serve as a gauge of progress on a project. Some characteristics of a good milestone are:

- Represents a decision point in the project
- Represents a dependency point on the critical path (i.e., other tasks cannot proceed until the milestone is accomplished)
- Represents a point where certain project members will begin to participate or, conversely, complete their tasks, thus becoming available for other assignments
- Represents critical dates by which time certain things must happen
- Marks some percentage of project completion or resource consumption
- Represents a point where related projects interface with this project (Carstens 1996)

A milestone is the *successful* conclusion of a major activity that produces a tangible deliverable. We emphasize the word *successful* because an incomplete or inaccurate deliverable of one milestone will surely impact the completeness and accuracy of other milestones that follow. As Ed Carstens states, "A milestone must have a tangible output measurable or observable. It is binary; it is either done or not done." (Carstens 1996)

It is important to remember that in data warehouse projects we have multiple parallel development tracks, each with its own sets of milestones. The back-end ETL process may have a milestone of source data identified, which may coincide with the front-end data delivery's milestone of tools selected, while the repository navigation's milestone repository testing completed is scheduled for two weeks later, and the technical infrastructure's milestone hardware installed a week later yet. In other words, all the different milestones for all the different development tracks will not necessarily fall on the same calendar dates or in a straight sequence of order. You are in fact managing and controlling multiple parallel subprojects with their own project schedules, even though you show them all on one project plan Gantt Chart.

12.2.4   Deliverables

A deliverable is a tangible product. (Carstens 1996) Most milestones will have a major deliverable, such as a selected tool, a tested application, or a loaded database. Every task will also have a deliverable. A task deliverable could be as large as a documented set of user requirements, a fully attributed logical data model, or a completed user training class. A task deliverable could also be as small as an observable event, such as a scheduled meeting, a published agenda, or a resolved issue. Task deliverables are used to monitor the progress and the status of the project and are generally a buildup to the milestone deliverable, but not always.

While significant scope changes would affect the major milestone deliverables, smaller adjustments often affect only the planned task deliverables. This means that the project manager's best means of controlling a dynamic project is on the task level. Adding, eliminating, or modifying the tasks and their associated deliverables can often accommodate small changes to user requirements without jeopardizing the major milestone deliverables or the project schedule on the whole. Needless to say, this must be strictly controlled through traditional impact analysis and change control procedures.

12.2.5   Schedules

An *accurate* schedule for the entire project with associated cost estimates can be developed only after requirements have been defined and all required work has been identified, but nothing remains static. Changes always have to be made, situations are clarified, personnel are shuffled, and we learn new information about the users and the data. Therefore any initial project plan will have to be periodically refined. (Carstens 1996)

Unfortunately, data warehouse schedules are often set before a project plan has been developed. This is often driven because management must make an initial determination if the project is to be funded, how much resource it will take, and when the project may be expected to complete. These preliminary schedules may become the de facto schedule by which the project manager has to live. It is the process of creating a detailed project plan with tasks, durations, and assignments, as well as task and resource dependencies that determines how long a project will take. Without such a plan, assigning a delivery date is, at best, wishful thinking and, at worst, setting you up for an unattainable deadline. An unrealistic schedule pushes the team into the mode of taking shortcuts that ultimately impact the quality of the deliverables. A good project plan is a powerful tool for resisting unreasonable target dates.

What about those who say, "We need a stake in the ground. Otherwise the project manager will have nothing to shoot for, and the project will go on indefinitely." This approach does not give the project manager any credit for developing a Project Agreement, producing a project plan, or managing the project. If imposing a delivery date is the only way to get the project manager to deliver, you have the wrong project manager. Once the plan is correctly completed, you have a manageable date—it simply has been set with reasonable expectations and proper task durations in mind.

The users would like the data warehouse to be delivered very fast. In fact, they have been told by countless vendors that a data warehouse can be delivered in an unrealistically short time, sometimes as short as 90 days. What the vendors fail to include are the following:

- Understanding and documenting the data. They assume the data is well understood and documented before their product is deployed for the building of the application.
- Cleansing the data. They assume the data is clean or that the cleansing is accomplished before their product has to work with it.
- Integrating data from multiple sources. They assume one source— that is, that the integration and associated translation have already been done in a process prior to invoking their product.
- Dealing with performance problems. They assume performance is someone else's problem or can be dealt with at a later time; besides, the vendors want to implement with a small subset of the data warehouse.
- Training internal people so they can enhance and maintain the data warehouse. They commit only to the development, not to the maintenance, of the system.

What gets delivered in short periods of time are small data marts that are not industrial strength, not robust enough to be enhanced, and of not much use to more than a handful of people from one small group in a department. We have thus come full circle and are back at a swim lane approach to data warehouse development (reread Chapter 1, "Introduction to Data Warehousing").

The opposite of quick-and-dirty development is not a monolithic effort to build the entire data warehouse universe. On the contrary, a data warehouse lends itself nicely to phasing. This means that increments can be developed and delivered in pieces without much of the traditional difficulty associated with phasing an operational system. An increment could be a subset of the source files, a subset of the data elements in the source files, or a subset of the eventual target set of users. Typically, an operational system is not fully functional unless all of its components are implemented. This is not true for data warehouses. Each data warehouse increment can be an independent project with its own schedule, but there should be an overall high-level schedule that incorporates all of the increments, and this approach must have a data architecture as its foundation. This effort should be coordinated not only with the business and developers but also with the stewards of the data—the administrators and architects who will ensure the integrity of the multiple overlapping projects is maintained.

12.2.6 Resources

The most challenging job for the data warehouse project manager is recruiting internal skilled personnel. Your organization's competent workers are almost always very heavily involved with other projects. Pulling them into the data warehouse world takes a very creative and well-connected project manager who can sell both management and the targeted team member.

It may be possible to recruit employees skilled in certain aspects of the data warehouse, but it means knowing who they are, where they work, and how best to approach their management to release them for the time required on the assignment. If the person doing the recruiting is new to data warehousing, he may be easily fooled by the current buzzwords and may be overly impressed with knowledge in some specific area of data warehouse, such as familiarity with a data delivery, Web delivery, or OLAP tool. Experience in writing queries does not equate to skills in data warehouse database design. To keep from getting fooled, a data warehouse-experienced consultant—internal or external—could aid in evaluating the candidate and should be part of the interview process. A good project plan can help identify needed skills and identify when those skills are needed.

While it may be expedient to engage consultants for advice and direction and to engage contractors for specific tasks, the organization should plan to grow the data warehouse skills in-house. You may choose to bring in hired guns, but you don't want them around after they have cleaned up the town.

Another key resource is budget. Without an adequate budget, the project manager has no hope of hiring good people, choosing the best products and tools, acquiring the right hardware, and hiring consultants and contractors. What should a data warehouse cost? The cost will be a factor of the following:

- The size of the database—remember to include estimates of space for indexes, summaries, and working space, and capacity planners must also include the space anticipated for future growth. It will grow.
- The complexity and cleanliness of the source data—this will determine the effort required to cleanse the data, and how sophisticated the transformation tool needs to be.
- The choice of tools—the more sophisticated the tool needs to be, the more expensive it will be and the greater the learning curve of your staff. Some tools run only in certain environments and may require other supporting software to be installed on the client, server, or both to run properly.
- The number of source databases and their characteristics—integrating source data is difficult and time-consuming.
- The number of users, their level of expertise, and their location.
- The network requirements.
- Training requirements—will courses be conducted at a vendor location or in-house? Will the vendor develop a customized training package, or will that be the responsibility of an internal training organization? How customized does the training need to be?

- The difference between the required and the available skills—the associated training to bring the team up to speed.
- The amount of IT resources (people and hardware) needed.
- Length of the project.

It is impossible to develop an accurate budget without a good project plan as its base. The project plan will help identify the people resources; from that you can estimate people costs. The project plan will also bring to light the complexity of the system, and from that you can estimate tool and technology expenses. See Chapter 6, "Cost Benefit."

12.2.7   Developing the Project Plan

With only a few changes most of the following steps, which are generally followed to develop a project plan, will look familiar to the reader (Carstens 1996):

- With the sponsor, identify objectives, project costs and benefits.
- Document planning assumptions.
- Determine tasks and deliverables to be produced—create the work breakdown structure.
- Remember to include the "looping activities"—as described in Chapter 9, "Methodology." These are tasks from prior activities that you anticipate will have to be revised or redone.
- Estimate average effort time for each task. If this is your first data warehouse project, this is one of the areas where the advice of an expert is required. There will be some tasks that are new to you, so you will have no historical experience on which to base your estimates.
- Note dependencies between tasks or between tasks and external events.
- Identify project milestones and, if appropriate, time-reporting categories for all parallel development tracks.
- Define roles and responsibilities and gain concurrence from management.
- Assign resources to tasks, and adjust effort estimates depending on a person's skill and experience level as well as knowledge of the subject matter and knowledge of the organization.
- Note dependencies between tasks and available resources and between resources and events (vacation time, etc.) to ensure that available staff are fully scheduled without being overloaded in any particular time period.

- Calculate duration time, taking into account any required training, time for project reviews and walkthroughs, weekly meetings, presentations, administrative time (computer downtime, maintaining another system, etc.), and nonproject time (illness, jury duty, e-mail, voice mail inboxes, etc.).
- Construct a Gantt Chart or network chart (Bubble or Pert) reflecting all dependencies and parallel activities.
- Understand and document the risks associated with the project, and develop contingency plans if the risks should materialize.

An alternative approach is to draw on your own development experience. At a fairly high level, write down a list of what has to be done to deliver your project. For each item on your list, write down some details of what must be done to complete the item. Every task should produce some kind of deliverable (in other words, a tangible product that can be viewed by others such as a document, data model, or prototype). Generally, tasks and deliverables are two aspects of the same thing; every task should produce a deliverable, and every deliverable is the result of a task. This philosophy helps avoid useless tasks that take time and produce nothing of value.

12.2.8 Maintaining the Project Plan

Developing any project plan means coming up with one's "best guess" as to effort and time needed for a project. In operational systems, your best guess is probably more accurate because it is based on your experience with similar systems. In data warehousing, it is almost impossible for anyone's best guess to be accurate because regardless of experience with prior systems, data warehouses have a very dynamic nature with constantly changing requirements. Add to that the cultural change, the shifted roles and responsibilities, the possible plethora of new technology, and the dynamic looping activities throughout its development cycle, in addition to the anticipated and unanticipated roadblocks. This all makes for a development environment that is difficult to control and difficult to estimate.

The answer is not to forget about project planning—the answer is to tighten it up. That means that you cannot continue the practice of creating the initial project plan and then track progress against it when your staff's status reports come in every Friday afternoon. After a very short period you would be tracking progress against a project plan that no longer reflects the activities on the project. Instead, you must adjust your project plan on an ongoing basis. In order to do that you must know, at the task level, what activities and what deliverables are being worked on, how complete they are, what types of problems the staff is running into, what changes the users are requiring, and so on.

It should be obvious by now that the controlling and managing of a data warehouse project is a full-time job and cannot be done a few hours a week from a back office. If the project manager has other administrative duties that take up the majority of his time, the ongoing project management activities (planning, controlling, adjusting, and negotiating) must be delegated to an assistant or lead person. Otherwise the project manager runs the risk of losing control over the project.

12.3 ESTIMATING

Here are a few more guidelines on estimating. The job of estimating how long a task should take, the work effort, and the duration are difficult at best and almost always too optimistic. There are many factors that should be taken into account in the estimating process.

12.3.1 Experience

Skill/Experience level. A DB2 or Oracle database administrator (DBA) with skills and experience in data warehouse will have already made the big mistakes and, hopefully, will have learned from those mistakes and will not repeat them on your project. It will take the experienced DBA far less time to create the database design; he will make far fewer missteps and backtracks. He will require less research time, and he will be more confident, thereby cutting down on wasted effort, reducing the learning curve and hesitancy in unsure situations. A DBA with skills and experience may be anywhere from two to six times more efficient than one who is new to the job.

Knowledge of the Organization. A person who is newly hired will take some time to learn how things work in your organization and will take some time to familiarize himself with the standards and procedures specific to your organization. Most important, it will take him some time to learn the people organization, the power structure, who honors their commitments, who is competent, and who is ally or foe.

Documentation. Another aspect to experience is the accurate, documented knowledge of the data, the processes of the systems, and the organization. The completeness, accuracy, and availability of this documentation will impact the work that needs to be done.

12.3.2 Dependencies

Some tasks are dependent on the completion of others, whereas other groups of tasks may be done concurrently.

Task Dependencies. When you are building a house, you have to lay a foundation before you start the framing. By the same token, you must understand the user requirements before much else can be done. For example, the logical data model must be fairly complete before work is started on the physical model. Most tasks will have a dependency on a preceding task, and it is critical to identify and understand these dependencies as the project plan is built. The task dependencies will determine the critical path of the project plan.

People Dependencies. Tasks have associated resources—that is, skilled people who are either primarily or secondarily responsible for a task. Let's assume that two tasks are independent and can be performed in parallel, but you have only one person who has the skill needed to perform either task. In this case you cannot take advantage of scheduling the tasks to be worked on in parallel because both tasks are now dependent on one person. In addition, people are not always available as scheduled. They become ill, go on unscheduled leave, or get committed to some other project (as is so often the case). Obviously, the tasks assigned to them will not be completed according to the original start and completion times on the project plan. People resources must be constantly reviewed and revised for you to stay on top of the plan.

Decision and Sign-off Dependencies. Many decisions, sign-offs, and validations are made in the course of a data warehouse project, both by management and by the technical people. We have seen projects slip due to the inability, unwillingness, or inattentiveness of decision makers to make decisions. This has resulted in schedule impacts from key decisions that have not been made in a timely manner. If the real decision maker is not in the meeting where the decision is supposed to be made, the schedule may also be impacted. The stand-in may not have the authority or knowledge to make the decision, and so, time is lost. The people responsible for the decisions and sign-offs must be made aware of the impact of their indecision, their unwillingness to delegate authority, and the impact of their not attending a decision-making meeting.

12.3.3   Industry Standards

There are no real standards for how long it should take to perform any data warehouse task. Some of the project management tools have suggested times, but these times should be taken only as guidelines and must be modified for the project, the team, and the environment. The suggested times are best used to alert the project manager to a possible misunderstanding of what the task involves. If a suggested time is 35 hours and the project manager was about to estimate 3 hours, it alerts the project manager to a discrepancy in an understanding of the depth of the task.

Because of the absence of standards due to the high variability between data warehouse projects and the high risk of a data warehouse project, it is essential that the project manager has some prior experience in managing large dynamic projects. A data warehouse is not a training ground for a rookie project manager.

12.3.4   "In the Best of All Possible Worlds"

If estimates are derived with the idea that everything will go perfectly, the software will install without any problems, meetings will happen on time, and decisions will always be made in a timely fashion, then the work effort and especially the duration will be grossly underestimated. If your organization's experience of installing software from a particular vendor has been a problem in the past, it will probably be a problem with your project. In your organization, if meetings usually start late, are postponed, or are unproductive, they will probably start late or be postponed and be less than efficient with your project. If your business sponsor has a reputation for not making decisions, you should factor in the delays as you estimate duration.

12.3.5 Hours and Elapsed Time

Except for small, contained tasks, elapsed time will almost always exceed the work or effort hours. Activities are usually multitasked with personnel working on multiple tasks at the same time, and occasionally the same task may be assigned to multiple (usually no more than two) people. Events that are non-project related will absorb both work hours and durations. Events such as meetings unrelated to the project, company outings, weather-related problems, illnesses, holidays, vacations, personal time, World Series, titillating Senate Committee hearings, earthquakes, pestilence, floods, and countless other interruptions mean you will be unable to predict accurately, and these events must be taken into account. Due to these types of interruptions, some project managers will consider using only five or six hours each day to be allotted to productive project and non-project activities. Other managers give an overall 25 percent to 30 percent bump to the overall project estimate and schedule.

Do not initially schedule work for weekends, holidays, or any of your team's scheduled vacations. Toward the end of the project, a few weekend days may be necessary, but do not include them in your initial project plan. Although it may not have occurred to some readers to have their staff scheduled to work seven days a week, we have seen this practice.

12.3.6 Rework

The reality of projects is that some tasks will need to be redone—hopefully, not more than once. A design review may uncover flaws that require the task to be reworked. Tests may indicate problems with design, with a vendor's product, or with the user interface. Circumstances with the sponsor, with the organization, with competition, or with new regulations may cause the results of some tasks to be scrapped and the task to be reworked under the constraints of new requirements or a new direction. Estimates should include the time and effort for rework, even though it is not possible to predict where the rework will be required or how much will have to be redone.

What about the role of those wonderful data warehouse tools? Shouldn't they have a positive impact on the productivity of the team and, therefore, the schedule? They should have a positive impact, but the usefulness of the tools will be determined by how well-trained your people are. Do not believe the productivity representations of the vendors. Even when they use real situations with real productivity improvements, the examples are almost always taken from the best of the best. Your situation may not be as fortunate. Also there is the learning curve that usually results in an initial loss of productivity.

As a final note on estimating, a mentor once suggested coming up with a best estimate for each task and then doubling it. At the risk of appearing terribly imprecise, this technique has worked for many project managers.

12.4 CONTROLLING THE PROJECT

12.4.1 When Things Go Wrong

Every project has problems. Some can be controlled and contained by the project manager and the sponsor; some cannot. Don't forget that your sponsor is in desperate need of the data warehouse and will be a strong ally, or perhaps even the lead, in dealing with major problems. Some situations are hopeless or, at least, they appear that way initially. When the project has no chance for survival, an exit plan will salvage some of the team's morale and perhaps a sliver of your reputation. It's important to be able to recognize if the project is on life support and when it might be time to pull the plug.

12.4.2 Change Control

The nature of the data warehouse is such that new requests will constantly be added. These requests may come in the form of wanting new or additional data from current source files, new data from external data sources, new or differently formatted canned reports, a different delivery vehicle (maybe on the Web), the integration of new source files, or access by more users.

Most project managers add some amount of fat to their estimates to be able to accommodate unforeseen activities and small-scope changes. Sometimes, the small changes begin to creep in to a point where the existing schedule can no longer handle the additional requirements. This is scope creep. When the requests are for large changes, new and complex source data, or some new technology implementation, it is referred to as scope gallop.

If the schedule derived from the project plan was realistic, a major change or enhancement cannot be accommodated within the existing schedule. Other factors that might impact the schedule are the loss of key personnel or new information about the quality of the source data (this type of news is almost always bad).

The following project characteristics can be affected by a scope change:

- Functionality—capabilities that were scheduled to be delivered and data that must be delivered for the business users to consider the project complete.
- Resources—this includes budget, availability of skilled personnel, and management commitment.
- Quality—an unrealistic schedule may push the team to take shortcuts such as incomplete data analysis, no data cleansing, minimal testing, incomplete or nonexistent documentation, and inadequate training.
- Team health—some managers believe they can drive their team 12 hours each day, seven days each week. This can work for only a short time. After that, the team may be physically present, but their productivity and work quality suffer greatly.

12.4.3 Managing Risk

Every data warehouse project will have a degree of risk. The goal of the project manager is to recognize and identify the impending risks and to take steps to mitigate those risks. Since the data warehouse may be new to the project manager, the risks may not be as apparent as in operational systems. For an exhaustive discussion of risk, read Chapter 4, "Risks."

The loss of a sponsor is an ever-present risk. It can be mitigated by identifying at least one backup sponsor who is interested in the project and would be willing to provide the staffing, budget, and management drive to keep the project on track. Keeping user and IT management informed of the progress of the project along with reminding them of the expected benefits can also lessen the risk.

The user may decide not to use the system. This problem can be overcome by having the user involved from the beginning and through every step of the implementation process, including source data selection, data validation, query tool selection, and user training.

> The data warehouse manager for a large clothing manufacturer was describing his system. He was proud of the size (over 500 gigabytes), of the state-of-the-art tools they were using for extract/transform/load and data delivery, and of their response time. When asked how the users liked the system, he admitted the users were not using it. Apparently, IT decided they knew what the users would want, so they went off and built the system without almost any user involvement. When the users finally were shown the system, it was not to their liking, and they walked away.

The system may have poor performance. Almost every large data warehouse has some types of performance problems. The most demanding performance problems emerge in the extract/transform/load process, but there are often significant performance problems on the query side as well. Good database design with an understanding of how the query tools will access the database and the types of queries that will be performed can help hold performance problems in check. Active monitoring can provide the clues to what is going wrong and the associated queries that are being executed. Trained DBAs must be in place first to monitor and then to take corrective action. Well-tested canned queries made available to the users should minimize the chances of them writing *The Query That Ate Cleveland*. Training should include a module on performance and how to minimize problem queries. Understand that there is always a potential for a giant query that will bring the system to its knees. It is the DBA's job to monitor and deal with those situations.

> One Thursday afternoon, we encountered a user who complained about his query response time. When asked how bad it was, he told us that he launched the query the previous Monday. We knew we had a problem.

12.4.4 Project Management Tools and Methodology

While project management methodologies and software tools are no substitute for good project management, there are a few that can set an organization on the right track and some that have project-planning capabilities specific to data warehouse. The methodologies developed for operational systems are not appropriate for data warehouse. Those who have tried to force-fit an operational methodology onto a data warehouse project had many extraneous tasks that had to be deleted (with some difficulty) and had left out many critical tasks that are not included in traditional operational methodologies. Some of the large consulting organizations have data warehouse methodologies and project planning, but they are typically not sold separately from their consultants.

12.5 FIRST PROJECT SELECTION

The selection of the first data warehouse project is critical. If the project is a success, more data warehouse initiatives will follow. If it is a failure, management will take some serious convincing before they agree to fund the next potential failure. What you are looking for is a project that will give you a quick win, a project that can be shown to be successful in a reasonably short period of time. Recognizing that management may have already selected the project, and it appears that there is no room for the project manager to be involved in the selection, the opportunity for influencing the decision may still be available.

If you do have a choice to select the first project, here are some additional guidelines for the ideal first data warehouse project. A more comprehensive list can be found in Chapter 9, "Methodology."

12.5.1 Sponsor

The ideal sponsor is placed high in the organization and is powerful, politically astute, smart, informed, and aware; he is accepting of problems, has a sense of humor, and a good singing voice. The sponsor should have a major stake in the success of the project and be willing to devote some time and attention to the project. The ideal sponsor is one who can make quick decisions. You want this sponsor to be with you for the duration of the project and not be transferred to some other department in the middle of it.

12.5.2 Value

The project should have some real value to the organization. The project should contribute to the goals of the organization (improved quality, greater customer satisfaction, more revenue, lower cost, the demise of a hated competitor, etc.). Any project that has only marginal value is risky as it may be canceled and may not attract the requisite resources and management attention. Ideally, the project will contribute to a major organization initiative, such as positioning the company to be an attractive initial public offering.

12.5.3 High Profile

This characteristic is highly controversial. Those who like to play it safe would like the project to be treated as a secured skunkworks, invisible to anyone outside the team. Only after the project is complete would they be willing to advertise its existence. The problem with this approach is that you will be missing the attention and buy-in of management and the business as the project progresses. You will not be able to command their involvement when you need it. The danger with a low-profile application is that a project that no one really cares much about will be built. A high-profile application, on the other hand, will put your project on the front page of the company newsletter. The people you want will be eager to work on a visible project. If the project has the requisite value aspect noted in Section 12.5.2, it will probably also be a highly visible project.

12.5.4 Measurable

Many of the benefits of a data warehouse project are intangible and very difficult or even impossible to measure. A sponsor may be willing to attest to the intangible benefits of a data warehouse and provide a testimonial. While it is important to get testimonials from the sponsor, you also want to measure and report on the tangible benefits of the project. Select a project where you can show tangible user productivity, greater customer penetration, or a more effective relationship with suppliers. These are benefits that have high dollar values associated with them. See Chapter 6, "Cost Benefit," for more on this subject.

12.5.5 Reasonable Size

The project should not be so small as to be considered inconsequential either by the business or by IT. If the database is very small and there are very few users, there will be very little learned from the process. On the other hand, a very large database and a large number of users will very likely put the project in jeopardy. A large data warehouse will always have performance problems primarily in the ETL process. Some projects have failed because of excessive load times, unacceptable update time frames required, or terrible user response time. A large number of users can also put a strain on training and user support, and it puts a major load on the server and the network. Be sure to establish separate databases to be used only for training. This will minimize training's impact on production query response time.

12.5.6 Noncontroversial

If a project is highly controversial, or if there are assassins waiting in the wings to defame the project, its team, and its sponsor, you have an uphill battle. Someone important in the organization may have taken a position in opposition to your project—also known as a negative stakeholder. In these situations, you will spend an inordinate amount of time justifying the project; you may lack the cooperation of a critical person or department. It makes far more sense to choose a project that has minimal impact on anyone's empire, reputation, or position taken. All projects encroach on someone's territory, and you can do only your best to reduce the stress created by the invasion.

12.5.7 Reasonable Time Expectation

Management should not have unreasonable time expectations for the project. If management believes the project can be completed in 3 months, but the project plan schedule looks more like 12 months, it will be difficult to convince management of the competence of the data warehouse team. It's best to choose a project that does not carry any preconceived baggage of unreasonable time expectations.

12.5.8 Not Too Complex

The first project should have a minimum amount of complexity in the sources of the data, in the required cleansing, in the transformations, and in the data integration process. For example, the source data should have been well documented either in the source system or in the metadata repository before the project begins. Do not try to satisfy too many different types of users, each with his own set of needs, all at once. Keep the goal of the data warehouse as singularly focused as possible.

12.5.9   The Project Is Already in the Ditch

You may be asked to manage a project that is already in trouble. The trouble may be that the project is far behind schedule, is riddled with serious personnel or morale problems, or has a sullied reputation. These types of projects are rarely rehabilitated. If at all possible, politely decline, and choose a project that you will be able to define and control.

12.6   COMMUNICATION

Probably the most neglected aspect of a data warehouse project is keeping everyone informed. This includes the extended project team as well as the sponsors, user representatives, and other stakeholders. People's memories are short. Periodic formal and informal communications should be an integral part of every data warehouse project plan, especially large data warehouse projects.

12.6.1   Team Meetings

A method we have employed successfully at the onset of a project is to pick a day of the week and a consistent time, such as Tuesday, 9:00 A.M., after checking with team members and users for their most available and most convenient time slots. We then preschedule a weekly meeting in the project room or a conference room. It is most effective if the sponsor sends a memo to all extended team members and user representatives announcing the weekly meeting and asking them to clear their calendar for every Tuesday, 9:00 A.M., for one hour. Be sure to mention that the duration of each meeting and the frequency of meetings will be adjusted as needed and that the attendees will be notified of these changes ahead of time. Also mention that they will receive an agenda for each meeting at least one day prior to the meeting, and give them a standard process for submitting topics for addition to the agenda. Understand that other side meetings will come out of the main meeting as subtopics arise and require a specific subset of people to participate. The subgroup should then report their findings or actions back to the main team at the next session. This is a common practice when implementing both an enterprise data warehouse and an associated data mart in parallel.

12.6.2 Management Presentations

The project plan should include more formal—possibly monthly—presentations to sponsors and user executives. Each presentation should include the following:

- A quick review of the objectives and deliverables of the project
- A "we are here" on the project timeline
- A discussion of any issues that have been difficult to resolve—frequently one of the attendees can help cut through these tough obstacles
- A frank discussion of any activities that are behind schedule or have problems
- A high-level review of the coming month's activities and priorities, including actions and assignments
- Any contingency plans to make up time and address problems, including additional resources or schedule relief, if needed
- An open question-and-answer period
- A summary and conclusions wrapup

12.6.3 Newsletters

Unfortunately, not everyone with an interest in the project can attend the formal presentations. A semimonthly newsletter containing highlights can be circulated to every stakeholder. An Intranet Web site and e-mail are also common delivery mechanisms.

12.6.4 Honesty

We are compelled to end our communication discussion with a few words on honesty, or the lack of it, as we have observed on some projects. We have seen many disingenuous reports that gloss over problems and paint an incomplete, very pretty, and overly optimistic version of the truth. We were told it was "not safe" to tell the truth. Project managers, when reporting on their progress to their superiors, have often painted a rosy picture to avoid unpleasant interrogations.

It is imperative that communications be honest. You should feel safe to communicate the truth. Dishonest notices will result in a staff becoming cynical; they will start to question the truthfulness of any project communication. Your reputation will be in danger of being tarnished. If a heart-to-heart talk over lunch with your sponsor does not change your perception of safety, you may want to reevaluate your desire to manage this project.

Always be sure not to represent the project as being able to deliver more than possible, sooner than possible, or with fewer resources than possible. Be sure never to leave the users with expectations that cannot be fulfilled.

Data warehouse projects are generally very expensive, involve a lot of people over the long term, and include many activities that are not familiar to sponsors, users, or developers. This being the case, data warehouse projects generally need all of the good will they can get. Honesty and a well-executed communications plan can generate or preserve this good will and help keep harmful rumors and bad press to a minimum.

12.7 SUMMARY

Keep in mind that there are only four dimensions to a project: functions, schedule, resources, and quality. If you expand the functions, the schedule must be extended. If you expand the functions and maintain the schedule, the quality will slip. There may be a fifth dimension, and that is the health of the team. A team that is expected to work twelve hours a day, and seven days a week will suffer morale problems, health problems, and family problems.

Good project planning and management are usually the differentiators between a successful and a disastrous data warehouse implementation. It's naive to believe that since data warehouses are different and more dynamic than operational systems, we don't have to concern ourselves with project plans, schedules, resources, risk, project agreements, and change control because we can fix "it" later. "It" may be a ten-terabyte database that could easily take weeks to unload and reload as part of that fix. The truth is just the opposite. Since data warehouses are more dynamic than operational systems, you need to be more stringent with project planning and control to have a successful project.

A CAUTIONARY TALE

Project Took Forever and Never Did Complete

This was the project that took two years and three project managers to "complete." In fact, it was never completed—only about 30 percent of the original functionality was delivered. The scope was constantly changing. Actually, there was no Project Agreement, and so the project was free-floating to the whims of whatever influence management wanted to exert. There was no commonly accepted vision for a data warehouse charter; there were no accepted goals and objectives and no established criteria for success. The project managers were sent out on a suicide mission with no chance to succeed.

12.8 WORKSHOP

12.8.1   Rate Your Project's Probability for Success

1. Sponsor

    A. Strong and smart sponsor, politically well-positioned, accepting of problems.

    B. Average sponsor, not too smart, not in the strongest position in the organization, and somewhat rattled when problems occur.

    C. Weak or no sponsor.

2. Importance of the project to the organization

    A. This project clearly supports the strategic goals of the organization.

    B. The project has some value.

    C. The project has no discernible value to any department and certainly not to the enterprise.

3. Are the benefits of the project measurable?

    A. We expect tangible benefits from this project, and we have the metrics to do so.

    B. Not all the benefits are tangible, but we feel that we can measure some of them.

    C. All the benefits we are expecting are intangible, and we have no way to measure them.

4. Reasonable size

    A. Our data warehouse is somewhere between 50 and 500 gigabytes.

    B. Our data warehouse is either less than 50 gigabytes or between 500 gigabytes and a terabyte.

    C. Our data warehouse is over a terabyte.

5. Noncontroversial

    A. The project has the support of all the lines of business. There is no one who believes the project should not progress.

    B. There are some concerns voiced about the project.

    C. There are one or two highly placed assassins who do not feel the project has value and who would like to see it fail.

6. Reasonable time expectation

   A. Management is accepting of the schedule as dictated by the project plan.
   B. The schedule is challenging but doable.
   C. Management is under the delusion that the project can be completed in an unreasonably short time and has dictated a very short delivery schedule.

7. Complexity

   A. The project is not too complex. There is a small number of source files, and the transformations are well understood.
   B. There are some complexity and some anticipated challenges with the transformation process.
   C. The source data is dirty, there is a large number of source files, the data is undocumented, and we don't really understand what we have to clean, transform, or integrate.

8. Status of the project

   A. Either the project is just starting out, or you are taking over a well-run and on-target project.
   B. The project has had some problems and some schedule slippage, but you feel the project can be brought back into line.
   C. The project is behind schedule and over budget, and there are severe morale problems. Management's disgust is becoming apparent.

Scoring: A = 3 points; B = 1 point; C = 0 points.

15–24 Your project has a good chance to be successful.

10–14 You will have to work hard and address the looming problems and issues for you to succeed.

0–9   The project is doomed. Run!

12.8.2   Create a Communication Plan

1. Create a list with addresses, phone numbers, and e-mail addresses of your stakeholders.

2. Establish a schedule, and develop vehicles for communicating with stakeholders—for example, newsletters, status reports, and notification of demonstrations.

3. Build a set of scripts for your team for each phase of the implementation—for example:

    - "We have just selected Brio for our query tool. Would you like to see a demo?"

    - "The pilot is up and running. We have five users. We are having some problems with connectivity, but we should have those problems resolved pretty soon."

4. Create an agenda for periodic stakeholder meetings.

REFERENCES

Carstens, Ed. MapXpert™, *A Methodology for Data Warehouse Projects.* Newport Beach, Ca.: Xpert Corporation 1996.

APPENDIX

Please note: Appendix numbers match their corresponding chapters. Not all chapters have associated appendices, which accounts for the gaps in the numbering.

4.A   DATA WAREHOUSE APPLICATIONS BY INDUSTRY

Many of these are not truly applications but ways in which the data warehouse (including data mining) is used by the following industries.

- Consumer Goods
- Distribution
- Finance and Banking
- Finance—General
- Government and Education

  — Federal Government
  — State Government
  — University

- Health Care
- Hospitality
- Insurance
- Manufacturing and Distribution

  — General
  — Appliance
  — Automobile
  — Clothing
  — Computer
  — Food
  — Pharmaceutical
  — Steel

- Marketing
- Multi-Industry (conglomerates)
- Cross-Industry
- Retailers
- Services
- Sports
- Telephone
- Transportation
- Utilities

Consumer Goods

Consumer Goods 1

- Forecasting
- Inventory replenishment
- Effects of marketing campaigns, advertising, coupons, and store displays

Consumer Goods 2

- Market research
- Sales and marketing analysis

Consumer Goods 3

- Sharing information with distribution sites, business partners, and product managers

Packaged Goods

- Identify required product features

Distribution

- Supply chain analyses
- Understand pipeline issues

Finance/Banking

Bank 1

- Evaluating business concentration and risk exposure leading to modified credit policies and loan loss reserves
- Consumer asset data
- Spot market trends
- Government regulation reporting
- Marketing
- Mergers
- Geographic overlap and saturation
- Information for government regulation and approval

Bank 2

- To support management planning, marketing, and financial decision making
- Ability to track and cut costs
- Manage resources more effectively
- Provide feedback to bankers regarding customer relationships and profitability

Bank 3

- Information on spending patterns on a segment of issuing members' card base (cobrand)

    — Target marketing
    — Promotion performance

- Members' use to analyze performance by product, geography, interchange rates; volume by merchant, location, promotions, operational performance
- Cardholder spending by state and merchant classification to develop direct mail promotion with key merchants
- Ability to select better marketing partners, build innovative and successful new product, and build brand loyalty
- Cobranding—determining where cards (i.e., Sierra Club) are being used and developing target marketing plans
- Combine with proprietary data to determine purchase patterns to develop marketing programs

- Agent alerts
    - Early warnings for changing spending patterns
    - Opportunity for special offer based on abnormal cardholder activity
    - When response rate to promotions hits target
- Can test promotional opportunities
- Their member banks or cobrands can add data from the DW to their own proprietary databases

Bank 4

- Mortgage loan portfolio
- New loans in process (pipeline)
- Secondary marketing

Bank 5

- Customer defection prediction

Credit Cards 1

- Identify new customers
- Manage and control collections
- Develop new products
- Determine optimal marketing efforts for new products
- Manage customer service performance
- Identify potential risk of default

Brokerage, Commodity Trading

- Identify target investment services, products, and promotions
- Risk management
- Quality of trader transactions

Financial Services

- Tracking investment managers

Personal Trust

- Tracking managers on performance relative to indexes
- Tracking managers on the types of stocks they purchase

Data Mining

- Product analysis
- Customer segmentation
- Customer profitability
- Target marketing campaigns
- Fraud detection (credit cards)

Finance—General

- Expense evaluation—trends

Customer Information Systems

- Customer profitability
- Fee tolerance

Government and Education

Federal Government 1

- Compliance research

State Government 1

- Accounting
- Payroll
- Procurement
- Human Resources

State Government 2

- Auditing and fraud investigation of social services

University 1

- Provide information to be used in a grant proposal

University 2

- Provide information on ethnicity statistics for a grant proposal
- University finances
- Human resources
- Student demographics
- Financial aid
- Room and course scheduling

University 3

- [Data would be captured on the characteristics/demographics of students to understand retention and success among minorities better.]

Government—Social Services

- Fraud detection
- Effectiveness of services
- Profiles of who is using what services

Government—Taxes

- Auditing tax records for patterns and anomalies

Government—Health Information

- Program policy effectiveness (cost and outcomes)
- Provider care adequacy

Government—Police

- Patterns and trends of criminal activity
- Justice resource deployment
- Consolidation and integration of data from multiple agencies
- Effectiveness of programs and patterns of policing

Health Care

Health Care 1

- Financial
- Clinical
- Strategic and outcomes data
- Helps measure and track and analyze how well the hospital is providing services
- Reports on percentage of patients being fed intravenously
- Compares physicians to peer group on how long their patients occupy a bed and the cost of surgery by the physician
- Finance department gets statistics by patient type, revenue code, and insurance carrier
- What percentage of a hospital's billings are from Medicare, Medicaid, and each major insurance company
- Ability to be more proactive about research

- Can respond to managed care contracts more knowledgeably
- Ability to track costs and cut costs, manage resources more effectively, provide feedback to physicians regarding outcomes and the cost of realizing these outcomes.

Health Care 2

- Outcomes analysis
- Providing feedback to physicians on procedures and tests

Health Care 3

- Using data mining, detecting inappropriate tests
- Reports to doctors of testing trends and practices within their specialty
- Results of study given to doctors so they can refine their decisions for ordering tests

Health Care 4

- Evaluating service to determine if it should be provided or outsourced (for example, dialysis, organ transplantation)
- Nosocomial analysis
- Continuing education and certification of health care professionals

Health Care—General

- Pairing clinical to financial records to determine cost effectiveness of care
- Utilization review
- Contract management
- Financial analysis
- Data mining to identify data patterns that could predict future individual health problems
- Data mining to identify patients who will probably not respond well to specific procedures and operations
- Discover "best practices" to improve quality and reduce costs
- Analysis of care delivery
- Research (prescribing patterns, use of antibiotics)
- Physician performance
- Resource utilization

- Sell data to medical suppliers (pharmaceutical and medical device manufacturers)
- Information for bids on managed care contracts
- Information to support audits and external reports
- Disease state support (cardiovascular, end-stage renal, etc.)
- By illness, cost of treatment
- Patient mix by provider
- Risk management profiles
- Statistics on length of stay
- Utilization management
- Provider profiling

Pharmaceutical

- Market share analysis
- Testing analysis—product safety
- Disease management
- Competitive analysis
- Plans for new drugs
- Outcomes analysis
    — Doctor access

Hospitality

Hotels, car rental, timeshares

- Cross-brand promotions—target customers with promotional offers tailored to their demographics and travel patterns
- Estimate response to promotions and products through demographic analysis
- Cross-market

Insurance

Insurance 1—Established subject areas (claims, marketing)

- Incorporate both internal and external data (information on competitors and insurance industry trends)
- Forecast and monitor changes in the industry, thereby allowing better positioning in the marketplace
- Identify characteristics of profitable business

- Analyze information related to retention of business at renewal (including patterns of customers who do not renew), determine reasons why, and resolve issues that will assist in retaining valued clients

Insurance 2

- Accurate, consolidated view of customer portfolios

Insurance 3

- Analysis of profitability by customer, product, geography, and sales hierarchy
- Analysis of sales offices for profit and loss

Property and Liability Insurance

- Data mining review of claims by actuarial department

Workers' Compensation Insurance

- Recommend health insurance deductibles
- Analysis of claims by the employer, cause of injury, body part injured, and the percentage of employees who have suffered similar injuries
- Fraud analysis using data mining

Health Insurance

- Provider evaluation

  — Physicians' profiles
  — Cost
  — Length of hospital stay
  — Procedure evaluations

- Impact on subscriber services and cost
- Employee costs per employer
- Service usage
- Fraud detection
- Actuarial analysis
- Patterns of insurance usage

Health Insurer 1

- Fraud detection—Searching for claims where the service has not actually been provided; looking for patterns that would suggest further inquiry into the claim
- Abuse detection—Searching for patterns indicating that certain providers are performing unnecessary procedures, prescribing expensive medication where a less expensive drug would be as effective, performing unnecessary tests, and keeping a patient in the hospital longer than necessary

Health Insurer 2

- Analysis of claims
- Providers analysis
- Reporting to groups, government agencies, trade associations
- Analysis of quality of care and costs
- Marketing managed-care contracts
- Actuarial
- Underwriting
- Financial analysis (actual expenses vs. planned expenses)
- Profitability of managed-care arrangements
- Capitated contract performance
- Fraud analysis based on the provider's health care specialty and the geography of the claim

Pharmaceutical Insurance

- Sales and marketing
- Provider profiling
- Government reporting
- Utilization
- Claims
- Actuarial
- Integrating pharmaceutical information with medical claims
- Cost analysis by patient demographics and geographical distribution
- Cost analysis by provider, provider specialties, and treatment protocols
- Analysis by diagnosis/prescription
- Generic/brand name drug comparisons

Insurance Research

- Claims information

Manufacturing and Distribution

Company M&D 1

- Analyze emerging business trends
- Examine product bookings
- Determine product shipments, backlogs, and cancellations
- Better manage product portfolio
- Sharper contract negotiations
- Better manufacture forecasting
- Earlier detection of warning conditions
- Ability to eliminate products from portfolio
- Allows product mangers to identify more quickly product lines that are no longer required or profitable
- Information about margins, product backlogs, or historical sales data to critical decisions
- Visibility to its customers—on an individual customer level, what products the company sells, where it sells the products, and at what price point
- Worldwide view of marketing developments
- Common global language

Company M&D 2

- Departments that would use the DW: Sales, Marketing, and Finance
- Marketing executives are better able to manage their product lines
- Better visibility into product and customer profit margins
- Information on customers, products, costs, invoices

Company M&D 3

- Access to market demand data (orders and shipment data) by both finance and materials groups
- Legal department used DW to substantiate trademark claims in foreign markets

Company M&D 4

- Sales analysis for product movement
- Sales decision support

    — Are the company's products not being stocked?
    — Market share
    — Competitor's market share
    — When our company increases its share of the market, is it coming from competitors, or are we cannibalizing our own line?

Company M&D 5 (Computer Component Manufacturer)

- Provide selected DW access to both customers and suppliers
- Extensive measurements of the quality of the product, and the quality of the components supplied by their vendors
- Extensive feedback from customers on quality of the products

Company M&D 6

- Sales history/sales trends
- Customer profitability

Company M&D 7

- Plant capacity management
- Variances between standard and actual product costs
- Inventory turnover
- Human resources
- Core competency, skills, and distribution of skills

Company M&D 8

- Analysis of production patterns to improve inventory and pricing practices
- Demand forecasting to determine optimal inventory
- Analysis of product pricing to establish discounts and margins

Automobile Manufacturer

- Tracks assembly and warranty quality information by supplier
- Plans to use this information for product planning and design
- Supplier quality information to give the manufacturer a better position for negotiation with supplier

- Plans to provide suppliers with information on their products through the Internet. The goal is to give them enough information so they will improve the quality of their products. (The supplier could be provided with data on the cost of defective parts to the automobile manufacturer.)
- Provides a quantitative measure of quality for both the manufacturer and the supplier

Appliance Manufacturer

- Customer service
- Suppliers' quality
- Negotiation with suppliers

Clothing Manufacturer

- Analyze sales and product trends by location to understand customer buying patterns
- Analyze sell through—what was selling at retailers
- Analyze and understand cancellations—the reasons for the cancellations to identify steps to remedy manufacturing problems

Computer Manufacturer

- Market demand projections

Food Manufacturer

- Measure against competition
- Ability to project how a new product will do
- Sales analysis by region and by store
- Ability to show grocery managers how product is selling at competitive stores, at stores within the same chain, and against competitive products
- Using agents, monitors conditions that require attention including variances in prices and volumes in company's and competitors' products
- Analyzes fixed costs, equipment utilization
- Analyzes manufacturing costs and performance
- Analyzes productivity
- Analyzes inventory levels
- Planning and forecasting

Pharmaceutical Manufacturer

- Analysis of physicians (along with managed-care connections) and their prescribing patterns
- Target marketing
- Identify emerging prescribing trends

Pharmaceutical Manufacturer

- Generate reports for preclinical approval stage
- Measurement of toxicology parameters
- Research analysis
- Testing analysis

Steel Manufacturer

- Control (reduce) inventory
- Understand item-level detail by cost, revenue, profit, inventory, customer, location
- Analysis of production problems
- Reduce accounts receivable
- Understand profitability by customer
- Understand margins and profitability by manufacturing facility leading to decisions about where to manufacture each item
- Evaluate possibilities for renegotiating contracts with customers
- Identify opportunities for new products
- Identify opportunities for new locations
- Compare plans to actual performance
- Improve product and customer mix
- Item level detail by cost, revenue, customer, location

Data Mining

- Quality analysis
- Profitability and problems with suppliers
- Profitability and problems with customers

Manufacturing—General

- Supply chain measurement and analysis
- Customer profitability
- Product profitability analysis

- Strategic partnering—negotiating with suppliers, customers
- Customer purchases to identify who should get new Material Safety Data Sheets
- Contract negotiation
- Profitability by business
- Facility specific analysis for productivity and quality

Marketing

- Comparing product lines
- Media research

Retailers

Retailer 1

- Tracking an item's contribution to margin for its category
- Tracking how promotions and one-time buys are doing, including using trend analysis
- Buyers using it to analyze sales data
- Allowing slow-selling lines and items to be dropped from the stores, while giving their shelf space to more profitable items

Retailer 2

- Better understand customers and their buying patterns

  — Drives promotions—by having access to all data, marketing staff can make more accurate and effective promotion decisions

  — Feeds targeted and mass mailings

  — Enables retailer to develop a relationship proactively with its best customers or individuals that should be buying more than they currently are

- Marketing staff can ask "What if" marketing questions and get fast response
- Meets the objectives of increasing sales, increasing profit, increasing marketing analyst productivity, and decreasing mail expense and promotion cycle time
- Mail promotion effectiveness easily and quickly quantified

Retailer 3

- Sales analysis
- Target marketing
- Cardholder base
- Evaluate technician training
- Evaluate maintenance tool and equipment inventory

Retailer 4

- Merchandising
- Inventory management
- Flow of goods management
- Relationship marketing
- Supplier integration

Retailer 5

- Marketing strategy
- Buying strategy
- Merchandising strategy
- Sales tracking by item

Retailer 6

- Sales analysis
- Forecasting
- Inventory tracking
- Market basket analysis—Do products on sale generate other sales?
- Individual items' contribution to profits
- Vendors (suppliers) have access to how their products are selling

Retailer 7

- Shelf space allocations
- Effectiveness of promotions, advertising
- Product analysis

    — Restocking
    — Profitability
    — Inventory turns
    — Price changes

- Category management (determining the optimal product in each category and the optimal price for that product)
- Merchandising strategy—sales tracking

  — Analysis by SKU by store
  — Trend analysis

- Competitive analysis

Retailer 8

- Understanding complaints, claims, and returns

Retailer 9

- Analyze customer contacts to determine preferences, attract and retain profitable customers
- Understand customer and predict behavior

Retailer 10

- Goal—improve gross margins

  — Better merchandising
  — Better buying decisions

- End-of-season vendor negotiations
- Inventory management
- Price management for markdowns and promotions
- Vendor analysis

Retailer 11

- Analyze information early in new product's sales cycle
- Identify problems in inventory flow
- Determine the right level of inventory for forthcoming promotions

Retailer 12

- Inventory management
- Pricing
- Buying

Retailer 13

- Analyze product mix
- Analyze effectiveness of promotions

Department Store 1

- Merchandising and buying decisions

Department Store 2

- Information to negotiate on end-of-season merchandise
- Inventory and price management for promotions and markdowns
- Vendor analysis

Automobile Convenience Store

- Better product mix by location and demographics
- Understanding price zones, profit, margins
- Understanding the competition
- Understanding customers—images of the customers (who they are)

    — Results of surveys
    — Brand recognition
    — Customer demographics
    — Price sensitivity

- New locations
- Modeling/testing profitability of new items, different product mixes
- Effectiveness of advertising and promotions
- Understanding shrinkage by product, location
- Understanding product tie-ins (coffee and doughnuts, hot dogs and soft drinks, gasoline and oil, smog check and tune-up) and trying ways to exploit those tie-ins
- Shelf allocation
- Use of ATM cards vs. cash (Are credit cards being considered?)
- Effectiveness of alternative business controls
- Statistical sampling when not all data is available
- Suppliers/vendors

    — Price
    — Support/service
    — Delivery

— Profitability
— Quality
— Alternative suppliers
— Supplier negotiations
— Joint promotions
— Demographic data from suppliers

Fast Food

- Analysis of food costs
- Analysis of labor costs
- Analysis of sales data
- Service quality
- Customer information

Data Mining

- Advertising effectiveness
- Market basket analysis
- Profitability

Retailing—General

- Product profitability analysis
- Merchandise planning
- Analyze sales fluctuations
- Selling marketing data to suppliers
- Markdown management
- Identify markets to target for newspaper advertising inserts

Catalog

- Identify low profit products

Services

- Finance
- Revenue
- Purchase orders
- Human resources
- Customer profiles
- Materials management

Sports
- Winning player combinations
- Analyzing strategies, patterns of plays, defenses, players involved
- Player negotiation
- Internet statistical searches by fans

Telephone

Telephony 1

- Fixed asset analysis

Telephony 2

- Facility for sales reps to market to volume customers different long-distance packages based on their latest calling patterns

Telephony 3

- Integrated customer and financial data
- Work request tracking

Telephony 4

- Customer information systems

  — Exploring product "churn"
  — Managing strategic accounts
  — Building customer loyalty
  — Market segmentation
  — Target marketing

- Product development
- Risk and fraud assessment

Telephony 5

Customer analysis

- Which customers are most likely to respond to an offer

  — Which customers are likely to accept new technology
  — Which customers are likely to respond to competitors' offers
  — How much can we expect customers to spend on various products
  — Which prospects (noncustomers) are likely to accept our offers

Telephony 6

- Identifying deadbeat customers and not marketing to these customers
- Identifying potentially profitable market segments

Telephony 7

- Fee tolerance
- Telemarketing
- Predictive modeling
- Merge lifestyle and demographic data to existing customer information

Data Mining

- Analyzing customers most likely to switch to another carrier
- Understanding customers
- Understanding customers' desires and expectations in contrast to what they have ordered and what the company can provide

Transportation

Transportation 1

- Target marketing
- Understanding customer requirements

Railroad 1

- Customer satisfaction
- Train performance
- Derailment prevention
- Crew management

Railroad 2

- Fleet management, locomotive information
- Customer financial analysis

Railroad 3

- Rate analysis
- Profitability analysis
- Fleet maintenance analysis
- Identify tax-exempt purchases
- Understanding competitor's cars on railroad's line

Airline 1

- Customer service program—financial data

Airline 2

- Cargo volume analysis to understand source of revenue

Airline 3

- Fraud analysis—issuing tickets on bad credit cards

Airline 4

- Adjust pricing and flight schedules in response to competitive changes

Multi-Industry (conglomerates)

- Planning and forecasting
- Make comparisons to plans

Cross-Industry

- Legacy system retirement
- Reliability of sales forecasting
- Call centers—evaluating productivity and costs associated with varying responses to customer problems
- Control of property and income tax
- Financial

    — Budgets
    — Uncover problems in financial numbers before they are reported to upper management

Utilities

   — Pricing
   — Supply chain
   — Asset management

- Human Resources—Medical benefits package evaluation
- Finance—Wholesale pricing models
- Accounts Receivable—Maximizing collections for customers who missed a payment

- Accounts Receivable—Analyzing processes to maximize collections for overdue accounts
- Fixed Assets
- Customer Information Systems

  — Marketing
  — Customer Satisfaction
  — Financial
  — Conservation

Marketing Queries

- Determining customer usage
- Understanding demographics and usage by demographics
- Tracking marketing programs
- Modeling a new program
- Cost justifying a new program
- Commercial customers—price sensitivity
- Data mining—looking for patterns that may be marketing opportunities
- Data mining—looking for patterns that predict delinquencies

Customer Satisfaction Queries

- Tracking customer comments and complaints

  — By demographics
  — By psychographics

- Tracking customer surveys
- Reporting to the Utility Commission and the press
- Data mining

Financial Queries

- Customer profitability
- Evaluating relationship pricing
- Assessing alternative delivery channels
- Assessing outsourcing possibilities
- Tracking profits across divisions

Conservation Queries
- Monitoring conservation programs by customer
- Identifying pattern of customer (demographics) that could be candidate for conservation program
- Identifying customers who have (or have not) signed up for special programs
- Peak-period air conditioner disabled
- Old refrigerator surrender
- Fluorescent bulbs

5.A   USER RESPONSIBILITY PROBLEM

Problem: My user sponsor doesn't attend my meetings, doesn't answer my voice mail, and doesn't respond to my e-mail. He will not validate the materials given to him. What do I do?

Answer: Document in your status report (that goes to the sponsor, among places) the issue of delay due to the lack of response to a specific question. Ask the sponsor's secretary for a 45-minute meeting. The topic of the meeting (because the secretary needs to specify the reason for the meeting) is issues and problems with the project. At the meeting be direct. Make it clear to the sponsor that you will never waste his time but that his lack of responsiveness will mean that certain project activities (tell him which ones) cannot and will not even begin. This means that the project will be delayed by at least the time it will take for this response. His suggestion that an underling (with little knowledge and practically no authority) should be acceptable to take his place can be addressed with questions about the appointee's authority to make decisions. If the underling lacks the authority to make decisions or if the decisions are likely to be overridden, explain again what it will do to the schedule and expenditures.

5.B   USER VALIDATION TEMPLATE

The users will be testing the system, and, based on their experiences, the project will be considered either a success or a failure. Users need a Validation Template against which to compare and judge. Without a framework, the testing and validation have no structure. A Validation Template is not the same as a test case or expected test result. Test cases and expected test results pertain to specific test runs, whereas the Validation Template is an overall assessment of the usefulness and validity of the system. The following template has sample responses.

Name _____

Department _____

Date _____

For example:

Criteria	Evaluation
Interface	Understandable, logical icons
Data quality	I don't believe the segmentation of the customers. Something's wrong.
Performance	Averaging 20 seconds. One query "Customer02" took over 30 minutes. I thought performance was going to be better.
Availability	It was working while I was testing. No problems.
Help desk	I had only one problem, and the Help Desk was able to resolve the problem over the phone.
Ease of use	OK
User Liaison Support	I didn't have to contact them.
Web delivery	No problem. The interface was clear and understandable.
Value of canned queries and reports	I ran two or three canned queries. They ran OK, and the results looked accurate.
Training	The training seemed pretty generic. It should have had more information about our data.
Repository	I looked at the repository. The definitions seemed to be correct, and it is easy to navigate.

5.C WORDS TO USE/WORDS NOT TO USE

This list of words should not be considered politically correct versions but rather words and phrases that either will make the user uncomfortable or will resonate and draw the user into your way of thinking. Assume the user has asked for something that cannot reasonably be done. You will be discussing and negotiating with the user. Your goal is not to show you are smarter, more knowledgeable, or just plain correct, or to show the user that he is wrong. The goal is to come to an understanding, a solution, and a plan where both of you feel good about the outcome.

Wrong	Right
No! Forget it!	Let me get back to you with what your request will mean in terms of time, additional money, and additional resources we will need from your department.
Are you crazy? You can't do that!	We can do that, but if we do, it will delay the project by at least two months.
What a stupid idea!	Hmm. Let's explore that option.
(The vendor has just convinced the user to buy something that is absolutely wrong.) You bought what? Boy, that was dumb!	Vendors sometimes exaggerate their products' capabilities. We want to be sure that their product will work well in our environment and that we can properly support it.

5.D   SAMPLE LETTER TO INTERVIEWEES

To: Interviewee

From: Sponsor

As you know, we will be starting a data warehouse project for our Marketing Department. We need to know your requirements for a Marketing Data Mart. We want your input on what information you and your department could use to make your folks more productive, to make better decisions, and to market to our customers more effectively. Please keep in mind that requirements will have to be prioritized and that some requirements may never be satisfied. Therefore please indicate your most important information needs and, if possible, prioritize them.

Harold Schmedlap will be contacting you to arrange an appointment for a one-hour interview. You will be the only one scheduled during this time. Feel free to bring anyone on your staff who you feel could help us understand your marketing requirements.

Just a final note—don't limit your requirements to the information you are getting today.

If you have any questions, please contact Harold at ext. 3097.

Sincerely,

5.E INTERVIEW RESULTS TEMPLATE

Date _____

Department _____

Interviewee(s) _____

_____

Requirements

  1.

  2.

  3.

Findings

  1.

  2.

  3.

Issues

 1.

 2.

Opportunities/Other

 1.

 2.

5.F   **USER SATISFACTION SURVEY**

Note: To increase the percentage of questionnaires returned, bribes and guilt can be useful. Movie passes, tickets to sports events, or entry in a drawing will increase the number of responses. You can either clip the movie passes to the questionnaire (guilt approach) or send the passes when the question-naires are returned. Some users will want to remain anonymous, or they may not be so candid if their identity is known, and so clipping the bribe to the questionnaire is more appropriate.

The data warehouse team has as one of its primary objectives the continual improvement of the data warehouse. We need your help. Would you give us your candid assessment of the data warehouse and your use of it.

I am in the _____ Department.

I consider myself   A power user _____

Quite capable with the query tool and the data _____

A casual user _____

Technologically challenged _____

I am accessing the _____ data warehouse/data mart

I use   Brio _____

Business Objects _____

SQL _____

Impromptu _____

SPSS _____

SAS _____
Excel _____
Essbase _____
Other _____

I write _____ of my own queries/reports per month (indicate the number).

I launch _____ parameterized queries/canned reports per month (indicate the number).

I run _____ regularly scheduled reports per month (indicate the number).

On the average, my response time is

(give the number of) _____ seconds
_____ minutes
_____ hours
_____ days

My impression of the query/report tool is Excellent _____
Very good _____
Good _____
Poor _____
Very poor _____
Impossible to use _____

What don't you like about the tool?

_____
_____
_____

What additional functions would you like to have?

_____
_____
_____

My impression of the Web delivery is   Excellent _____
                                        Very good _____
                                        Good _____
                                        Poor _____
                                        Very poor _____
                                        Impossible to use _____

What don't you like about the Web delivery?

_____

_____

_____

During the last month, I experienced _____ minutes
of downtime when I could not access the system.

I rate my IT support as Excellent _____
                         Good _____
                         Fair _____
                         Poor _____
                         I didn't know I had support _____

What could be done to improve support?

_____

_____

_____

I find the quality of the data in the data warehouse to be   Excellent _____
                                                              Good _____
                                                              Fair _____
                                                              Poor _____
                                                              Terrible _____

If the quality of the data is anything but "Excellent" or "Good," please
provide specifics.

_____

_____

_____

What three things should we do to improve the data warehouse?

1. _____

2. _____

3. _____

Please fill in your name and phone number if you would like us to respond directly to your comments.

Name _____

Phone _____

Thank you for your time. Respondents to this questionnaire will have their names automatically entered in a drawing for an all-expense-paid weekend for two in Duluth.

5.G USER SCORECARD

User name _____

Department _____

1. Importance of the data warehouse to the user

   a. Critical

   b. Important

   c. Nice to have

2. Reasonableness of the user

   a. Reasonable in what is expected (schedule, function, availability, performance)

   b. Somewhat reasonable

   c. Unreasonable

3. Understanding of the data warehouse

   a. Good understanding of the data warehouse

   b. Some understanding

   c. Not a clue

4. Availability of business user to participate in the project

   a. Will be available and will participate

   b. Will be available and will participate whenever possible

   c. Refuse to participate and claim there is no time

5. Sophistication of PC-literate users

   a. Active users comfortable with PC,

   b. Somewhat comfortable

   c. Believes the PC is evil and is part of Bill's plot to control the galaxy

6. Time allowed for users to be trained

   a. Adequate time set aside for user training—has time on the job to become familiar with the product

   b. Some time and time on the job have been allocated for user training.

   c. Users expected to be able to use the tool without training

`6.A`   BENEFITS ANALYSIS FOR HEALTH CARE

Copyright Xpert Corporation, 1997

The data warehouse has a remarkable potential for benefits in the health care industry. The benefits will be both tangible and intangible. For the tangible benefits, an organization should be able to estimate specific cost savings and increases in revenue. This template indicates potential benefits and suggests the formulas for calculating those benefits.

This analysis of benefits is aimed at organizations that provide health care and organizations that insure health care.

Tangible Benefits

Increase Membership

The organization will be better able to market to employer groups by having more information on the following:

- Coverage
- Costs
- Outcomes
- Member utilization

The organization will be better able to recruit and retain members by knowing more about the following:

- Membership
- Satisfaction
- Outcomes

The organization will be better able to enroll more groups and more members and to retain groups and members by being able to provide more and better information to employer groups.

The organization will be able to identify marketing opportunities by analyzing demographics and integrating this analysis with existing members.

The organization will be better able to enroll and retain more groups and more members by giving employer groups access to information about their members through the Internet.

Benefit = Profit/member × Additional members

Increase Revenue

The organization will be better able to negotiate with employer groups by having more information on the following:

- Coverage
- Costs for each category of care
- Outcomes

The organization will be better able to bid on managed care contracts by having more information on the following:

- Coverage
- Costs for each category of care
- Outcomes

The organization will be better able to increase revenue income from providers by knowing more about the following:

- Providers
- Revenue generated
- Referrals
- Fees paid to providers
- Outcomes

The organization will be better able to recruit and retain providers, groups, and members by being able to measure the following:

- Results
- Outcomes
- Provider productivity

The organization will be better able to collect a higher percentage of claims by having better information on claims.

Marketing will be able to present more acceptable packages and will be able to recruit and retain groups and members by being able to target the right set of alternatives.

Benefit = Increased Revenue $\times$ (Number of Employer Groups $\times$ Average Number of Employees/Group)

Benefit = Increased Revenue/Provider $\times$ Number of Providers

Benefit = Revenue/Provider $\times$ Additional Number of Providers

Benefit = Revenue/Member $\times$ Additional Number of Members

Benefit = Increased Revenue/Claim $\times$ Number of Claims

Cost Control

The organization will be better able to understand and control costs by knowing costs per member per month and knowing these costs by the following:

- Demographics
- Preexisting conditions
- Diagnosis

The organization will be better able to negotiate with providers and control costs by knowing more about the following:

- Providers
- Revenue generated
- Hospital referrals
- Provider compensation
- Outcomes.

The organization will be better able to control inventory, charge for supplies, and negotiate with suppliers by knowing more about the following:

- Supplies
- Suppliers
- Costs
- Inventory

By knowing more about costs, the organization can better determine which procedures, practices, and services to outsource (lab, pharmacy, surgical procedures, dialysis, help desk, administrative functions, etc.).

By providing better information to physicians and encouraging them to follow protocols, the total cost of treatment can be reduced.

By having better HR information, the organization will be better able to negotiate with unions and employees for the following:

- Wages
- Working conditions
- Hours
- Benefits

Incorrect payments—searching for patterns of claims, incorrectly paid, incorrectly denied, or incorrectly administered that can suggest changes in claims processing procedures.

Abuse detection—searching for patterns indicating that certain providers are performing unnecessary procedures, prescribing expensive medication where a less-expensive drug would be effective, performing unnecessary tests, and keeping a patient in the hospital longer than necessary.

Fraud detection—searching for claims where service has not actually been provided; looking for patterns that would suggest further inquiry into the claim.

Benefit (Material Management) = Cost Savings for Supplies

Benefit (Outsourcing) = Cost Savings/Procedure × Number of Procedures Outsourced

Benefit (Protocols) = Average Cost Savings by Following Protocols × Number of Protocols Followed

Benefit = Average HR Cost Savings × Number of Employees

Benefit = Administrative Costs Resulting from Errors in Payments

Benefit (Abuse) = Average Cost of Procedures × Number of Unnecessary Procedures

Benefit (Fraud) = Average Cost of Claim × Number of Fraudulent Claims

Increase Provider Base

The organization will be better able to recruit and retain providers by knowing more about the following:

- Providers (specialty, boards, credentials)
- Revenue generated
- Referrals
- Fees paid to providers
- Outcomes

By being able to measure results, the organization will be better able to recruit and retain providers.

By being more proactive in research, the organization will be able to improve its reputation and attract and retain more and better providers.

Benefit = Revenue/Provider × Additional Number of Providers

Facilities Utilization

By knowing more about utilization of facilities (bed occupancy, type of bed, etc.), the organization will be better able to schedule and more fully utilize existing facilities.

Benefit = Additional Revenue from Greater Facilities Utilization

Outcomes Analysis

By knowing more about outcomes, the organization will be better able to do the following:

1. Develop protocols
2. Ensure that physicians follow protocols
3. Understand physician performance
4. Analyze protocol variance
5. Improve reputation of organization
6. Recruit and retain providers
7. Generate more physician hospital referrals
8. Deliver more cost-effective treatment
9. Have fewer readmissions
10. Have less-expensive drug therapy
11. Have less-expensive and fewer lab orders
12. Deliver a higher quality of care to members

By running "What if" scenarios, the organization will be able to analyze the effectiveness of various protocols.

Benefit = Revenue/Provider × Additional Number of Providers

Benefit = Profit/Hospital Admission × Number of Additional Hospital Referrals

Benefit = Cost Savings/Episode × Number of Episodes

Benefit = Cost Savings/Readmission × Number of Readmissions

Benefit = Revenue/Provider × Additional Number of Providers

Benefit = Average Laboratory Costs × Number of Inappropriate Lab Orders

Benefit = Medication Cost Savings × Number of Less-expensive Prescriptions

Analyst and Programmer Productivity

Analysts today spend between 50 percent and 90 percent of their time gathering data; the remaining time is spent actually performing the analysis. With the data warehouse, organizations have found the numbers to be reversed, giving the analysts far more time on productive work.

It has been estimated that 50 percent of requests to IT are for new reports and changes to existing reports. A number of organizations that primarily buy application packages are using the data warehouse to generate needed reports not produced by the application packages.

By giving users the ability to create their own reports, the productivity of both IT and analysts should increase.

By having a data warehouse capability, the production of both internal reports and external reports for government agencies will require less development time.

Benefit = Cost Reduction/Report × Number of Reports/Year

Benefit = Reduction of Number of Hours/Report × Fully Burdened Rate of IT or User-Analyst Hour

Benefit = Improvement in Programmer Productivity × Number of Programmers × Fully Burdened Rate

Risk

By providing better information, the organization can be more proactive identifying potential for medical malpractice and correcting problems before they occur. In addition, better information and more extensive development and use of protocols should result in less exposure to lawsuits or mandatory arbitration as protocols are accepted and followed.

Benefit (Fewer Lawsuits) = Cost of Defending the Lawsuit × Reduced Number of Lawsuits

Benefit (Lawsuits Successfully Defended) = Number of Lawsuits × Average Judgment

Benefit (Smaller Judgment Awards) = Reduction in Awards × Number of Awards

Intangible Benefits

Not all benefits can be quantified. Even without hard dollar justification, the intangible benefits should be identified whenever possible.

- One accepted source of data
- Consistent reports and answers to queries
- Easier access to data
- Consistent, accepted data definitions stored in a repository or dictionary available to everyone in the organization
- Better decisions, both operational and strategic
- Better quality of information, cleaner and better understood data, better reporting procedures
- More timely information so that decisions are more timely; reducing reluctance to make decisions
- Higher personnel morale as employees are more comfortable with their decisions, take greater pride in their work, and feel good because the organization provides good tools and capabilities. Workers should do a better job, and the retention rate should be higher.
- Better information about the members should result in being more responsive to the members, providing better service, the right service from the member's perspective, and a better community image.
- By understanding billings for Medicare, Medicaid, and insurance companies, the organization will be better able to understand profitability in a variety of categories (home health care, urgent care, hospitals), diseases (diabetes, epilepsy, cardiovascular disease), and so on.
- By understanding costs for Medicare, Medicaid, and insurance company patients, the organization will be better able to understand profitability in a variety of categories, diseases, and so on.
- By running "What if" scenarios, the organization will be able to analyze various business strategies.

The benefits in this section can be approximated by asking the users what they are willing to pay for the following:

1. Having their reports available n days earlier than they are getting them today

2. Having cleaner data than they are getting today (this would have to be done with specific examples of higher-quality data)

3. Information that will now allow them to make decisions based on fact

4. Being able to analyze alternatives without actually having to implement them

Another approach is to evaluate the funding of projects. As an example, if users are willing to fund a project that will give them more timely information (and nothing else), the amount of the funding may be considered as the benefit the user places on the improved timeliness.

Postproject review

It would be unusual if the resulting benefits were as predicted. It's important to review the benefits to determine the accuracy of the predictions. Armed with the results of the review, more accurate predictions can be made in each category, and the prediction process can be improved with more accurate benefits projected for future projects. More accurate benefits analysis can aid in prioritizing data warehouse projects.

6.B BENEFITS ANALYSIS FOR FINANCE

Copyright Xpert Corporation, 1997

The data warehouse has a remarkable potential for benefits in the finance industry. The benefits will be both tangible and intangible. For the tangible benefits, an organization should be able to estimate specific cost savings and increases in revenue. This template indicates potential benefits and suggests the formulas for calculating those benefits.

This analysis of benefits is aimed at banks, thrifts, and other financial institutions.

Tangible Benefits

Increase the Number of Customers

The organization will be better able to recruit and retain customers by knowing more about the following:

- Relationships
- Accounts
- Activity
- Channel utilization
- Customer demographics

The organization will be able to identify marketing opportunities for products and services by analyzing demographics and integrating this analysis with existing and potential customers.

The organization will be better able to enroll and retain more customers by giving customers access to information about their accounts and the products and services available to them.

$$Benefit = Profit/Customer \times Additional\ Customers$$

Increase Revenue

The organization will be better able to increase revenue by cross-selling to existing customers by knowing more about the following:

- Relationships
- Accounts
- Activity
- Channel utilization
- Customer demographics
- Revenue generated
- Fees

The organization will be better able to market to new customers by being able to measure the following:

- Revenue
- Profit
- Channels available

- Customer demographics

The organization will be better able to collect on loans by having more information about the customers.

The organization will be better able to generate loans by having more information about their customers.

Benefit = Revenue/Customer × Additional Number of Customers

Benefit (for Each Product and Service) = Increased Revenue/Product/Service × Number of New/Retained Products/Services

Cost Control

The organization will be better able to understand and control costs by being familiar with the costs to service accounts and customers and by knowing the following:

- Type of account
- Channel
- Customer activity

The organization will be better able to control inventory and negotiate with suppliers and vendors by knowing more about the following:

- Suppliers and vendors
- Services (airline, hotel, travel agencies, copying and printing, consulting, etc.)
- Outsourcing services
- Capital expenditures
- Costs

By knowing more about costs, the organization can better determine which activities to outsource (lock box, data processing, help desk, cafeteria, administrative functions, etc.). *Note: The impact on the quality of service and the reduction in the organization's core competencies must be examined along with any cost savings.*

By having better HR information, the organization will be better able to recruit and retain employees.

Fraud detection—searching for fraud, both internally and externally

Benefit = Cost Savings

Benefit = Better Contracts with Suppliers and Vendors

Benefit (Outsourcing) = Cost Savings

*Benefit = Average HR Cost Savings to Recruit and Train New Employees ×
Number of Employees*

*Benefit (Channels) = Savings/Transaction × Number of Transactions on
Less-expensive Channels*

Facilities Utilization

By knowing more about utilization of facilities (office space, fixed assets,
etc.), the organization will be better able to schedule and more fully utilize existing facilities.

Benefit = Additional Revenue from Greater Facilities Utilization

Analyst and Programmer Productivity

Analysts today spend between 50 percent and 90 percent of their time
gathering data; the remaining time is spent actually performing the analysis. With the data warehouse, organizations have found the numbers to
be reversed, giving the analysts far more time on productive work.

It has been estimated that 50 percent of requests to IT are for new
reports and changes to existing reports. A number of organizations that
primarily buy application packages are using the data warehouse to generate needed reports not produced by the application packages.

By giving users the ability to create their own reports, the productivity of both IT and analysts should increase.

By having a data warehouse capability, the production of both internal reports and external reports for government agencies and community
requests will require less development time.

Benefit = Cost Reduction/Report × Number of Reports/Year

*Benefit = Reduction of Number of Hours/Report × Fully Burdened Rate of
IT or User Analyst Hour*

*Benefit = Improvement in Programmer Productivity × Number of Pro-
grammers × Fully Burdened Rate*

Intangible Benefits

Not all benefits can be quantified. Even without hard dollar justification, the intangible benefits should be identified whenever possible.

- One accepted source of data
- Consistent reports and answers to queries
- Easier access to data
- Consistent, accepted data definitions stored in a repository or dictionary available to everyone in the organization
- Better decisions, both operational and strategic
- Better quality of information, cleaner and better understood data, better reporting procedures
- More timely information so that decisions are more timely; reducing reluctance to make decisions
- Higher personnel morale as employees are more comfortable with their decisions, take greater pride in their work, and feel good because the organization provides good tools and capabilities. Workers should do a better job, and the retention rate should be higher.
- Better information about customers should result in being more responsive to customers, providing better service, the right service from the customer's perspective, and a better community image.
- By running "What if" scenarios, the organization will be able to analyze various business strategies.

The benefits in this section can be approximated by asking the users what they are willing to pay for the following:

- Having their reports available *n* days earlier than they are getting them today
- Having cleaner data than they are getting today (this would have to be done with specific examples of higher-quality data)
- Information that will now allow them to make decisions based on fact
- Being able to analyze alternatives without actually having to implement them first

Another approach is to evaluate the funding of projects. As an example, if users are willing to fund a project that will give them more timely information (and nothing else), the amount of the funding may be considered as the benefit the user places on improved timeliness.

Postproject Review

It would be unusual if the resulting benefits were as predicted. It's important to review the benefits to determine the accuracy of the predictions. Armed with the results of the review, more accurate predictions can be made in each category, and the prediction process can be improved with more accurate benefits projected for future projects. More accurate benefits analysis can aid in prioritizing data warehouse projects.

7.A DESIRED TYPES OF REFERENCES

If you do not tell the vendors the types of references you want, they are likely to give you some that are of no value. Tell them what you want and what you do not want. Some vendors want to participate in the call. The information from the references will be much less candid with the vendor involved. Decline this arrangement. The following are some suggestions for the types of references you want to call.

1. The reference site does not have to be local (you will be using the phone, not visiting), and it does not have to be in your industry.

2. The reference should have been actively and productively using the product under consideration for at least six months. You don't want anyone in the throes of implementation, and you don't want anyone who is just playing with the product.

3. If you are interested in a specific release, you want to talk with a reference that is using that release.

4. You want the reference to be on a similar platform (operating system and RDBMS) as you intend to use. Don't accept an NT reference if you plan to be on Unix.

5. You want a reference that has at least as many users as you intend to have and has a database of at least the size you plan. *Note:* This is to verify performance, not function or ease of use, so you will want at least one of this type.

6. You don't want a reference that has a financial or marketing association with your organization.

7. If possible, ask for references that have the same products as you have already chosen. For example, if you are a DB2 shop and are evaluating

query tools, you would ask the query tool vendors for references that are also on DB2.

7.B   QUESTIONS FOR THE REFERENCES

Before you talk with the references, you want to know what questions you will ask, you want your questions to be consistent, you want to be sure all the important questions are asked, and you don't want to waste the references' time. The questions will vary based on the tool category. Don't ask questions if you already know the answers. Ask only questions that will make a difference in your decision. The following are a set of sample questions you can use to build your own set of questions.

1. What hardware, operating system, RDBMS, network topology, and so on are used?

2. If you are using multiples of the above, do you experience any differences in performance or availability?

3. What are your hours of scheduled availability?

4. Do you have service level agreements (SLAs) for performance? For availability?

5. How long does it take to perform specific operations? (In an RDBMS or ETL comparison you will want to know load/update/refresh times.) What is the data rate?

6. What is the size of your entire data warehouse? What is the largest table? (You may give the size in gigabytes or number of rows. If one answer is given, ask for the other as well.)

7. What is your average response time?

8. How do you measure response time (tools, utilities)?

9. How many queries are run each day, week, month?

10. What other tools did you consider in this category?

11. What were your criteria for selection?

12. What was your opinion of the other tools?

13. As a rule, do you continue to evaluate other tools?

14. What other similar tools are installed and being used?

15. How long have you had the tool in production?

16. If you use both a Web implementation and a standard implementation, what differences have you seen, especially involving function?

17. What was the composition of the team that installed the tool?

18. What is the composition of the team that supports the tool?

19. What training was given to the users?

20. Who provided the training?

21. What is your assessment of the quality of the training?

22. How do you evaluate the effectiveness of the training?

23. How many users were trained on the tool?

24. How many active users do you have?

25. If you have significantly more trained than active users, what might be the reasons for some of the trained users not actively using the tool?

26. How would you characterize your users (power, casual, report reader, executive, etc.)?

27. How does each type of user like the tool?

28. Have you measured user satisfaction?

29. How satisfied are the users? Any specifics?

30. What do they like about the tool? What do they dislike?

31. Do you have canned queries and reports available to the users? Are these canned queries and reports being actively used?

32. What kinds of problems did you have with implementing the tool? How were those problems resolved?

33. What kinds of problems do you have with ongoing maintenance?

34. What comments do you have on vendor support (Help Desk, etc.)?

35. Did you require consulting support for the product? Was the support from the vendor? What was the quality of their consulting staff?

36. What general comments do you have on the vendor?

37. On your Help Desk, what types of questions are asked?

Trip Report

If you do decide to visit a reference site, you will want to write a trip report. The following are suggestions for the trip report outline:

1. Reason for the trip

2. Who went on the trip?

3. What site was visited?

4. Why was this site chosen?

5. Whom did you talk with at the site?

6. General observations

7. How effectively is the site using the tool?

8. Conclusions about the tool

9. Recommendations

7.C   VENDOR RULES OF ENGAGEMENT

Most vendors are anxious to sell you their products. They have been doing it for some time and have methods that can waste your time, lead to confusion and hard feelings within your organization, and may even lead to the wrong decision. The following is a form letter and a suggested set of rules by which the vendors should be asked to play.

Dear Vendor:

Your product _____ has been selected for evaluation by our organization. To expedite the evaluation and selection process, we have a set of rules we want you to follow. Those vendors who don't abide by these rules will not make the "short list" and will be dropped from consideration. We suggest that all your representatives have a copy of these rules and review them before meeting with us.

1. Your only contact(s) in our organization is/are _____.
   This includes contacts for demos, questions, phone calls, e-mails, and written and printed materials. Your contact will distribute your materials to the other stakeholders as appropriate. This means you are not to contact users or anyone else in our organization without our prior written approval.

2. We are interested in hearing about your company and your product. We do not want to hear your opinion of the competition. Your view of your competitors will only confuse us. We will not disclose your competition.

3. We want to hear about product features that are generally available. In your presentations, do not mix what is available today with what will be available in the future. While information about future releases may be of interest, meetings on future releases should be scheduled separately.

4. You may never misrepresent anything to anyone in our organization—IT or business users—either by omission or commission. Don't let anyone walk away from a meeting with the wrong impression of your product.

5. When asked if your product can perform a certain function, understand that we have no interest in knowing if your product can theoretically do something. We want you to show us a proven track record. This means we can be shown that the function is actually being performed by one of your customers and that you provide us with client references.

6. We will be sending you the notes from our meetings. If anything is incorrect, confusing, or misstated, please inform the contact immediately. If we don't hear from you, we will assume all statements are accurate.

7. We will inform you of our schedule for evaluation and selection, and we will try to hold to these dates. While we appreciate your need for meeting certain dates for recording sales, it will not impact our own selection schedule.

We will not tell you who in our organization will be involved in the decision. You may assume it will be those individuals who attend your presentations and demonstrations.

7.D PLAN TO SELECT PRODUCTS

1. Convene the selection committee (keep it small).

2. Document your data warehouse architecture.

3. Prioritize the tool categories, and select which one(s) to evaluate.

4. Establish criteria for selection, and solicit suggestions from stakeholders.

5. Research which vendors and products you want to consider, and create your long list.

6. Create a request for information (RFI), request for proposal (RFP), or an information package for the vendors to let them know what you are looking for.

7. Contact the vendors and give them your architecture, timeframe, the RFI, RFP, or information package and your rules of engagement.

8. Compile a list of references from the vendors and from other sources.

9. Research the products.

10. Call the references, document their comments, and distribute the notes to the selection committee.

11. Reduce the number of products to two or three for the short list.

12. If appropriate, ask the vendors to demonstrate their products and present their solution to your project and to your organization.

13. Depending on the type of product, your exposure, and the price of the tool, you may want to have the vendor perform a proof-of-concept to prove the effectiveness of the product with your data in your environment.

14. Solicit comments from the stakeholders, and, using your criteria for selection, determine your first and second choices.

15. Negotiate price and terms with the vendors, and make your final selection.

16. Sign the contract, and celebrate a milestone.

7.E DATA WAREHOUSE PRODUCT CATEGORIES

- *Data Mining.* Discovery process of unknown or unsuspected patterns of data, not hypothesis testing
- *Data Modeling.* Tools that support logical and physical modeling and the ability to store data requirements and business rules

- *Data Quality.* Tools that analyze the source data for noncompliant values and will sometimes clean the data
- *Extract/Transform/Load.* Tools that extract selected data from source systems, transform portions of the data, aggregate data from multiple source files, create derived data, calculate summarized data, and load the data to the data warehouse
- *Front-end Query.* Tools that provide access to the data warehouse without the need to write SQL. These tools usually provide a Web interface.
- *Multidimensional/Online Analytical Processing (MOLAP).* Tools that allow users to analyze the data along multiple dimensions such as time, region, product, and salesperson. These products have their own proprietary databases.
- *Relational Database Management System (RDBMS).* The physical store, the databases where the data warehouse resides
- *Relational Multidimensional (ROLAP).* Multidimensional query tools that access relational databases rather than having their own proprietary databases
- *Repository, Dictionary, Directory.* Stores metadata, including information about the models, the data in the data warehouse, information about the source files, and the transformation rules used in the ETL process
- *Data Warehouse Industry Models.* Models that are specific to industries such as property and casualty, banking, health care, and telephony
- *Outsourcer.* A company that will develop and run a data warehouse without much assistance from the client organization
- *Methodology.* Tools that provide a road map with tasks, deliverables, and suggested roles to perform the tasks along with project plan generation
- *Performance Measurement.* Provides metrics to determine machine and database resources used, response time, and information on who is running queries and reports
- *External Data.* Data that can be purchased from vendors who capture retail and business data that is typically not captured in an organization's operational systems

8.A   ORGANIZATIONAL STRUCTURES

We show three organization structures; they all work. We have seen these and variations of each in numerous organizations. The structures all have certain roles: the data warehouse architect, security, and the Help Desk, with dotted line responsibility to the project manager. It is rare that the project manager has these roles reporting directly to him. There are pros and cons to each of the three structures.

Organizational Structure A, as seen in Figure 8.A.1, has the database administrator and the data administrator reporting directly to the project manager. This arrangement gives the project manager much more control over the time and activities of these people and helps to ensure they will be 100 percent dedicated to the project in hours, interest, and incentive. The project manager does not have to go begging for their time, and there is less risk that they will be pulled off to work on something else. There may be overriding reasons that you cannot obtain them. The Database Administration and data administration managers may be very possessive, powerful, and unwilling to relinquish control.

Organizational Structure B, as shown in Figure 8.A.2, has the database administrator and data administrator reporting to their respective managers with dotted lines reporting to the data warehouse project manager. The benefit of this structure is the possible pool of expertise in the larger group of DBAs and DAs. When there is a problem, the DA or DBA has more direct resources available for consultation. See Organizational Structure A for the downside.

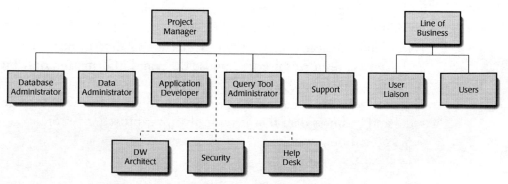

Figure 8.A.1: Organizational Structure A

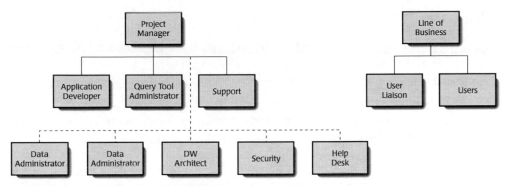

Figure 8.A.2: Organizational Structure B

Organizational Structure C, as in Figure 8.A.3, is the ideal structure. By having the line-of-business project manager joined at the hip to the IT project manager, there is little chance that the users will not get what they want. There will be few or no unrealistic expectations from the users, as they will always be current and clear on what they will be getting and when. This structure helps assure the availability of the right users for their respective tasks. By having the users involved all the way through, the communication is far superior, issues can be resolved much more quickly, and tolerance for problems is enhanced.

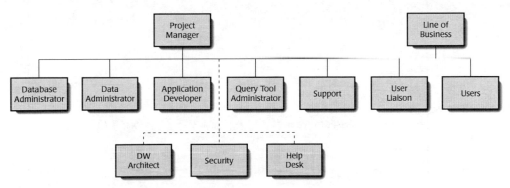

Figure 8.A.3: Organizational Structure C

8.B   **SALARY SURVEY**

The following figures represent the average base salaries for data warehouse project managers in the labor markets indicated. This data is
excerpted from the First Quarter 2000 "*Market-Priced IT Salary Survey
Benchmarks Report,*" published by Foote Partners LLC, collected January
2000 – March 2000 from more than 8400 IT workers in over 680 companies. For in-depth information on this benchmark, contact Foote
Research Group at *www.footepartners.com.*

<u>City</u>	<u>Average Salary</u> *
Atlanta	$115,275
Austin/San Antonio	$108,117
Baltimore	$105,213
Boston	$103,871
Charlotte	$96,952
Chicago	$113,106
Cincinnati	$93,385
Cleveland/Akron	$97,350
Columbus	$96,651
Dallas	$106,075
Denver	$93,498
Detroit	$102,734
Green Bay, WI	$84,758
Hartford	$95,917
Houston	$98,209
Indianapolis/Fort Wayne	$84,773
Kansas City	$89,346
Long Island, NY	$101,775
Los Angeles	$116,771

continued

City	Average Salary *
Louisville	$92,558
Lower Fairfield County, CT/ Westchester County, NY	$104,419
Miami	$100,616
Milwaukee	$92,924
Minneapolis	$99,481
New Jersey/Northern, Central	$111,708
New York City	$129,325
Omaha, NE/Des Moines, IA	$79,963
Orange County, Southern CA	$119,289
Orlando/Tampa	$95,505
Philadelphia	$95,691
Phoenix	$88,415
Pittsburgh	$90,069
Portland	$111,036
Raleigh/Durham/Greensboro	$94,958
Salt Lake City	$100,964
San Diego	$119,588
San Francisco	$121,159
Seattle	$114,241
St. Louis	$96,674
Upper Fairfield County/New Haven, CT	$108,717
Washington, DC	$112,806

* with 8–10 years of progressive, broad-based IT experience, 5 or more years managing systems and/or relevant business unit experience, and 2 years of experience in data warehousing planning and development

9.A **SERVICE LEVEL AGREEMENT STANDARDS**

Response Time

Usually the first thing users ask for is an SLA for response time, but this will be the last SLA IT can commit to for a number of reasons. First, there are usually more ad hoc queries written against a data warehouse than prewritten reports. Second, the usage of the data warehouse is fairly unpredictable at the beginning and must be monitored for a while to give the DBA an opportunity to tune it properly. Therefore response time SLA will be established only for a small number of the canned queries and reports that have well-defined operating parameters with a nonvariable expectation of the number of I/Os and amount of calculation. By monitoring the performance of standard queries and reports, degradation in performance would be observed, and proactive performance activities would be initiated.

An example would be "Report 'Monthly Group Health Sales' will complete in less than 30 minutes."

Scheduled Hours of Operation

The scheduled hours of operation would generally include normal working hours. Extended hours may be scheduled at month end, quarter end, year end, or as necessary and possible. Extended hours would support long-running queries and reports or international users who are in different time zones. The days per week would generally include the normal workweek and any additional days on the weekend.

An example would be "18 hours/day, 6:00 A.M. to midnight, 6 days/ week, Monday through Saturday."

Availability of Updated Data

The availability of the load/refresh is a function of the completion of the load run and availability of the source data as well as the extract, transform, and load time.

An example of availability of updated data would be "Monday morning before 6:00 A.M.," following a weekly load/refresh.

Availability During Scheduled Hours

No system can be up 100 percent of the time. Availability will be dependent on the stability of the system and how well it is tested and controlled. It is dependent on the backup and recovery procedures established by Technical Services and by the DBA.

An example would be "The system will be available 97 percent of the time during scheduled hours."

Response to Problems

This SLA is for those who support the users. Although it is not possible to commit to a resolution time to problems, it is possible to commit to a response time to problems.

Examples would be "Users will be notified of the status of their problem within four hours after proper notification."

11.A QUESTIONS FOR EXTERNAL DATA VENDORS

Many of you will be bringing in external data and combining it with your own data to create your data warehouse. The external data is often incomplete, dirty, and difficult to integrate with your own data. The following is a list of questions you will want to ask your external data vendor.

1. What have you done to certify the quality of the data you are sending us?

2. What reports do you produce on the quality and completeness of the data?

3. Can we see these reports?

4. Do you use any tools to analyze the quality and completeness of the data?

5. Are these tools also available to us?

6. How complete is the data (for example, will you have demographic data for 80 percent of our customers)?

7. How complete are the columns for the rows you are providing—that is, are any of the fields blank, and, if so, which ones?

8. What do you do to ensure that each column contains only valid values?

9. What do you do to ensure that each column has the right data type and length?

10. How timely is the data—that is, is it current as of last Friday or the end of the month?

11. How soon after the close of a period will we be receiving the data?

12. What procedures do you have in place to ensure that each new external file you send is complete and accurate?

13. How much advance notice will we be given when you change the format or content of your data?

14. Are there any privacy landmines we should be aware of?

12.A PROJECT PLAN TASK TEMPLATE

This template is appropriate for each task and subtask and should be completed and maintained by the person with the primary responsibility for the task. It will be part of the project documentation set.

Task name: _____

Task description: _____

Notes: _____

Required skill to support the task: _____

Primary responsibility: _____

Secondary responsibility: _____

Predecessor tasks/higher-level tasks: _____

Critical success factors: _____

Dependencies: _____

Deliverable: _____

Criteria for acceptance: _____

Design review required? _____

Issues associated with this task: _____

Expected effort: _____

Expected duration: _____

Task Template Instructions

For each task where you are listed as the primary person accountable (i.e., your name is listed first on the project plan), please use the following process to evaluate what is needed for that task.

- Task name—short name/explanation that will appear on the list of project tasks.
- Task description—clearly explain what the task is, including the following:
  - Notes—detailed explanation of task (this will be input in the Notes section in the project plan).
  - Primary and secondary responsibility—understand the roles of others assigned and plan to coordinate the involvement of all. Since you are completing this form, you are likely the Primary. List all others involved under Secondary.
  - Predecessor tasks/higher-level tasks—identify specific tasks in the project plan that must precede this task. Be sure to list the task name rather than the number, as task numbers will change when tasks are added/deleted.
  - Dependencies—identify any conditions or events that are dependent on each other. Examples include having standards in place and team members having sufficient skills. Be sure to flag additional skills/training needed.
  - Deliverables—consider what concrete deliverables should be produced as part of this task (e.g., evaluation matrix, recommendation document, request for proposal).
- Criteria for acceptance—what needs to happen to show that the task was successfully completed? This may include review or other valida-

tion by specific team members, steering committee, business analysts, and so forth.

- Design review required—specifically list any review required, in terms of what will be reviewed and who will review.
- Issues associated with this task—list specific issues identified with this task, if any. These may also need to be included in the formal team issue log.
- Expected effort—stated in terms of hours of actual work effort (*not* the same as duration). Consider three cases: best, worse, and most likely (i.e., realistic). Communicate the most likely/realistic.
- Expected duration—length of time you expect before task is completed. This will consider wait time and other workload considerations, non-project-related commitments, and meetings in addition to the expected work effort. Consider three cases: best, worse, and most likely (i.e., realistic). Communicate the most likely/realistic.

The following are some other factors to consider:

- You may want to break down the tasks into smaller subtasks. Rule of thumb is to break down further if the task is greater than 40 hours of effort.
- Think about communication and needed knowledge transfer to other team members; specifically build these into your tasks/subtasks. Example: Demo of technology learned; communicate logical data model to DBA, ETL manager, and so on.
- Consider documentation that explains what was done and/or what decision was made; may need to include a narrative to explain diagrams.

You should go through this general process for each of your tasks. However, depending on the complexity of the task and/or how well defined it is, you may or may not want to document all aspects formally.

Task Template Sample

Task description: Receive and review data delivery proposals

Notes:

Vendors will be notified (possibly sent an RFP) with a description of our environment and what we are looking for in a data delivery (OLAP) tool. They will be given our rules of engagement and time frame.

Primary responsibility: Harold Schmedlap

Secondary responsibility: William Nott

Predecessor tasks/higher-level tasks:

- Recommendations from Pieter Mimno on acceptable A&A tools from Pieter's class
- Feedback from departments already using data delivery tools

Dependencies:

- Enterprise-wide data delivery standards
- Skills of the evaluation team

Deliverable:

Deliverables will be in subtasks.

Design review required? No

Issues associated with this task:

- Do we need more than one finalist?
- Responsiveness of vendors.
- Need for demonstrations unknown.
- This may take longer than the time we have scheduled.
- This may involve more effort to do the research than we had allocated.

12.B SAMPLE PROJECT PLAN

From PlanXpert for Data Warehouse

The following high-level project plan is excerpted from *MapXpert for Data Warehouse* published by Xpert Corporation. This project plan lists the main activities for each major development step, including looping activities, which occur in most steps. For a detailed data warehouse project plan, which includes a more complete set of tasks and subtasks, contact Method Focus Inc.: *www.methodfocus.com*.

Work Breakdown Structure	Effort–Hours	Start	End	Deliverable	Lead Role Title
Project Agreement					
Project preparation					
Gather information				Memo	Data warehouse architect
Define objective				Data warehouse objectives	Project manager
Prepare Project Agreement				Project Agreement document	Project manager
Prepare project plan				Project plan	Project manager
Define business requirements					
Define business requirements (data & access)				Business requirements	Data warehouse architect
Obtain sponsor approval				Memo	Data warehouse architect
Model the data					
Identify candidate entities				Entity candidate list	Data administrator
Create preliminary conceptual data model				Conceptual data model	Data administrator
Conduct modelling sessions					
Create the logical data model				Logical data model	Data administrator
Define entities				Entity definition	Users
Define relationships				Relationship definition	Data administrator
Define data elements				Data element definition	Users
Define security requirements				Security specification	User liaison
Populate repository				Metadata in repository	Data administrator
Identify data sources					

continued

Work Breakdown Structure	Effort–Hours	Start	End	Deliverable	Lead Role Title
Determine sources of data				Selected source files	ETL developers
Assess quality of source data				Data quality exceptions list	Data quality analyst
Determine technology architecture					
Identify technology requirements				Technology model	Data warehouse architect
Determine alternatives				Solution alternatives	Data warehouse architect
Define project standards				Project standards	Project manager
Review/refine architecture				Review report	Data warehouse architect
Update project plan and estimates					
Analyze risk				Risk analysis	Project manager
Replan project				Updated project plan	Project manager
Prepare deliverable completion log				Deliverable completion log	Project manager
Estimate costs				Cost analysis	Project manager
Identify benefits				Benefits analysis	Project manager
Review plans and specifications				Results report	Project manager
Establish Technology Platform(s)					
Project initiation					
Project kickoff meeting				Agenda–memo	Project manager
Establish change control procedures				Project change log	Project manager
Establish status reporting procedures				Memo	Project manager
Establish test procedures				Test log	Delivery application developers
Train team on tools				Training (delivered)	Training coordinator

continued

Work Breakdown Structure	Effort–Hours	Start	End	Deliverable	Lead Role Title
Select vendors/products					
Define tool selection criteria				Selection criteria document	Data warehouse architect
Create short list of potential vendors/products				Short list	Data warehouse architect
Call references				Reference interview notes	Data warehouse architect
Choose final vendors/products				Memo	Project manager
Purchase product				Purchase order	Project manager
Install product				Installed product	Technical support
Test product				Test log	Delivery application developers
Complete the step					
Review project plan estimates				Results report	Project manager
Review changes				Memo	Sponsor
Revise Project Agreement document				Updated project agreement	Project manager
Update risk analysis				Updated risk analysis	Project manager
Database & ETL Development					
Planning session for this step				Memo	Project manager
Build the database					
Complete the logical data model				Logical data model	Data administrator
Complete source data quality assessment				Update ETL process specs	Data quality analyst

continued

Work Breakdown Structure	Effort–Hours	Start	End	Deliverable	Lead Role Title
Complete data access/delivery requirements				Updated data access requirements.	Database administrator
Create the physical data model				Physical data model	Database administrator
Create database structures				Data definition language (DDL)	Database administrator
Code physical view definitions				Physical view definitions	Database administrator
Prepare extract/transform/load specs					
Create extract/transform/load specs				ETL process specs	Lead ETL developer
Review ETL process specs				Review results report	Review team
Define ETL tests				ETL test specs	ETL developers
Describe ETL test cases				ETL test cases	ETL developers
Plan test activities				Test plan	ETL developers
Design/prototype ETL software					
Prepare ETL process flow diagram				ETL process flow diagram	Lead ETL developer
Design ETL modules to be coded				ETL module definitions	ETL developers
Walk through program specs				Results report	Review team
Revise/review				Updated results report	ETL developers
Build ETL process					
Code ETL software, including reconciliation totals				Program code	ETL developers
Conduct walk throughs				Walk through results report	ETL developers
Conduct unit tests				Unit test data	ETL developers

continued

Work Breakdown Structure	Effort–Hours	Start	End	Deliverable	Lead Role Title
Test ETL software					
Create ETL test data				ETL test data	ETL developers
Execute ETL processes				ETL test data	ETL developers
Verify/log results, including reconciliation totals				Test log	ETL developers
Revise/retest				Test log	ETL developers
Complete the step					
Review project plan/estimates				Results report	Project manager
Review high-level changes				Memo	Sponsor
Revise Project Agreement document				Updated Project Agreement	Project manager
Update risk analysis				Updated risk analysis	Project manager
Review/revise logical data model				Updated logical data model	Data administrator
Review/revise physical data model(s)				Updated physical data models	Database administrator
Change database structures				Updated DDL	Database administrator
Review/revise ETL process specs				Updated ETL process specs	Lead ETL developer
Update metadata repository				Updated metadata in repository	Data administrator
Query/Reporting Development					
Planning session for this step				Memo	Project manager
Build/prototype queries & reports					
Design/prototype queries				Prototype	Delivery application developers
Test special query/reporting features				Prototype	Delivery application developers

continued

Work Breakdown Structure	Effort–Hours	Start	End	Deliverable	Lead Role Title
Correct and reexecute				Test log	Delivery application developers
Document canned queries				Query descriptions	Delivery application developers
Design/prototype reports				Report descriptions	Delivery application developers
Review results/revise/reexecute				Test log	Delivery application developers
Document reports				Report descriptions	Delivery application developers
Establish support infrastructure					
Develop metadata delivery application				Metadata delivery application	Delivery application developers
Develop capacity plan				Capacity plan	Technical services
Develop usage monitoring				Usage monitoring plan	Delivery application developers
Develop performance monitoring				Performance monitoring plan	Database administrators
Define organization impacts				Organization plan	Project manager
Identify needed policies, standards, procedures				Policies, standards, procedures	Data warehouse architect
Prepare implementation plan				Implementation plan	Project manager
Document procedures					
Prepare operations procedures				Operating procedures	Delivery application developers
Prepare user help desk procedures				Help desk procedures	Delivery application developers
Prepare training material				Training material	Delivery application developers
Provide training					
Train help desk				Training (delivered)	Training coordinator
Train users				Training (delivered)	Training coordinator

continued

Work Breakdown Structure	Effort–Hours	Start	End	Deliverable	Lead Role Title
Conduct acceptance tests					
Execute ETL processes				Populated databases	ETL developers
Execute report and query processes				Reports and Queries	Delivery application developers
Conduct user acceptance tests				Test log	Users
Log/report user acceptance tests				Test log	User liaison
Revise/retest				Test log	User liaison
Prepare for implementation					
Review documentation				Review results report	Project manager
Update data models				Updated data models	Data administration
Prepare implementation specs				Implementation specs	Project manager
Complete the step					
Review project plan/estimates				Results report	Project manager
Review high-level changes				Memo	Sponsor
Revise Project Agreement document				Updated Project Agreement	Project manager
Update risk analysis				Updated risk analysis	Project manager
Review/revise logical data model				Updated logical data model	Data administrator
Review/revise physical data model(s)				Updated physical data models	Database administrator
Change database structures				Updated DDL	Database administrator
Review/revise ETL process specs				Updated ETL process specs	Lead ETL developer
Update meta data repository				Updated metadata in repository	Data administrator

continued

Work Breakdown Structure	Effort–Hours	Start	End	Deliverable	Lead Role Title
Implementation					
Install system components					
Move ETL programs into production				Executable code in production	ETL developers
Move reports/queries into production				Executable code in production	Delivery application developers
Create databases in production				Executed DDL in production	Database administrator
Load production databases				Loaded databases	Database administrator
Test programs against production databases				Test log	Developers (ETL & delivery)
Turn over system documentation					
Provide users with documentation				User documentation	User liaison
Provide computer operations instructions				Operations documentation	ETL developers
Promote all software to production status				Memo	Technical support
Initial production processing					
Begin production operations				Memo	Computer operations
Provide follow-up support				Memo	Developers
Close the project					
Disable/remove obsolete components				Memo	Computer operations
Prepare project close report				Project close report	Project manager
Obtain final sponsor sign-off				Project close report	Project manager

continued

Work Breakdown Structure	Effort–Hours	Start	End	Deliverable	Lead Role Title
Ongoing project management					
Report project status				Project status report	Project manager
Report individual status				Status reports	Team members
Coordinate project activities				Project plan	Project manager

12.C   DISASTER EXAMPLES

All of the following examples were taken from real life. Descriptions have been altered to protect the innocent and the semi-innocent. All of these disasters could have been avoided. Each has a reference to the chapters that would have addressed the situation.

1. A daily load took 27 hours. (Chapter 4, "Risks")

2. All operational data was "sucked" out of operational systems and "plunked" into the data warehouse indiscriminately, producing a large database with mostly dirty and useless data. (Chapter 2, "Goals and Objectives")

3. A data warehouse delayed for six months because of dirty data. (Chapter 11, "Data Quality")

4. An interface that was much too difficult for the user (and the user didn't use the system). (Chapter 5, "Satisfying the User")

5. A project that never completed—only about 30 percent of the original function was delivered. (Chapter 12, "Project Planning")

6. A project that took two years and three project managers to complete. (Chapter 12, "Project Planning")

7. Standalone "data marts" were built using the swimlane approach and were costly to integrate afterward. (Chapter 1, "Introduction to Data Warehousing")

8. The hardware to run the system was grossly underestimated. (Chapter 6, "Cost Benefit")

9. The software was so complex; the cost for consultants and contractors was three times the cost of the software—and the consultants are still there. (Chapter 7, "Selecting Software")

10. The sponsor lost faith in the team, a new team was brought in, who, of course, redid everything. (Chapter 5, "Satisfying the User" and Chapter 12, "Project Planning")

11. Disparate data marts produced reports that were inconsistent, and they still have to reconcile the disparities. (Chapter 1, "Introduction to Data Warehousing")

12. Expensive software that is essentially sitting on the shelf was bought. (Chapter 7, "Selecting Software")

13. Critical members of the team became disheartened and were lured away by other companies to build their data warehouse. Nothing was documented, and there is no one left who knows the software, the system, or why decisions were made. (Chapter 8, "Organization and Cultural Issues")

14. A key software vendor had financial trouble, it was sold to a stronger company, and the product is no longer being enhanced or even supported. (Chapter 7, "Selecting Software")

Belcher, Lloyd, and Hugh Watson. "Assessing the Value of Conoco's EIS." *MIS Quarterly*, September 1993.

Bruce, Thomas A. *Designing Quality Databases with IDEF1X Information Models.* New York, N.Y.: Dorset House Publishing, 1992.

English, Larry P. *Improving Data Warehouse and Business Information Quality.* New York, N.Y.: John Wiley & Sons, 1999. ISBN 0-471-25383-9.

"The Foundations of Wisdom: A Study of the Financial Impact of Data Warehousing." Toronto: *IDC*, 1996.

Hackney, Douglas. "Data Warehouse Delivery: How about 0% ROI?" *DMReview*, Volume 9, Number 1, January 1999.

Huang, Kuan-Tsae, Yang W. Lee, and Richard Y. Wang. *Quality Information and Knowledge.* Upper Saddle River, N.J.: Prentice Hall, 1999.

Inmon, William H. *Building the Data Warehouse.* Second Edition. New York, N.Y.: John Wiley & Sons, 1996.

Inmon, William H., Claudia Imhoff, and Ryan Sousa. *Corporate Information Factory.* New York, N.Y.: John Wiley & Sons, 1997.

Maglitta, Joseph E. "Beyond ROI." *Computerworld*, October 27, 1997.

Manual for Data Administration. March 1994.

Marquez, Jay. *"Creating a Business Case in Data Warehouse,"* *Practical Advice from the Experts,* Joyce Bischoff and Ted Alexander, eds. Upper Saddle River, N.J.: Prentice Hall, 1997.

Menagh, Melanie. "Warming Up to Your Non-IT IT Boss," *Computerworld,* September 20, 1999.

Simsion, Graeme. *Data Modeling Essentials: Analysis, Design, and Innovation.* Boston, Mass.: International Thomson Computer Press, 1994.

Reingruber, Michael C., and William W. Gregory. *The Data Modeling Handbook, A Best-Practice Approach to Building Quality Data Models.* New York, N.Y.: John Wiley & Sons, 1994.

Yourdon, Edward. *Death March: The Complete Software Developer's Guide to Surviving "Mission Impossible" Projects.* Upper Saddle River, N.J.: Prentice Hall, 1997.

INDEX

Addison-Wesley Information Technology Series
Capers Jones and David S. Linthicum, Consulting Editors

The information technology (IT) industry is in the public eye now more than ever before because of a number of major issues in which software technology and national policies are closely related. As the use of software expands, there is a continuing need for business and software professionals to stay current with the state of the art in software methodologies and technologies. The goal of the **Addison-Wesley Information Technology Series** is to cover any and all topics that affect the IT community. These books illustrate and explore how information technology can be aligned with business practices to achieve business goals and support business imperatives. Addison-Wesley has created this innovative series to empower you with the benefits of the industry experts' experience.

For more information point your browser to www.awprofessional.com/itseries

Sid Adelman, Larissa Terpeluk Moss, *Data Warehouse Project Management.* ISBN: 0-201-61635-1

Sid Adelman et al., *Impossible Data Warehouse Situations: Solutions from the Experts.* ISBN: 0-201-76033-9

Wayne Applehans, Alden Globe, and Greg Laugero, *Managing Knowledge: A Practical Web-Based Approach.* ISBN: 0-201-43315-X

David Leon Clark, *Enterprise Security: The Manager's Defense Guide.* ISBN: 0-201-71972-X

Frank P. Coyle, *XML, Web Services, and the Data Revolution.* ISBN: 0-201-77641-3

Kevin Dick, *XML, Second Edition: A Manager's Guide.* ISBN: 0-201-77006-7

Jill Dyché, *e-Data: Turning Data into Information with Data Warehousing.* ISBN: 0-201-65780-5

Jill Dyché, *The CRM Handbook: A Business Guide to Customer Relationship Management.* ISBN: 0-201-73062-6

Patricia L. Ferdinandi, *A Requirements Pattern: Succeeding in the Internet Economy.* ISBN: 0-201-73826-0

David Garmus and David Herron, *Function Point Analysis: Measurement Practices for Successful Software Projects.* ISBN: 0-201-69944-3

John Harney, *Application Service Providers (ASPs): A Manager's Guide.* ISBN: 0-201-72659-9

International Function Point Users Group, *IT Measurement: Practical Advice from the Experts.* ISBN: 0-201-74158-X

Capers Jones, *Software Assessments, Benchmarks, and Best Practices.* ISBN: 0-201-48542-7

Ravi Kalakota and Marcia Robinson, *e-Business 2.0: Roadmap for Success.* ISBN: 0-201-72165-1

Ravi Kalakota and Marcia Robinson, *Services Blueprint: Roadmap for Execution.* ISBN: 0-321-15039-2

Greg Laugero and Alden Globe, *Enterprise Content Services: Connecting Information and Profitability.* ISBN: 0-201-73016-2

David S. Linthicum, *B2B Application Integration: e-Business-Enable Your Enterprise.* ISBN: 0-201-70936-8

David S. Linthicum, *Enterprise Application Integration.* ISBN: 0-201-61583-5

David S. Linthicum, *Next Generation Application Integration: From Simple Information to Web Services.* ISBN: 0-201-84456-7

Sergio Lozinsky, *Enterprise-Wide Software Solutions: Integration Strategies and Practices.* ISBN: 0-201-30971-8

Anne Thomas Manes, *Web Services: A Manager's Guide.* ISBN: 0-321-18577-3

Larissa T. Moss and Shaku Atre, *Business Intelligence Roadmap: The Complete Project Lifecycle for Decision-Support Applications.* ISBN: 0-201-78420-3

Bud Porter-Roth, *Request for Proposal: A Guide to Effective RFP Development.* ISBN: 0-201-77575-1

Ronald G. Ross, *Principles of the Business Rule Approach.* ISBN: 0-201-78893-4

Dan Sullivan, *Proven Portals: Best Practices for Planning, Designing, and Developing Enterprise Portals.* ISBN: 0-321-12520-7

Karl E. Wiegers, *Peer Reviews in Software: A Practical Guide.* ISBN: 0-201-73485-0

Ralph R. Young, *Effective Requirements Practices.* ISBN: 0-201-70912-0

Bill Zoellick, *CyberRegs: A Business Guide to Web Property, Privacy, and Patents.* ISBN: 0-201-72230-5